THE DARKROOM:

A Complete Guide to Processing and Printing Color and Black-and-White Photographs

by

Tom Grimm

In Collaboration with
Jerry Burchfield and Mark Chamberlain

PHOTOGRAPHS BY
TOM AND MICHELE GRIMM
AND JERRY BURCHFIELD

A PLUME BOOK
NEW AMERICAN LIBRARY
TIMES MIRROR
NEW YORK, LONDON AND SCARBOROUGH, ONTARIO

NAL BOOKS ARE AVAILABLE AT QUANTITY DISCOUNTS
WHEN USED TO PROMOTE PRODUCTS OR SERVICES. FOR
INFORMATION PLEASE WRITE PREMIUM MARKETING DIVISION,
THE NEW AMERICAN LIBRARY, INC., 1633 BROADWAY,
NEW YORK, NEW YORK 10019.

Library of Congress Catalog Card Number: 78-51650

PLUME TRADEMARK REG. U.S. PAT. AND FOREIGN COUNTRIES
REGISTERED TRADEMARK—MARCA REGISTRADA
HECHO EN WESTFORD, MASS., U.S.A.

SIGNET, SIGNET CLASSICS, MENTOR,
PLUME, MERIDIAN and NAL BOOKS
are published *in the United States* by
The New American Library, Inc.,
1633 Broadway, New York, New York 10019,
in Canada by The New American Library of Canada Limited,
81 Mack Avenue, Scarborough, Ontario M1L 1M8
in the United Kingdom by The New English Library Limited,
Barnard's Inn, Holborn, London EC1N 2JR, England

First Plume Printing, October, 1978

5 6 7 8 9 10 11 12 13

PRINTED IN THE UNITED STATES OF AMERICA

For Michele,

a great companion in the dark.

Contents

condensor-diffusion and cold-light, lamps, lenses, lens coating, common focal lengths, f/stop openings, negative carriers, Newton's Rings, focusing methods, support columns, baseboard, filter drawer, filter types: variable contrast, color printing and color compensating, color heads, dichroic filters, voltage regulator/stabilizer

5 Considering Black-and-White Papers and Processing 72

6 Making Black-and-White Contact Prints Step by Step 90

11 Processing Color Films Step by Step 153

12 Preparing to Make Color Prints 177

negative-to-positive printing, positive-to-positive reversal type printing, internegative, white light subtractive exposure method, tricolor additive exposure method, filtration, color balance, color photo papers, primary/complementary colors, emulsion layers, filter density

Equipment for Making Color Prints 180
list of items for color printing

Enlarger 181
filter drawer, color head, dichroic filters

Color-corrected Enlarger Lens 185

Color Printing Filters 185
CP and CC types, ultraviolet (UV) filter, filter list for tricolor printing, filter list for white light printing

Heat-absorbing Glass 186

Enlarging Timer 187
electronic type, standardizing exposure time

Processing Devices 188
tube-type processors, sizes, loading, solution capacity, motorized devices, processing trays, paper emulsion, agitation, temperature control, drum processor, basket-and-tank processing, continuous-roll processing

Thermometer 191

Processing Timer 191

Color Print Paper 191
Type A, Type B, Ektacolor RC, Ektachrome RC, Cibachrome, weight, surfaces, sizes, storage, handling, fogging

Processing Chemistry 192
types, temperature control, contamination, storage life, sizes, processing kits

Rubber Gloves 193

Towels 193

Safelights 194

Voltage Regulator/Stabilizer 194

13 Processing Color Prints Step by Step   199

14   Exposing Color Print Papers   226

THE BASIC
DARKROOM BOOK:
A Complete Guide to
Processing and Printing Color
and Black-and-White Photographs

It's Magic

"It's magic!" That's a frequent exclamation in my beginning darkroom classes at the University of California, Irvine, when students first see an image appear on the paper they've slipped into a tray of chemicals. Indeed, there is a thrill, and a feeling of creativity, as a photograph develops before your eyes.

In advanced darkroom classes, long after the thrill has diminished, the feeling of creativity remains. In fact, that is the main reason many photographers insist on doing their own developing and enlarging—they have total control over the results. Other photographers feel darkroom work is too technical and tedious, and they leave their film and print processing to commercial laboratories.

Can you be a good cameraman—and get the photograph you desire—without doing your own darkroom work? Many photographers say yes. Besides, they argue, there's not enough time to become proficient and prolific with *both* camera and enlarger. How can a photographer's shooting improve if he's always in the darkroom?

Others contend that you can't get the best possible photograph unless you take it *and* make it yourself. They question why you should trust someone else to finish what you've started.

These conflicting philosophies often depend on whether a full-time professional or a part-time amateur is talking. Certainly the pros must be knowledgeable about both photographing and printing. Consider Ansel Adams, a master photographer *and* printmaker. Through years of work with film and paper, he developed camera and darkroom skills that brought him artistic and financial recognition worldwide.

Should amateur photographers be as concerned about knowing how to operate an enlarger as well as a camera? For those who demand complete photographic control and perfection, the answer is yes. For others who prefer to spend their time shooting and are content with commercially processed results, perhaps not.

However, every photographer should have a basic understanding of the complete photographic process—from the time light first strikes his film to the time he displays the finished print.

This book offers these basic facts and procedures, as well as advanced

1. *Photographers have a chance to show their creativity in the darkroom. For this image, a high contrast copy negative was made of a print of two roll film developing tanks with reels and sheet film hangers. Then it was printed several times on the same piece of enlarging paper, using different exposure times to produce various gray and black tones.*

darkroom techniques. Both black-and-white and color photography are covered in detail. Film processing, contact printmaking, and enlarging are fully described. So are special darkroom effects, such as solarization, vignetting, and reticulation.

The book also features photographs and drawings to illustrate darkroom techniques. And there is a glossary to help you become familiar with the terms of a darkroom technician.

Regardless of how complicated darkroom procedures may seem initially, they are quite simple once you understand them. You should have no worries about ruining your film. In fact, doing your own darkroom work will enable you to produce prints of better quality than commercial labs might be making for you now. That is a goal of this book. Another is to familiarize you with creative darkroom techniques that are not even offered by commercial processors.

Although several chemical solutions are involved in darkroom work, you don't need to be a chemist to understand, mix, or use them. And you'll learn more than just basic processing, including how developing can be "pushed" to save films that were accidentally underexposed.

While some photographers spend as much money for their darkroom equipment as for their camera gear, processing and printing can be relatively inexpensive. A discussion of the various types of equipment available will help you decide what investment is required for your darkroom needs. Did you know, by the way, that a darkroom is not required to develop films?

Many helpful tips and practical ideas are included in the following pages. For instance, rubbing "oil" from the side of your nose onto a scratched negative will help prevent the scratches from showing in your print.

The chapters on color processing and enlarging will help you discover new excitement in photography, even if you are already familiar with black-and-white darkroom work. When you make your first color print, it may really seem like magic.

But like magicians who must know how their tricks work, photographers should read this entire book to learn how to process and enlarge in both black-and-white and color—and to enjoy some of the artistic innovations that are popular in today's darkrooms.

This guide is a companion volume to my book about camera equipment and photographic techniques, *The Basic Book of Photography*. It has valuable information that will help you take better pictures, including ways to improve composition and make correct exposures, so your negatives and transparencies will be worthwhile processing and printing.

1

Understanding the Photographic Process

The first photographers, those of the 1800s, faced many hardships. They had the laborious task of coating paper, glass, or metal plates with light-sensitive chemicals that would record an image. And even under the brightest of conditions, full sunlight, an exposure could take minutes. Processing was also troublesome and tedious.

Not so for today's photographers. We can quickly load our cameras with films that record as many as thirty-six exposures, use fast lenses and shutter speeds to capture almost any subject, and then process and print the film with ease and confidence. No wonder amateurs alone are estimated to shoot more than six billion pictures every year!

How did photography evolve to where it is today—little more than 150 years since the first-known photographic image was made? Some historical highlights are both interesting and helpful for understanding the photographic process.

The Beginning of Black-and-White Photography

Initially, man made a drawing or painting to record something. Much later he learned that if light was allowed to enter a darkened room through a tiny hole in one of the walls, the scene outside the room would appear upside down on the opposite wall. This is the principle of the *camera obscura,* which was popular with artists who wanted to record details of nature in accurate perspective.

After 1568, when a lens was first used to make sharper and brighter images, all kinds of unique cameras obscura were made, including portable models. Soon, people wanted something to record permanently what the camera obscura projected; a light-sensitive material was needed to capture and hold these images.

In the first-known photographic research, Johann Schulze, a German professor of chemistry, discovered in 1727 that silver salts darkened when

2. *A tintype made shortly after the Civil War.*

exposed to sunlight. Other experimentation was done at the turn of the century by Thomas Wedgwood, whose father was the famed British potter. Using paper soaked in silver nitrate, Wedgwood obtained negative images after placing lace over the sensitized paper and exposing it to light. The problem was that neither Schulze nor Wedgwood nor anyone else had found a way to make lasting images—eventually the images all turned black.

Finally, in 1826, the first permanent photographic image was made by Frenchman Joseph Niépce. He discovered a way to reproduce engravings onto pewter plates by using a certain type of bitumen and lavender oil. Then he tried this process with a camera obscura, making an eight-hour exposure from the window of his home in Gras.

Another Frenchman, Louis Daguerre, with similar interest in photographic images, formed a partnership with Niépce, but Niépce died before word of their research was published in Paris in 1839. A year earlier, the first successful *daguerreotype* had been made, on a silver-coated piece of copper. The process was tedious, and exposures originally were as long as 40 minutes (although improvements soon reduced exposure time to less than a minute). Other drawbacks were the daguerreotype's delicate surface, its small image size, and the fact it was a one-of-a-kind direct positive image.

About the time daguerreotypes were becoming well known, Englishman William Henry Fox Talbot perfected another photographic method called the *calotype*—for which he is credited as being the father of modern photography. Talbot coated fine writing paper with light-sensitive emulsion, put it in a camera obscura, and got a reverse image (naming it a "negative"). By placing this negative in contact with another piece of sensitized paper, he could reverse the image back to a positive. Importantly, he could repeat this second process, making as many positives as he wanted from the same negative.

At first Talbot had trouble making his images permanent, as had Daguerre, until it was discovered that soaking the prints or plates in hyposulfite permanently fixed the photographic images. (The "fixer" used by photographers today is still often called hypo, although its real chemical name is sodium thiosulfate.)

Even though Talbot's negative/positive process is the basis of today's photography, it wasn't well received by the public because prints were made from a paper negative and they lacked sharpness. Also, they resembled drawings.

Eventually another Englishman, Frederic Archer, announced a process involving a chemical substance called *collodion* that enabled emulsions to be coated onto glass plates. This became known as the *"wet plate" process* because collodion-coated glass plates were dipped in a light-sensitive silver nitrate solution and exposed by the camera while wet. The wet plates produced sharp images, which made photography more popular. The collodion process was adapted to other materials, including metal plates that produced photographs called *tintypes*. Numerous other photographic inventions culminated with George Eastman's 1888 announcement of the first Kodak camera, and roll film, which made black-and-white photography available to amateurs everywhere.

Summarizing Black-and-White Processing and Printing

There are three general steps in processing black-and-white photographs. The first is to develop the film, which results in the *negatives* from which prints are made. The second step is to make *contact prints* of the negatives in order to see what the image will look like as a positive. The third step is to make an *enlargement* which represents the final photograph as you desire it.

For photographers who learn to "read" negatives and can readily visualize the image as a positive, or for those in a hurry, the intermediate step of making a *contact proof sheet* often is eliminated. However, such proof sheets, if filed with your negatives, will serve as an excellent catalog of all the black-and-white pictures you've taken.

Developing black-and-white film is quite simple. Extensive or elaborate equipment is not required, nor is a special darkroom. Basically, here's what happens. A film's emulsion is a coating of light-sensitive chemicals, silver halides. When light coming through your camera lens strikes this emulsion, an image is formed. However, it is called a *latent image* because it cannot be

3. The final positive image, an enlarged black-and-white photograph with a full range of gray tones.

seen until the emulsion is acted upon by another chemical, the *developer*. This developer turns the portions of light-struck emulsion to metallic silver, which is black or shades of gray, depending on the intensity of the light. Where little or no light has struck, as in dark or shadowed areas of the original scene, the emulsion is hardly affected by the developer.

After a predetermined time in the developer, the film is immersed in a chemical solution called *stop bath*. As you might have guessed, this stops the action of the developer, and rinses off the developer so it will not contaminate the next chemical in which the film is immersed, the *fixer*. The fixer preserves the image and dissolves the unaffected silver halides that are no longer needed. Water is used to wash away the fixer, and the film is then hung up to dry. The images you now see will be preserved. The dark or black areas of the original scene will be clear, while the white or bright areas will be black. That is why the developed film is now called a *negative*.

To see the images correctly as positives, a print must be made. Contact proof sheets are made by placing the negative on top of light-sensitive photographic paper which is then exposed to light. As with film, a latent image is formed. And as with film, the paper is then run through three chemicals to produce a visible image. First the paper goes in the developer (usually a different type from the film developer), then stop bath, and finally the fixer, after which the print is washed and dried. The negative images have reversed again to become positives, and reproduce the scene as you photographed it. The print, of course, is in black and white and various shades of gray.

To produce a picture larger than the size of the negative, an enlarger is used. This projects the negative image in almost any size you desire onto photographic paper. The chemicals and processing steps for enlarging are the same used to make contact proof sheets. To be sure, it is quite exciting to see the first roll of negatives you've processed, but watching an enlargement emerge in a tray of chemicals is even more thrilling.

2

Considering Black-and-White
Films and Processing

There are many types of black and white films. Films for general photography record a full range of tones, while graphic arts films eliminate the in-between gray tones and produce images only in blacks and whites. And infrared films record not just the visible (light) waves of electromagnetic radiation, but invisible (infrared) rays as well. Although most black-and-white films produce negatives from which prints are made, some will make black-and-white transparencies (slides), which are called *diapositives*.

Film Characteristics

Regardless of the type of black-and-white film, each has certain characteristics that help determine the quality of the image it produces. Words frequently used to describe film characteristics include light sensitivity, grain, resolution, definition, sharpness, color sensitivity, density, contrast, and reciprocity. Before discussing them, it is worth knowing a little about the physical make-up of films.

Modern black-and-white sheet and roll films consist of six layers, measuring a total of about .005 inches thick. Color films have the same basic characteristics of design and reaction to light, but contain several more layers in order to register the different colors of the light striking the film.

The layers in black-and-white films—from top to bottom—are:
1) a scratch-resistant coating of hard gelatin to protect the emulsion
2) the emulsion itself, a gelatin in which the light-sensitive silver halide crystals are suspended
3) an adhesive, a layer of gluelike gelatin to adhere the emulsion to its base
4) the film base, a strong but flexible cellulose-acetate to support all the other layers
5) a second adhesive, between base and backing
6) the *antihalation backing*, a dye coating that prevents light passing

through the film from reflecting off the camera's film pressure plate back onto the emulsion. Without it, "halos" would be created around bright areas of the image.

The emulsion layer, composed of about 60 percent gelatin and 40 percent silver halide crystals, is the most complex part of the film. This is where an electrical/chemical chain reaction takes place, triggered by light, which ultimately forms the negative (or positive) image by converting silver halides to particles of metallic silver.

The *light sensitivity,* or *speed* (ASA), of any film is directly related to the size and number of the silver halide crystals suspended in the emulsion. Larger-sized crystals are more sensitive to light than smaller ones. Thus films with large crystals have higher ASA ratings; they are considered "fast" films. Such high speed films have a problem that is also related to the size of the silver halide crystals in the emulsion: the large crystal structure produces what photographers call "grainy" results.

"Slow" speed films have smaller and therefore more silver halide crystals distributed throughout the emulsion layer. Because of the greater number of crystals, there is a finer grain texture in the negative.

Because the speed of film is an indication of the grain that will be evident in the final image, it is very important to choose the type of film that will yield the results you want in a print. Generally when big enlargements or fine detail are desired, it is advisable to use a slower (fine grain) film when there is adequate light. A fast film, on the other hand, permits shooting under low light levels, plus greater creative choices during exposure (i.e. using a smaller lens opening for better depth of field, or a faster shutter speed to stop action). But the graininess of the film will be more evident in the final print. Of course, sometimes high speed film is used purposely for the effect its large grain structure gives.

Grain structure reveals another characteristic of all films, *resolution,* which also is determined in part by the nature of the film's silver halide crystals. The resolution, or resolving power, of a film is best described as its ability to distinguish between finely-spaced lines of similar tone or density. This is important to the clarity of the image. An advantage to using slower, fine-grain films is that they give higher resolution.

Resolution and grain contribute to what is described as a film's *definition,* which indicates the quality of detail that is evident everywhere in the photograph. *Sharpness* between the edges of details in the picture is one indication of the film's definition. When the line between a dark and light subject area appears sharp, rather than an edge that blends from one area to the other, the film is considered to have good definition.

Another distinguishing characteristic of black-and-white film is its *color sensitivity,* because not all films react the same way to colors. Unless the silver halide crystals in the emulsion are treated with certain dyes, they will react only to shorter wavelengths of light. That is why the early black-and-white films, which lacked such dyes, were overly sensitive to ultraviolet, violet and blue, while being relatively insensitive to red and green.

With the discovery that dyes could be added to the emulsion, *orthochromatic* films were produced. They gave better rendition of greens and yellows, but reds and oranges were still recorded in tones that were unnaturally dark.

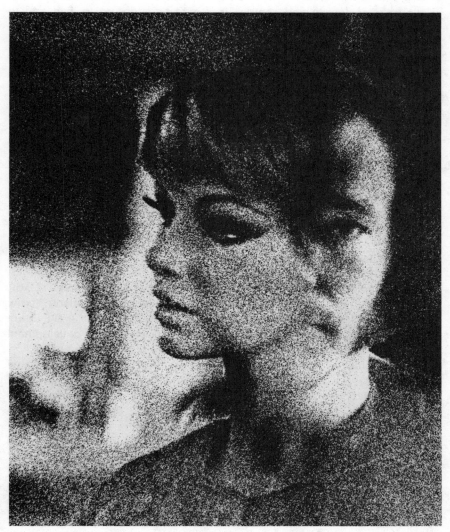

4. *Grain is very evident in this photograph of a female mannequin that includes a partial portrait of the photographer reflected in the store window. Film was shot at night in low light and overdeveloped.*

Later, films were improved so they would be sensitive to all colors in the visible spectrum. These films are called *panchromatic,* and they are the type of black-and-white films commonly used today. They reproduce colors with brightness which is similar to that seen by the human eye. And with the use of different *filters* on the camera lens, panchromatic films can be modified to enhance or exaggerate any color.

You should also understand another important characteristic of film, the relationship of density and contrast in regard to exposure to light and to developer. In general, *density* is the degree of silver metal built up in a negative; it is directly related to the amount of light to which the film is exposed and to the length of time the film is in the developer. The choice of film and developer also determines the amount of density.

Contrast in film is the range between different tones of gray, specifically the difference in density between the thinnest and densest parts of the negative. A high contrast film indicates a greater span between the gray tones, and therefore fewer shades of gray. A low contrast film yields more gray tones with a shorter span between them.

Examples of films possessing relatively high contrast are commercial process films, certain orthochromatic films, and general panchromatic films with low speed, like Panatomic X, rated ASA 32. Another example is graphic arts film like Kodak's Kodalith, where as few as two tones (black and white) can be obtained; such high contrast film is used when distinct separation between tones is desired for graphic rather than realistic rendition of the subject matter.

At the other extreme are high speed films capable of revealing many tones, like Tri X, rated ASA 400. Films popular for portraits, like Plus X, rated at ASA 125, also produce a greater number of tonal values, particularly in the shadow areas. They allow greater latitide in exposure without a significant increase in contrast, although you can modify film exposure and development to achieve greater or reduced contrast.

Exposure has a special consideration, *reciprocity.* It means the same density can be achieved through *either* a change in intensity (brightness) of the light reaching the film *or* the length of time to which the film is exposed to light. That means, for example, you can get the *same* density on the same speed film when taking a picture at different exposure combinations. For instance, an exposure of f/16 at 1/125 second is the same as f/8 at 1/500 second in regard to the density recorded on the film.

This example of an exposure's reciprocal relationship shows that an increase of two stops in intensity of light (f/16 opened to f/8) will be balanced by a decrease of two stops in time (1/125 reduced to 1/500 second), and both exposures yield the same density. The exposure results will be the same because the *quantity* of light to which the film is subjected is identical for both exposures.

However, there are exceptions, and these are generally known as *reciprocity failure*. It occurs with two extremes of exposures: very short exposures (with strong light intensity) and very long exposures (with low light intensity).

The failure happens to most black-and-white and many color films when low levels of illumination require exposures of 1 second or longer to achieve normal density on the film. In such cases, an increase in exposure will not make a proportional increase in density. So the length of time must be increased in order to avoid underexposure. Also, the greater the length of exposure time beyond 1 second, the greater the compensation required.

The effect of lengthening the time of exposure also increases the contrast of the film, which can be used to good advantage if an increase in contrast is desired. But to avoid increased contrast produced by long exposures in low light levels, it's best to increase exposure by opening up the lens to a wider aperture (f/stop) when possible.

With very short exposures, because of high illumination, a similar reciprocity failure occurs. This usually happens with certain electronic flash producing exposures shorter than 1/10,000 second, resulting in a reduction in the density of the image on the film. You must compensate by opening up the lens aperture to let more light reach the film and provide proper density.

Film Sizes

The film size for 35mm cameras is 135. Standard lengths are for twenty, twenty-four, or thirty-six exposures, loaded in light-tight metal *cassettes (Kodak calls them magazines)*. Kodacolor II and Kodacolor 400 also are supplied in twelve exposure cassettes. Some 35mm film is available in *bulk*. Each bulk roll has one hundred or more feet of film, and the photographer has to load his own cassettes to use it in the camera. All 35mm film has sprocket holes bordering both edges of the film.

Rolls of film in larger sizes are commonly designated 120, 220, 620, or 127. Such film is wrapped with *paper backing* onto a spool. The backing prevents light from exposing or fogging the film before and after the film is used in the camera. Roll films will make eight, ten, twelve, fifteen, sixteen, twenty, or twenty-four exposures, depending on the camera's format (square or rectangular) and the length of the film roll. Size 120 roll film, for instance, allows twelve 2¼ x 2¼-inch or ten 2¼ x 2¾-inch exposures, while size 220 film gives twice as many exposures of the same size. Other spool-wound roll sizes include 828, 116, and 616.

Some film comes in plastic *cartridges* and is designed to drop in the camera for loading, as with Kodak's Instamatics. The larger cartridge film size is 126, while the smaller pocket Instamatics take 110 film. Cartridge films also use a

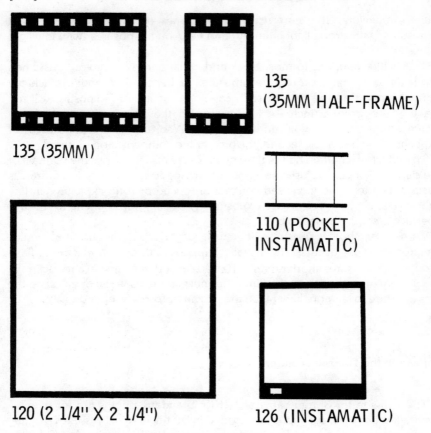

5. *The relative size and image area of popular films.*

light-tight paper backing to prevent fogging of the film. The exposure frame number is printed on this backing and appears through a window on the cartridge (and camera). They come in twelve-, twenty- and twenty-four-exposure lengths. A film speed code notch on the cartridge sets the appropriate ASA on automatic cameras when the cartridge is inserted.

There are also subminiature film sizes, usually 16mm or 9.5mm cartridges used in very small cameras like certain models of the Minox. They give eighteen, twenty, twenty-four, or twenty-six exposures.

In addition, film comes in *sheets* which are put in light-tight film holders to use with view, studio, or older press cameras. Sheet film sizes are measured in inches, and standard sizes are 2¼ x 3¼, 3¼ x 4¼, 4 x 5, 5 x 7, 8 x 10, and 11 x 14.

Also used in studio, view and older press cameras are *film packs,* each containing sixteen thin sheets of film that are attached to paper tabs which the photographer pulls to advance each sheet. Common film pack sizes are 2¼ x 3¼, 3¼ x 4¼, and 4 x 5 inches.

Not all types of films are available in all sizes, and some may just be available in sheets, pack, cartridge, 35mm, roll, subminiature, or bulk form.

Film Brands

Following is a list of black-and-white films that are popular with many photographers today. Included are manufacturer and brand names, ASA film speeds, and some of the available sizes.

In the chart, Cartridge film refers to 126-size unless asterisked (*) to indicate 110-size is available as well. Cassette refers to 135-size film for 35mm cameras. Roll film refers to 120-size only. And Sheet film indicates availability of 4 x 5-inch sheets only.

Subminiature cartridges are not indicated. These 9.5mm and 16mm cartridges often are loaded with some of the same films given below, and are available only from the manufacturer of the subminiature camera.

Film speeds (ASA) are indicated for Daylight or Tungsten use. The ASA is the same for either type of illumination unless a different ASA number appears in the Tungsten column.

BLACK-AND-WHITE FILMS

MANUFACTURER AND FILM NAME	ASA FILM SPEED Daylight / Tungsten†	FILM SIZES			
		Cartridge (126 or 110*)	Cassette (135)	Roll (120)	Sheet (4 x 5)
KODAK					
Panatomic-X	32		X		
Panatomic-X Professional	32			X	
Plus-X Pan	125		X		
Plus-X Pan Professional	125			X	X
Tri-X Pan	400	X	X	X	
Tri-X Pan Professional	320			X	X
Verichrome Pan	125	X*		X	
2475 Recording	1000		X		
Royal-X Pan	1250			X	X

BLACK-AND-WHITE FILMS (Cont.)

MANUFACTURER AND FILM NAME	ASA FILM SPEED Daylight / Tungsten†	FILM SIZES			
		Cartridge / (126 or 110*)	Cassette / (135)	Roll / (120)	Sheet (4 x 5)
High-Contrast Copy	/ 64		X		
Professional Copy	25 / 12				X
High Speed Infrared	50 / 125		X		X
ILFORD					
Pan F	50 / 40		X	X	
FP4	125 / 100	X	X	X	X
HP4	400 / 320		X	X	X
HP5	400 / 320		X	X	
AGFA					
Agfapan	25		X	X	X
Agfapan	100		X	X	X
Agfapan	400		X	X	X
H&W CONTROL					
VTE Pan	50 / 40		X	X	
VTE Ultra-Pan	16		X		
FUJI					
Fujipan K 126	125	X			
Neopan SS	100		X	X	
Neopan SSS	200		X	X	
SAKURA					
Konipan SS	100		X		
Konipan SSS	200		X		
LUMINOS					
Lumipan	100	X	X	X	
Lumipan Portrait Press	125				X

†Same as Daylight ASA Film Speed, unless indicated.

Film Care and Storage

All unprocessed photographic films can be harmed by high temperatures and relative humidities, and some gases. Color films are affected more than black-and-white films because of dyes that are incorporated in additional layers of emulsion. Proper storage is required before and after exposure, especially under hot and humid conditions.

Processed films also require proper storage to last a long time, but proper processing is important, too. Faulty agitation, excessive times in certain chemicals, and inadequate washing are some processing errors that can eventually cause defects in films (as well as prints).

Before use, films should be kept in their sealed foil packages, or plastic or metal cans, as in the case of 35mm cassettes. This gives the films considerable protection from high humidity and gases; it will not protect them from heat or from X-rays commonly used to inspect passenger luggage at airports. When traveling by plane, carry your film personally and insist on a hand security check. Regarding heat, keep films away from heaters, and never close them in a car that will be heated up by the sun. For car travel, place films in a cool styrofoam ice chest or insulated picnic bag.

Some photographers keep their films in refrigerators, or even freeze them, especially color films. However, those films should remain sealed in their original foil pouches or cans to protect them from water vapor; if necessary, seal films in a tightly capped jar.

Refrigerated films should be allowed to reach room temperature before opening them for use, or moisture may condense on the film surfaces and cause damage. For single rolls standing on end, figure one hour minimum warmup time, and at least 90 minutes' warmup if the film was in the freezer.

After film packages are opened, special attention to gases and high relative humidity should be given. Vapors from mothballs and cleaning solvents, as well as automobile exhaust fumes, are especially harmful.

Films should be processed as soon as possible after exposure, because the latent images are affected by heat and high humidity.

Beware of moisture condensation that can occur on films when going from a cool building or air-conditioned car into warm outside air, or when coming from the cold outdoors into a warm building or car.

Film becomes more brittle in cold weather, too, and it can crack or break if wound or rewound too rapidly in the camera. Sprocket holes in 35mm films may rip if film is advanced too quickly in cold conditions. In very dry situations when relative humidity is low, including the indoors during winter months, rapid winding or rewinding of film can produce static electricity that will damage the film with streaks, dots, or fogging.

After processing, films are less susceptible to damage when properly stored. Color films require more consideration than black-and-white negatives, but a general rule for all films is to keep them in a place that is dry, cool, and dark. Light and heat can cause the images to fade, and dampness may promote fungus growth on the films. Protect your negatives from physical damage by storing them in plastic sleeves, and keep mounted slides in slide boxes or files.

Some final advice: Always check the film's *expiration date* printed on the film box by the manufacturer. A film's characteristics, including speed, contrast, and color balance, may change considerably after that date. Even if the date indicates the film is still fresh, never purchase any film that you think has been subjected to damage, such as film displayed in a store window or kept on a shelf near a heater. Taking precautions with film, whether unexposed or processed, is important if you want the best photographs possible.

Film Processing Equipment

Processing your own film, particularly black-and-white, is far easier than most people imagine. More importantly, you have complete control over the results.

With small expense, nearly any kind of roll or sheet film can be processed at home. But to always produce top quality negatives or transparencies, you must know the proper developing procedures, and follow them consistently.

To begin with, here is a list of basic equipment for developing film (descriptions of these items follow).

Developing tanks or trays	Scissors
Thermometer	Sponge or squeegee
Measuring graduates	Washing device
Stirring rod	Film clips
Funnel	Drying cabinet
Storage bottles	Negative sleeves
Timer 49.95	Dark room or changing bag
Film cassette opener	Chemicals

Developing Tanks and Trays

There are a variety of daylight developing tanks, made of plastic or stainless steel, for use with single or multiple rolls of films in 120, 135, 126, 110, and other sizes. With these film tanks, after loading film onto the reel(s) and putting the reel(s) into the tanks in total darkness, the entire developing process can be done with the room lights on.

Relatively inexpensive plastic models often are designed only for single rolls but they can be adjusted for various film sizes. Agitation, however, may be restricted to twisting a center post connected to the tank's film reel, which is not the most effective method of agitation.

Stainless steel tanks, or high priced plastic tanks, are preferred by the pros. These require different reels for each film size, but the tanks and reels will last a lifetime. Many 35mm photographers purchase a double tank so they can process two rolls of film at one time. Larger tanks will accommodate several reels of the same or different sizes of film—some take up to eight rolls of 35mm, or four rolls of 120-size, or other combinations.

Stainless steel tanks and reels are easier to keep clean and therefore help

6. *Plastic and stainless steel tanks for developing film include models with adjustable and fixed reels for various sizes and amounts of roll film, and others that hold hangers with sheet film.*

prevent chemical contamination. They are unbreakable, too. Most importantly, they allow the most effective agitation because they can be inverted without chemicals dripping out.

For sheet film, trays or deep developing tanks are required. With tray processing, it is best to buy trays one size larger than the film size being processed to allow for easy interleaving of the individual sheets: use 5 x 7-inch trays for 4 x 5-inch sheet film, and 10 x 12-inch trays for 8 x 10-inch film sheets.

Tanks of plastic, hard rubber and stainless steel are available in ½-, 3½-, 5-, and 10-gallon sizes. Special stainless steel or plastic hangers are used to suspend the film. *Film hangers* come in standard sheet film sizes—2¼ x 3¼, 3¼ x 4¼, 4 x 5, 5 x 7, 8 x 10, and 11 x 14 inches. Some are made to hold two to four sheets of film, except the larger sizes.

Processing sheet film in tanks is preferable because there is a danger of scratching the film when processing it in trays. Also, agitation in a tray by interleaving film sheets requires practice, because the emulsion gets soft and is very susceptible to damage.

For 4 x 5-inch or smaller sheet film, tanks of either plastic or hard rubber are adequate and considerably less expensive than stainless steel. The half-gallon size will handle twelve 4 x 5 hangers without crowding, or fourteen hangers if you are careful. For sheet film processing, a tank must be purchased for each chemical used—at least three. Only one daylight developing tank is required for roll film processing.

Thermometer

An accurate thermometer should be used when mixing chemicals, and to check chemical temperatures before and during processing sessions. Photographic thermometers are best because of manufacturers' precautions in calibration. Metal-tipped, dial-face thermometers read faster and more accurately than the very cheap, glass-enclosed thermometers. The most useful photo thermometers are marked with both Fahrenheit (F) and Celsius (C) scales.

Graduates

Vessels for mixing and measuring chemicals are called graduates. Consider buying two of them, one for larger volumes, like 32 or 64 ounces, and another under 4 ounces for more accurate measurement of smaller volumes. Both can be used for print chemicals, too.

Glass graduates are best but more expensive than plastic. Because plastic is porous, don't allow chemicals to stand too long in such containers. Whether your graduates are plastic or glass, be certain to rinse them thoroughly after use with any chemical to avoid contamination of the next chemical. Buy graduates marked with both U.S. and metric measurements, indicated by oz. and ml.

Stirring Rod

To mix chemicals thoroughly, use a glass or plastic rod, never a wooden or metal one unless the latter is stainless steel.

Funnel

A glass or plastic funnel must be large enough to allow chemicals to be poured quickly to and from the developing tank or trays and storage bottles.

Storage Bottles

Dark-colored glass bottles are best for storing chemicals, particularly developers, because those solutions are deteriorated by light. You can spray ordinary glass bottles with black paint. Do not use plastic bottles unless they are specially made for photographic purposes; some plastics "breathe," and air that passes through them decreases the useful life of chemicals. Also, avoid such *oxidation* by having a variety of bottle sizes on hand so you can fill them to the top with the chemical. Otherwise, to raise liquid levels to prevent oxidation when storage bottles are partially full, some photographers add clean marbles to the bottles.

Timer

Timing each step in processing is important, especially when film is in the developer, and for agitation. A wristwatch or wall clock with a second hand are okay, but a darkroom timer is a worthwhile investment. Especially good is the kind that buzzes when time is up, like Gralab, and also can be used with an enlarger for timing the exposure of prints. It also has luminous markings that can be seen in the dark. Most processing timers, however, give readings in minutes and are not designed—or accurate enough—to be used for timing seconds when making exposures with an enlarger. The newest electronic timers feature solid-state circuitry, and some have digital readouts. A darkroom timer is especially important for color processing, where the steps are often quite short, frequent, and require accurate timing.

Film Cassette Opener

There are special gadgets for opening 35mm film cassettes, but an ordinary bottle cap opener will work as well. Without either, you can rap the protruding end of a 35mm cassette on a hard surface to open it. Use pliers if your fingers aren't strong enough to break open the plastic Instamatic-type film cartridges. Roll film does not require special openers; just use your thumbnail to break the seal.

Scissors

To cut off the leader of 35mm film when loading it on the reel of a developing tank, use a pair of scissors. The adhesive tape used to secure cassette or roll film to its spool can be cut with scissors, or torn carefully with your fingers.

Sponge or Squeegee

To remove excess water (or stabilizer in color processing) from the film before drying, use a clean sponge or chamois. Special photographic *film squeegees,* as well as viscose sponges and chamois, are sold in camera stores. Use them for nothing else but wiping wet film.

Washing Device

For washing film, a rubber or plastic hose can be inserted into the center of the reel in a developing tank, and attached to a water faucet. Or you can buy a special plastic or stainless steel film washer. Whatever the washer, water must be changed completely at least five times during the wash cycle. It is a good idea to agitate the tank or the film intermittently to remove air bubbles that may adhere to film. Without running water, pour water into the developing tank or tray repeatedly, and agitate the film before each draining.

Film Clips

Special clips are made for hanging up wet film to dry. They come in plastic or stainless steel, and the best ones are weighted to help keep roll films from curling while drying. Clothespins will work okay, but use enough at the bottom for adequate weight to prevent curling.

Drying Cabinet

You may wish to build a simple cabinet for drying film. It should be ventilated so moisture can escape, and prevent dust from circulating in the air. For fast drying, use a fanless electric heater, but never very hot or too close to the film. At the very least, find a relatively dust-free area in which to hang up film to dry, like a clean closet.

Negative Sleeves

It is a smart idea to devise a logical and safe manner of filing your negatives. Most photographers eventually do this, usually after going through the hassle of searching for a particular negative, and then finding it is not usable because of scratches or coffee stains. Start right now to protect all your negatives in glassine, paper, or plastic negative sleeves.

Kraft paper and glassine sleeves are adequate where permanence is not required, but for *archival* storage for negatives, either a high quality plastic or rag-content paper sleeve is preferable. In cheaper sleeves or envelopes, sulphur in both the paper and glue ultimately attacks and ruins the silver metal that forms the negative's image.

Clear plastic sleeves in the form of a three-ring notebook are ideal for negative storing and filing. Each will hold one roll of 35mm film (twenty or thirty-six exposures) or one roll of 120-size film. And they can be used directly when making contact proof sheets. A notebook, with pages of sleeved negatives and corresponding contact sheets, is an excellent filing system for most casual photographers.

Dark Room or Changing Bag

A darkroom, per se, is not required for processing roll film, but a totally dark room is needed for loading the film onto the reel that is placed in the light-tight developing tank. (For sheet processing, in a tank or tray, you will need a darkroom.) To check a room for light leaks, wait at least five minutes until your eyes become accustomed to the dark.

Without a dark place, a changing bag is very convenient for loading daylight tanks with roll film. The film, cassette opener if required, scissors, daylight tank and reel are zipped into this black, double-layered bag. You put your arms into the bag through two sleeve openings that have elastic to keep a light-tight seal. As long as the bag has not been damaged by careless handling, the inside provides total darkness. At first, you may feel awkward trying to load film on reels in a changing bag; practice with old unwanted rolls of film until you feel confident.

Film Processing Chemicals

Black-and-white negative films can be processed with just two chemicals, developer and fixer, converting the unseen latent image to a permanent visual image. Other solutions—stop bath, clearing agent, and wetting agent—are optional but useful for obtaining film processing results that are consistently good. Here are some details about these various chemicals.

Developer. The basic function of *all* photographic developers is to make a latent image visible. The action of developer upon exposed silver halide crystals within a film emulsion (or enlarging paper emulsion) frees crystals that have been exposed to sufficient light and converts them to silver metal particles. The concentration of silver metal is proportionately greater in those areas of the negative (or print) that have received greater illumination than those areas receiving less light. A certain amount of "fog density," where developer acts upon unexposed silver halide crystals, is inherent in all development processes, but developers are compounded to minimize this effect so the final image is not affected adversely.

Film manufacturers make recommendations for specific developers on the data sheets packed with their films. The graininess of a negative is an important consideration, especially when you plan to make big enlargements, because some developers produce finer grain results than others. Also, if films have been accidentally or purposely underexposed, some developers are designed to turn them into negatives of good contrast, without excessive graininess.

Following is a list of black-and-white film developers, by manufacturer and brand name, as well as their characteristics regarding grain in the resulting negatives: moderate or fine grain. Also indicated is whether the developer is packaged as a powder or liquid.

Read the developer's instructions regarding mixing and dilution (if required), and whether it is a one-shot type (to be thrown away after a single use) or re-usable type, and if it can be replenished.

Most photographers use one kind of developer for films, and a different kind for developing prints, but some *universal-type developers* will process both. These are marked with an asterisk (*).

BLACK-AND-WHITE FILM DEVELOPERS

MANUFACTURER AND DEVELOPER NAME	TYPE OF NEGATIVE RESULTS		PACKAGED AS	
	Moderate grain (M)	Fine grain (F)	Powder (P)	Liquid (L)
KODAK				
D-76	M		P	
DK-50	M		P	
HC-110	M-F			L
Microdol-X		F	P	
Polydol	M		P	
Versatol*	M			L
ILFORD				
Microphen	M-F		P	
Perceptol		F	P	
ID-11	M		P	
AGFA				
Rodinal	M			L
H&W CONTROL				
Maximal		F		L
Control 4.5	M			L
ACUFINE				
Acufine		F	P	
ACU-1		F	P	
Diafine		F	P	
ETHOL				
UFG		F	P	
UFG Liquid		F		L
TEC	M		P	L
90		F	P	L
Blue		F		L
EDWAL				
FG7		F		L
Minicol II		F		L
Super 20		F		L
BESELER				
Ultrafin FD1		F		L
Ultrafin FD2		F		L
Ultrafin 1 + 1		F	P	
Ultrafin FD5		F		L
Ultrafin FD7		F	P	

*Universal-type developer; can also be used for developing prints.

Of those listed, Kodak's D-76 is an excellent general purpose film developer that offers moderate grain and good shadow detail under normal exposure conditions. It is available in powder form. Another fine film developer for general use is Kodak's HC-110, which is similar to D-76 but offers shorter development times. It is available in liquid concentrate form.

Liquid concentrate developers are popular because they can be quickly and precisely mixed at the recommended developing temperature, and then used immediately.

Powdered developers are best mixed in advance, so they can stand for several hours until cooled, and until you're sure they are thoroughly dissolved. To mix, powdered developers must be stirred adequately at high temperatures, sometimes as hot as 125°F (51.5°C). It is important to use the exact temperature recommended for mixing. If too hot, some chemicals will decompose, and if too cold, some will not dissolve completely. If you are in a hurry, and just-mixed developer is to be diluted for use, you can mix the hot stock solution in cold water. But for better stability of the developer, you should normally avoid dilution at such temperature extremes.

Tap water is suitable for mixing most photographic chemicals, although some photographers insist on using distilled water. Hard water, by itself, has little or no effect on the development process. But if the water is known to contain sulphur of any type, it would be safer to use either filtered or distilled water for mixing the developer. This avoids changes in the normal sulphur content of the developer, which otherwise might create fog in the negatives.

Stop bath. The primary function of the stop bath, sometimes called an "acid rinse" is to halt the development process, and to remove excess developer from the film. Many photographers believe running water is sufficient for this purpose. The safest idea, however, is to use an acid stop bath because it quickly neutralizes the developer and prevents it from contaminating the fixer. The stop bath also removes the calcium and magnesium scum, present in hard water, that may form on the film during development.

The most commonly used film stop bath is an acetic acid solution. A concentrated acetic acid, such as Kodak Glacial Acetic Acid, is diluted three parts to eight parts water to make a 28 percent solution. Then, for use as a film stop bath, the 28 percent solution is diluted 1½ ounces to 32 ounces of water.

It is important to use the correct dilution, because a stop bath that is too strong may create blisters in the film. On the other hand, if the acid rinse is too weak, development may continue until the film is in the fixer, and this will speed up exhaustion of the fixer by allowing developer to contaminate it.

Prepare the acid stop bath just before using it, and discard it afterward, because replenishing a stop bath is not recommended. There are some prepared stop bath chemicals, however, like Kodak's Indicator Stop Bath, that signal you to throw them out by changing color when they are exhausted.

The time required for film in most acid stop baths is 15 seconds, with agitation. If water alone is used, at least two complete changes of water within 30 seconds is suggested.

Fixer. The primary function of fixer is to dissolve the undeveloped silver halide crystals within the film emulsion, forming a soluble salt compound that is subsequently washed away. The main ingredient of fixer once was sodium hyposulfite, and early photographers called the fixer solution "hypo." That name is still in use, although the chemical most commonly used today is sodium thiosulfate.

Some fixers use ammonium thiosulfate and act more quickly than others. These so-called *quick* or *rapid fixers* can save you time. For instance, films can be fixed in Kodak Rapid Fixer in 2 to 4 minutes, while Kodak Fixer requires a fixing time from 5 to 10 minutes. It is important to fix films, with agitation, for *only* the manufacturers' recommended times. Too much time in the fixer prevents complete washing and ultimately may cause stains on negatives because of excess fixer that can't be removed. Also, overfixing may bleach the image by dissolving silver in the low density areas of the negative or print, particularly when rapid fixers are used. If using a rapid fixer that requires dilution, be sure to use the dilution ratio for film, and not the dilution ratio for paper.

Clearing agent. After fixing, film must be washed clean of processing chemicals. This usually requires 20 to 30 minutes, with agitation, and a complete change of water at least every five minutes. Because concern for conservation and ecology are placing a greater premium on water supplies, it is worthwhile to reduce long and therefore wasteful washing times by use of a clearing agent, often called a *hypo neutralizer* or *hypo eliminator.*

This solution speeds up removal of the fixer, and allows more effective washing. For example, after a 1- or 2-minute bath in Kodak's Hypo Clearing Agent, films need only a 5-minute wash. With other brands of clearing agents, like Permawash, treatment and wash times are even less. It's best to give the prints a prerinse, as well as moderate agitation during the clearing step.

An alternative way to washing in running water is to simply fill your film tank with water, agitate it, then dump and replace the water a minimum of ten times. This is something to remember if your tap water source or supply is limited, or its temperature exceeds the recommended wash temperature of 70° to 75°F (21° to 24°C).

Films (and prints) can be washed successfully in sea water; in fact, the time required to remove the fixer is cut in half. However, the salt water wash should be followed by a 2- to 5-minute wash in fresh water.

Wetting agent. Use of a wetting agent is unnecessary, but it is a final step that helps you get the best negatives. Wetting agents, such as Kodak's Photo Flo solution, make the film's surface "wetter" so water flows off it smoothly, preventing water spots or streaks on the film. The film is bathed in it for one-half to 1 minute.

This is the last step before drying, and it is a good idea to use distilled water for diluting the wetting agent stock solution. Such a wetting solution helps prevent scratching of the film emulsion if a squeegee is used, and also eliminates the problem of particles in the wash water that otherwise may cling to the film during drying.

3

Processing Black-and-White Films Step by Step

With few exceptions, you can follow the procedure outlined below for processing all black-and-white roll films. For procedures regarding sheet film processing, see page 38. By mastering a few simple techniques, and by being consistent, processing your own film will be easy, economical, and satisfying—and assure you negatives of the best quality. (The equipment and chemicals you'll need are described in the previous chapter.)

Getting Ready

Because roll film processing in tanks does not require a photographic darkroom, any light-tight room (closet, bathroom without windows, etc.) can be used for loading the film on the developing reel, which must be done in total darkness. A light-tight room is one in which you see no light leaks after being in it approximately 5 minutes; after that, your eyes become more adapted and far more sensitive to any light than are most films.

If such a space is not available, or cannot be created by blocking windows or doors, a changing bag can be used. Be patient when using this light-tight bag, because the first few times you may find it awkward to load the tank's reel without inadvertently marking the film with fingerprints.

Next, gather the developing tank and its top, reel or reels, the film cassette opener (can be a bottle cap opener), scissors, and the exposed film cassette(s) or rolls. Arrange these items in an orderly manner so you can locate them easily in the dark or inside the changing bag.

Loading Roll Film

Unless you're using a changing bag, turn out the lights. With 35mm film, a bottle cap opener or film cassette opener is used to remove the flat end of the light-tight film cassette. This metal container cannot be used again so don't worry about damaging it. The film will emerge wrapped around a small plastic spool. Find the film's outer end, the *leader,* and cut off this first 5 or 6 inches with a pair of scissors. Load the film on the reel with the emulsion side inward, following instructions that accompanied the tank. When you reach the end, pull or cut the tape which secures the film to the cassette spool. Place the reel in the tank, and make sure the tank top is properly sealed. Now the lights can be turned on and the actual processing begun.

For other roll film, such as 120-size, once the lights are out, break the seal on the film's paper backing and separate this paper from the film as you load the film on the reel. Tear the piece of tape holding the film to the paper backing at one end. Be careful not to touch or scratch the emulsion side of the film while loading it on the reel. Once loaded and placed in the developing tank, and with the tank's top securely sealed, the lights can be turned on.

For cartridge-type film, such as 126-size, snap the plastic cartridge in two by putting your thumb in the middle and pulling back on the rounded ends. Separate the film from its paper backing and load it on the reel just as described above.

If you have never loaded film onto a developing reel, it's best to practice first with an unwanted, *undeveloped* roll. Practice by rolling it onto the reel with your eyes closed, emulsion side facing the center of the reel. The emulsion side of a film curves slightly inward.

Handle the film by its edges, since touching the emulsion may cause fingerprints on the negatives. Be sure your hands, and the reel and tank, are dry. The film must not touch itself while on the reel, or the chemicals will not be able to cover the entire film surface. Patience often is required when loading the reel, especially with thirty-six-exposure film, which is more than 5 feet long.

To test whether a stainless steel reel is being loaded properly, gently push and pull on the film: if loose, it is going on well; if binding or if you can feel a crimped edge, something is wrong. Try again. Start the film in the first spiral at the reel's core, then turn the reel while slightly bowing the film. Be certain with stainless steel reels that you're rolling in the direction of the wire spirals. On reels with a clip at the center to hold the film, you may find it easier to avoid the clip and insert the cut leader in the opening just before the clip.

If you are using a plastic reel that "walks" the film on as you alternately twist the reel's sides, be sure the leading edge of 35mm film is not cut across its sprocket holes—that end must be smooth and straight.

When loading bulk film of an unusually long length that goes beyond the end of the reel, it is possible to roll the film around the outside of the reel without damaging the last four to six frames—if you are careful when inserting the reel into the developing tank. This means you may be able to get as many as forty-two frames of 35mm film onto one reel.

When you think you have mastered loading the reel, get set for the actual

Steps (in the dark) for Loading Reels with 35mm Film for Processing in Tanks

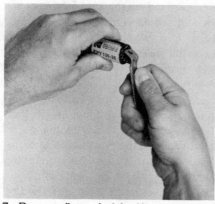

7. *Remove flat end of the film cassette with bottle top opener.*

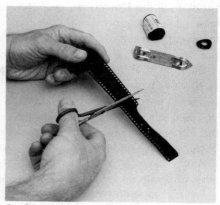

8. *Cut off film leader with scissors.*

9. *Curve film slightly, emulsion side inward, and slip into film clip in reel's center.*

10. *While maintaining slight curvature in the film, turn reel to wind film into the grooves, making sure it follows the direction of the reel's spiral (arrow).*

11. *For loading plastic reels, place film in the outside opening and "walk" the film into the grooves by alternately twisting each side of the reel.*

processing. Be sure you have at hand the bottles of chemicals (developer, stop bath, fixer, clearing agent, wetting agent), thermometer, graduate, funnel, timer (a watch or clock with a second hand will do), film clips, chamois or squeegee, and instructions for proper processing times given on the chemical packages and/or film data sheet.

Starting Development

Check the temperature of the developer; 68°F (20°C) is recommended, so cool or warm the developer accordingly. Ice can be packed around the developer bottle, or the bottle can be placed in cold or hot water, to adjust the temperature. The other chemicals, as well as wash water, should be of a similar temperature.

Determine the exact developing time according to the developer temperature, following the developer's instructions and/or film data sheet. If you use a "one-shot" developer, it will be discarded after one use. Other developers can be used again if the developer time is increased (see the developer's instructions), or if they are replenished.

Measure the required amount of developer into a graduate, and set the timer.

With small invertible tanks, remove the drain cap and tip the tank approximately 45 degrees to allow easy pouring and to prevent too many air bubbles from forming. Start the timer (or notice the time on your watch or clock) and rapidly pour in the developer without pause—which should take about 10 seconds. Once the developer is all in the tank, replace its cap, and begin agitation.

With large tanks that hold up to eight reels with 35mm film or four reels with 120-size film, prefill with developer and (in total darkness) quickly lower the reels into the chemical. A T-shaped wire supplied with large tanks is inserted through the centers of the reels and used for lowering and lifting the stack of reels. Cap the tank before turning on the lights.

Alternatively, with large tanks, you can pour in the developer once the film-loaded reels are in place, but do this in total darkness with the tank top off so the chemical will quickly cover the films. Pouring developer through the light-tight opening in the tank top is too slow a procedure to use with large tanks. Also, when developing time is up, remove the top in total darkness so you can quickly pour out the developer instead of letting it slowly drain from the light-tight opening.

Agitating

The primary purpose of agitation is to remove exhausted chemical solution from the immediate surface of the emulsion and allow fresh solution in its place. Improper agitation is a common source of trouble when developing your own film. It can result in ruined negatives, caused by problems like streaks or *surge marks, air bells,* or a significant change in contrast and graininess.

Methods for film agitation vary with different styles and sizes of tanks. Whatever technique you adopt, use it consistently, or your film negatives may vary from roll to roll.

For most developing tanks that can be inverted for agitation, the following agitation method is recommended. After the developer is in the tank and the cap is on, invert the tank and return it upright with fairly vigorous action. Inverting the tank, which takes about 2 seconds to turn over and upright, should be done continuously for the first 30 seconds of development.

In addition, you should rap the tank sharply against a firm surface 10 seconds after beginning, and again at the end of 30 seconds. This is to dislodge any air bubbles that have not been forced out by the agitation. If these cling to the emulsion, they'll prevent development—and cause tiny spots, called air bells, that ruin your negatives. To avoid streaks during agitation, rotate the tank one-quarter turn with every inversion.

After the initial 30 seconds of agitation, the film is agitated with the inversion procedure for 10 seconds of every minute (or 5 seconds every half-minute for small tanks). For even development, be sure to do this exactly on the minute (or half-minute).

With tanks that cannot be inverted because chemicals leak out, the procedure for agitation is different. After the developer is poured in, agitation is accomplished by sliding the tank back and forth over a 10-inch area, at about two cycles per second. Also rotate the tank one-quarter turn during each cycle.

Agitation is initially done for 30 seconds, then 10 seconds of every minute (or 5 seconds every half-minute). At the beginning, it is also necessary to rap the tank against a firm surface to dislodge air bubbles.

Certain noninvertible tanks have a center post that protrudes out of the tank to allow rotating the film for agitation. This can be used to turn the film, but should not be the only means of agitation. That's because back and forth rotation may set up a current within the tank and cause surge marks on the film. To avoid this, include the sliding agitation cycles described above.

When the clock indicates 10 to 15 seconds remain for developing, drain the tank quickly, funneling the developer back into its storage bottle (or drain it into the sink if it's a one-shot developer).

Stopping Development

If you are using a chemical stop bath, which usually is diluted acetic acid, premeasure it into a clean graduate.

After the developer is drained, as the clock or timer marks the end of the developing time, pour in the stop bath and agitate as before. It is important to introduce the stop bath precisely on time, because the developing action continues until the stop bath enters the tank and agitation begins.

The time of the stop bath step is brief. With a chemical stop bath, 15 seconds with agitation is adequate before draining it out of the tank. When running water is used for a stop bath, 30 seconds with agitation is sufficient, as long as two complete changes of water occur during that time.

Whether running water or a chemical stop bath is used, it should be within 5°F (about 3°C) of the developer temperature. Discard the stop bath after use, unless it is a type that indicates when it is exhausted (see page 27).

Fixing Negatives

Pour a premeasured amount of fixer in the tank. (Remember to wash the graduate before using it with different chemicals.) Agitate the film as before, and adhere to the times recommended for your particular fixer. In general, quick or rapid fixers take 2 to 4 minutes, while normal fixers require 5 to 10 minutes.

Too many photographers become lax about timing and agitation when film is in the fixer. They believe there isn't anything to worry about because development has already taken place. However, images on improperly fixed films may become bleached or stained. Stains often are the result of an exhausted fixer solution (and/or insufficient washing).

Developed films have a cloudy or milky appearance until the fixer clears it away. If you haven't kept a record of the amount of film processed in your fixer in order to know when the fixer is exhausted, make this test. Immerse a piece of developed film in the fixer, then turn on the lights. If the film's cloudiness doesn't clear within half of the manufacturer's maximum recommended fixing time, discard the fixer. Another way to test the fixer is with a product called Hypo-Check. Squirt a drop into the fixer; if it turns cloudy, the fixer is exhausted and should be discarded. Remember that fixing longer than the recommended time won't solve the problem of an exhausted fixer, and this can even cause bleaching of the image.

After draining the fixer back into its storage bottle, the developing tank's top can be removed and your results can be checked in the light. First, however, immerse the reel in water to rinse away excess fixer.

Washing

Eliminating all traces of chemicals from your negatives is an important step, and washing them in running water for 20 to 30 minutes will do the job. The water's temperature ideally should be between 70° and 75°F (21° to 24°C). Keep the film on the reel to allow uniform washing. It is important that the wash water be changed frequently and completely.

A hose attached to a faucet and pushed down to the bottom of the film tank through the center of the reels is adequate, *if* the tank is occasionally rapped to dislodge air bubbles. These tend to cling to the film surface and prevent fresh water from removing the fixer. It is also advisable to occasionally drain the tank by hand in order to remove the fixer-laden water from the bottom of the tank. Remember that just sticking the hose into the top of the tank does very little to remove the fixer; it merely dilutes it.

A simple and effective way to wash film is to manually fill, dump, and refill the developing tank a minimum of twenty times, with some agitation in between. The chief disadvantage is that such a washing procedure requires continuous attention and quickly becomes very boring.

There are a variety of commercial film washers. The best ones force aerated water uniformly over film that is placed in a special plastic or stainless steel tank.

To save time and water, and to be assured the chemicals are removed, many photographers bathe their films 1 to 2 minutes in a clearing agent. This so-called hypo neutralizer or hypo eliminator can reduce actual wash time to 5 minutes or less.

Adequate washing seems of minor concern to some beginning photographers, because damage to the film often is not evident for months or even years after processing. They are regretful later when some of their negatives have become unprintable because of fixer stain, bleaching, or fading—due to improper washing or processing.

Drying

To help prevent streaks and water spots on the negatives, you can soak film in a wetting agent before hanging the roll up to dry. With one type of wetting agent, Kodak's Photo-Flo Solution, bathe the film for 30 to 60 seconds.

If you also wipe the film to rid it of excess water or wetting agent, use a film clip to hold it securely. To avoid scratches, soak a dry sponge or chamois or squeegee in the wetting agent and wring it out before wiping the film.

Wipe the film slowly and steadily without applying too much pressure. If wiped properly, the film should be visibly free of moisture at the top by the time you reach the bottom of the suspended roll. If you apply too much pressure, the film will make a humming sound, and there's a danger of scratching the wet emulsion.

After the film has been wiped, a weighted clip should be attached at the bottom. If drying two or more rolls, be sure the films are spaced far enough apart to avoid contact with each other. Because film bows as it drys, all emulsions should face the same direction so they will not touch. Figure 2 to 4 hours for film to dry thoroughly in normal room conditions; it will feel dry to the touch sooner but the emulsion may still be soft.

Be certain dust is not stirred up in the drying area (close windows and doors, and turn off any fans). Dust in the air may become embedded in the wet emulsion, and once the film is dry, it is extremely difficult to remove these particles without resoaking the negative. If possible, construct a drying cabinet.

Cleaning Up

As your film is drying, you should begin an important but often overlooked part of darkroom procedure: careful cleanup. All the graduates, tanks, reels, funnels, and other items that have come in contact with chemicals should be thoroughly rinsed in hot water, drained, wiped, and stored. Rinse the tanks and reels particularly well, and as soon after use as possible. If chemicals are allowed to dry on them, a residue may build up and contaminate future processing.

Occasionally, reels and tanks should be soaked in warm soapy water, and sponged off. This will loosen any chemical residue which may be forming. A good rinse in very hot water will finish the job. Dishwasher detergents, like Cascade, do a good job; abrasive cleaners should be avoided because they can scratch smooth surfaces and actually contribute to the buildup of residue.

If you plan to process additional rolls of film immediately, make sure the developing tank's reel is *absolutely dry*. A hand-held hair dryer does a quick and thorough job. Any water on the reel will make it difficult to load the film, and can cause spots on the negatives.

Developing Sheet Films

You have a choice of using tanks or trays for developing sheet films. The chemical types and procedures are the same as for roll films. (See a description of sheet film tanks and trays and other equipment beginning on page 19.)

You can safely process more sheets of film in tanks than in trays. That's because stainless steel or plastic hangers are used to keep the films separated and suspended in the solutions. Also, some sheet film tanks have light-tight covers so room lights can be turned on between agitation cycles.

With *trays,* which is the most economical way to process sheet film, you use your hands to interleaf film for agitation. This limits the number of sheets that can be handled safely, and you must do everything in total darkness. However, if you just process sheet film occasionally, and only a few sheets at a time, trays are adequate.

For a single sheet, arrange three trays in order: developer, stop bath, and fixer. With the lights out, and in a totally dark room, remove the film from the camera film holder or light-tight storage box. Start the timer and slip the film into the developer emulsion side up so that the film's *code notch* will be on the lower right-hand side. Agitate the film continuously by rocking the tray, alternately raising and lowering each side.

When time is up, drain the film briefly, then transfer it with your fingers to the stop bath (water or acid rinse), and rock the tray as before, for a total of 15 to 30 seconds. Drain the film, and move it with your fingers to the fixer. For initial agitation, rock the fixer tray for the first 30 seconds. Agitate briefly in the same manner, at 1-minute intervals, until the recommended fixing time is up. Lights can be turned on after the film is in the fixer one or two minutes. If the film is still cloudy and does not "clear" in one-half the recommended fixer time, the fixer is probably exhausted and should be replaced.

After washing the first two trays, use them for the clearing agent and film washing steps. Finally, bathe the film in a wetting agent, squeegee carefully, and use a clothespin or a film clip to hang up the sheet by one corner for drying.

When several sheets of film are to be developed in trays, limit the number from two to six for uniform processing, and agitate them by *interleaving*. This means putting each sheet in a tray one by one, then pulling out the bottom sheet and placing it on top, and continuing the procedure with successive bottom sheets. Be careful to avoid finger marks or scratches; sheet film corners can dig into the emulsion of other sheets. When moving them to the stop bath and fixer trays, transfer the sheets in the order they were inserted in the developer; the first sheet in should be the first sheet out, and so on.

A *prewetting step* is recommended when tray processing several sheets, in order to keep film from sticking and air bells from forming. Place a tray of water before the developer tray; the water temperature should be the same as the developer's temperature, or within a few degrees.

With the timer set and the lights out, stack up the film to be developed. Immerse the film sheets one by one, emulsion side up, in the tray of water. Handle the film only by its edges, and make sure each sheet is covered by water before immersing the next one. To avoid water spots, keep one hand dry for picking up each sheet from the stack. Interleaf the sheets of film in the water, from bottom to top, at least two times.

Start the timer and transfer the films one by one to the developer, first draining each sheet briefly so the water will not significantly dilute the developer. (If too much dilution occurs, developer time should be increased.) Continue interleaving the film, bottom to top, until developer time is up.

Next, transfer them in order, one by one, to the stop bath. Avoid contamination of the developer by using one hand to pick up the films from the developer and the other hand to put them in the stop bath.

Continue interleaving the films in each of the remaining steps: stop bath, fixer, clearing agent, and wash. Follow the recommended times for each chemical and the wash.

For processing sheet films in *tanks,* film hangers are used to suspend the films and keep them separated. Load these hangers in total darkness, start the timer, and then immerse the films in the developer all at the same time, using an even motion. Rap the hangers a few times on the tank's top edge to dislodge any air bubbles from the film's emulsion.

For agitation, lift all the hangers from the developer, tilt one end of them to a 45-degree angle, then return them to the tank. While in the solutions, try to keep at least one-half inch of space between the hangers. Agitate in the previous manner every 60 seconds, but tilt the hangers in the opposite direction on alternate agitation cycles. Be consistent with the agitation procedure; don't just jiggle the hangers haphazardly. And do not overagitate, or the edges of your negatives will show uneven development where the developer flows in and out of the holes in the hangers.

When developer time is up, continue with the usual processing steps, stop bath and fixer. Washing procedures for sheet film differ from roll film. Washing tanks with film hangers are best, because the hangers allow water to flow safely and uniformly over the film. (Alternatively, you can "leaf" sheets of film in a tray of fresh running water, but periodically empty the tray and be careful not to scratch the film's emulsion.)

Films will dry faster if they are removed from the hangers and squeegeed. Suspend each sheet with a clothespin or film clip from one corner to dry.

After film is properly processed and dried, the resulting negatives are ready to be printed. You can make contact prints, which will be the same size as the negative images, and you can enlarge the negatives to much bigger sizes. Both kinds of printing require additional equipment, and a darkroom.

Push Processing Films

When low light conditions do not permit normal exposures, or if your film's ASA was incorrectly set on the exposure meter, you can still obtain acceptable results by making adjustments during film processing. You can "save" underexposed film by forcing development, which is more commonly referred to as *push processing*. That means that you increase the film development time to compensate for the underexposure. (Likewise, you can also save overexposed film by decreasing the film developer time.)

Push processing often compromises quality. But it allows you to get a printable result, despite increases in contrast and grain. (With color films, it can have a slight effect on color balance too.)

When film is exposed and processed normally, it has the capacity to record a wide range of tones—from the shadow areas to the highlights—and thus give a good *contrast ratio*. When film is push processed, there is relatively little change in shadow areas but highlights show a significant increase in density, thus increasing the contrast ratio. The reverse is true when you overexpose and compensate by reducing film development: you decrease the contrast ratio.

Many photographers use these principles to help them control contrast in a particular shooting situation: overexpose and underdevelop to reduce contrast, and underexpose and overdevelop to increase contrast.

A systematic approach to contrast control, the Zone System, was established by Ansel Adams, and has been interpreted in various ways by other photographers, including Minor White and Fred Picker. (For a brief summary of the Zone System and techniques for more control of your black-and-white photographs, see page 268.)

Push processing involves a change in developer time with normal film developers, and the following adjustments are suggested as a starting point; testing is best to determine the exact developer time for your particular developer and film and effective film speed.

Film Exposure	*Change in Developer Time*
4 times (2 f/stops) underexposure	increase by 75 percent
2½ times (1⅓ f/stops) underexposure	increase by 50 percent
2 times (1 f/stop) underexposure	increase by 35 percent
NORMAL ASA FILM SPEED	USE NORMAL TIME
2 times (1 f/stop) overexposure	decrease by 30 percent
4 times (2 f/stops) overexposure	decrease by 50 percent

If you are in a shooting situation where you know you will have to push process your film, set your exposure meter with the ASA film speed that is equal to the amount of under- or overexposure. For instance, for underexposures with ASA 400 film, like Kodak's Tri-X, set the meter's ASA to 800 for two times (one f/stop) under, 1000 for two-and-one-half times (1⅓ f/stop) under, or 1600 for four times (two f/stops) under. These will be the effective speeds of your ASA 400 film when you push process by the initial suggestion of a 35, 50, or 75 percent increase in developer time, as per the chart above.

For black-and-white films, there are some *high energy developers* designed to increase the effective ASA of film and produce better grain and contrast results than what you get by push processing in your normal developer. High energy developers, such as UFG, Acufine, and Diafine, enable you to increase the relative film speed two to four times the normal ASA. Tri-X, normally ASA 400, can be increased to ASA 800 or 1200 when processed in Acufine, and up to ASA 1600 when processed in Diafine. Kodak's 2475 35mm recording film can be shot as ASA 3200 when developed in Acufine, and at ASA 4000 when developed in Kodak's DK-50. Kodak's Royal-X 120-size film, when developed in Acufine, can also be shot at ASA 4000. These ratings are all approximate, and are suggested by the developers' manufacturer, so you should run your own tests to be sure you'll achieve the results desired.

Regardless of the film developer you are using, if you are uncertain that the film was properly exposed (and thus uncertain of the developer time), you may want to make a *snip test.* This means cutting off a few inches of exposed roll film, and developing it first. Use your normal developer time. If over- or underexposed, use the preceding chart to decrease or increase developer time. You may want to make another snip test at the revised developer time before processing the remainder of the roll.

You can also *develop by inspection,* but it is not easy to judge the film's development because you must do this with a dark green safelight (No. 3), kept at least four feet from the film. Also, your inspection should not begin until half the total developer time has elapsed, and it should last only a few seconds in order to avoid fogging the film with the safelight.

In total darkness, remove the developing tank top, pull out the reel, and unwind several inches of film. Turn on the safelight and look through the film to see if an image has appeared, or if the image is already quite dense. Extend or stop development accordingly. You may want to practice developing by inspection with a test roll in order to determine how to analyze the film quickly with a dim green safelight. Purposely make normal, as well as over- and underexposures, so you can view the different results with the safelight.

Errors in Exposure and Film Processing

After your negatives are processed, it's time to analyze them. Before considering negatives technically for film processing errors, check them generally for exposure.

Negatives that are dense or dark have been *overexposed;* too much light reached the film. With the proper photo paper and enlarging technique, however, acceptable prints can be made from many overexposed negatives. Overexposed negatives also can be reduced in density by a chemical process (see page 133).

Why are the negatives overexposed? It may be the result of using an incorrect, low ASA film speed with your hand-held or built-in camera exposure meter. Or perhaps you incorrectly aimed the meter when reading the light. Maybe you accidentally set the lens f/stop too wide, or the shutter speed too slow. If the exposure meter window of an automatic camera was blocked, it adjusted exposure for darker lighting conditions than actually existed. With overexposed flash pictures, the wrong flash guide number was used, or the flash was too close to the subject.

Negatives that are light or "thin" have been *underexposed;* not enough light reached the film. In many cases, however, underexposed negatives will produce acceptable prints if the proper photo paper and enlarging technique are used. Underexposed negatives also can be intensified by a chemical process (see page 133).

Underexposed negatives may be the result of too little light being available for shooting, or too high an ASA film speed set on your exposure meter. Perhaps you read the light incorrectly with your meter. Or you wrongly set the lens f/stop too small, or the shutter speed too fast. With underexposed flash pictures, the wrong flash guide number was used, or the flash was too far from the subject.

Sometimes your negatives will be completely clear, which indicates the film was *unexposed.* This often occurs when the film is not properly loaded in the camera and does not advance as expected, so no exposures are made. Or you may have processed an unexposed roll of film. To avoid this with 35mm film, make a practice of rewinding the film completely into the cassette after the final exposure. That way it cannot be confused with fresh film, which still has its leader showing. Unexposed film also results if the shutter does not open, the lens cap was left on, or the flash does not go off.

Sometimes the flash is simply not synchronized to fire when the shutter is open, and an unexposed negative results. With focal plane shutters common in 35mm SLR cameras, occasionally only a portion of the film frame is exposed. Again, faulty synchronization is the problem; the shutter speed was too fast. With electronic flash at X synchronization, focal plane shutters should be set no faster than 1/60 or 1/125 second, according to the camera's instructions.

Flash failure, and thus unexposed film, can be caused a number of ways. Batteries may be exhausted, uncharged, or dirty and not making contact. Connecting flash cords may be broken internally or improperly attached. The bulb, cube, or electronic flash unit itself may be faulty. Or flashcubes were used on cameras designed only for battery-less Magicubes.

Your negatives may reveal other problems that should not be considered processing errors. You might notice clear areas or fuzzy gray shapes in the negatives, indicating something blocked the light from reaching portions of your film. Often this is caused by dirt in the camera, including small pieces of film or lint. (Dust the inside of your camera carefully.) Other causes include a finger, part of the camera case, or your camera strap being in front of the lens. This frequently happens with rangefinder cameras, because the photographer sees the subject through a viewfinder while the film records it through another lens.

Dark streaks may show up in your negatives. These can occur when rays of sun, or bright lights, shine directly on the lens. (Keep the lens shaded.) Another reason for such streaks is that your film may be *"fogged."* This happens when light accidentally reaches the film, as when the camera back comes open unexpectedly, or when the camera is dropped and its light-tight body is damaged.

Sometimes, of course, your negatives will reveal mistakes made during processing, rather than camera-related errors. Some are subtle, such as incorrect contrast, but others show up as distinct and curious marks. Some of the more common ones are listed.

Half-moons are dark crescent shapes that appear in the negative where the film was wrinkled or creased, usually when loading it onto a reel for processing.

Cinch marks are parallel scratches on the emulsion, generally occurring when a roll of film is wound too tightly. This may happen if you drop an unprocessed film in the darkroom and decide to tighten it on the spool by pulling the end of the roll. (Cinch marks also can occur if you try to rewind a 35mm roll into its cassette and forget to press the camera's film rewind release button. Or if the film sticks in your camera and you try to advance or rewind it by force.)

12. *Careless handling during processing caused the scratches and chemical spots on a negative that are evident in this print. (Dust on the negative during printing added the white marks.)*

Static marks are lightninglike black lines caused by static electricity that is created when film is unrolled too quickly in a darkroom with low humidity. (Static marks also are caused in the camera when film is advanced or rewound too rapidly in dry weather conditions.)

Air bells are round, nearly clear spots formed where developer is unable to reach the emulsion because of air bubbles; rough agitation at the start of development prevents the problem by dislodging air bubbles. If the spots are yellow, the air bells occurred in the fixer; again, proper agitation is the only way to avoid this problem.

Surge marks are short dark streaks that can occur at the sprocket holes of 35mm film because of excessive agitation. They may also be noticed along the edges of sheet film processed in hangers, because excessive agitation causes the developer to surge through the hangers' holes.

Black spots often are foreign particles that become imbedded in the emulsion during washing or drying.

13. *Air bells, caused by improper agitation, kept developer from reaching the film emulsion uniformly; they show up as dark spots when the negative is printed.*

14. *Too much agitation in the developer caused surge marks to appear opposite the sprocket holes in this 35mm film.*

Minute clear spots are caused by dust on the film that blocks the light during exposure; keep the inside of your camera clean.

Brown or purple spots can be caused by particles of powdered developer that adhered to the film before processing; avoid this by mixing chemicals in another room or several days in advance of processing.

Water marks are gray spots that occur where water drops dry on the emulsion or back of a film. Use a wetting agent to help prevent them, and squeegee the film carefully, too. Spots with a dark outline are caused by water drops falling on the film after it has dried.

Clear or cloudy portions may appear if there is insufficient developer or fixer to completely cover the film during processing. Inadequate agitation may be another cause. If the clear or cloudy areas are irregular but distinct, portions of the film probably were sticking to each other during development or fixing. Usually that is due to loading film on the reel improperly. A milky appearance can be caused by a weak or exhausted fixer; refix the negatives in fresh fixer.

Mottle is blotchy, uneven development caused by lack of agitation, or the use of film that is past its expiration date.

Reticulation is an irregular cracking of the film's emulsion, which is caused by a drastic difference in temperature between one processing solution and another, or between the film and the processing solutions, including wash water.

Fogging can destroy the image, or part of it, by turning the negative black or gray. It can be caused by a light leak in the darkroom or developing tank or camera, or by exposure of the film to a safelight.

Fingerprints will be obvious, and you can tell when you got careless and touched the film. Moist fingers on a dry negative make distinct lines; fingers contaminated with developer leave a dark mark; and fingers wet with fixer make light fingermarks.

15. *When film is improperly loaded on a reel for processing, it may stick together and prevent chemicals from acting on portions of the emulsion, as indicated by the black mark in this negative.*

Evaluating Negative Density and Contrast

Negatives also can be evaluated for density and contrast. Density is determined by exposure, while contrast can be altered somewhat during processing, either by overdevelopment or underdevelopment. Sometimes a change from normal development (with a resulting change in contrast) is just a processing error, caused by using an incorrect developer time, or using developer temperatures that are too hot or too cold. Other times, overdevelopment or underdevelopment is done purposely.

You should "read" negatives to determine the reasons for their density and contrast. For instance, a negative of normal density, indicating correct exposure, has detail in both highlight areas and shadow areas. A dense negative has been overexposed, which means details in the highlights will be blocked up. A thin negative has been underexposed, which means there will be a lack of detail in the shadow areas.

Regarding contrast, a negative of normal contrast indicates normal development, a contrasty negative indicates overdevelopment, and a flat (uncontrasty) negative indicates underdevelopment.

Combining this knowledge about contrast and density, you'll be able to judge a negative—although it may take practice. For instance, a thin negative (lacking shadow detail) with other tones too contrasty indicates the film was underexposed and overdeveloped. A dense negative (no highlight detail) with other tones too contrasty means the film was overexposed and overdeveloped. A dense negative with flat (uncontrasty) tones indicates the film was overexposed and underdeveloped.

Always study your negatives for exposure and various film processing errors to help improve your camera and darkroom techniques.

Filing Negatives

Rather than leave a roll of film its full length, most photographers cut the film into manageable strips for proofing, filing, and use in the enlarger. For example, 35mm film is conveniently cut into strips of five or six frames, while 120-size is best cut into three or four frames per strip, depending on whether the images are 2¼ inches square or 2¼ x 2¾ inches. Such strips can be contact-proof printed easily, and will fill one 8 x 10-inch sheet of printing paper per roll of 35mm or 120 film.

16. Properly exposed and processed film yields negatives with good density and contrast, and they will produce prints with similar qualities. In this photograph, a migrating whale dives underwater along the southern California coast.

The negative strips should be stored in either glassine or clear plastic sleeves, which are available individually or in notebook-size pages. The pages are especially convenient because they hold a full roll, including thirty-six-exposure 35mm-size film cut into six strips. These pages can be filed in a notebook together with the proof sheets, which makes it simple to locate any negative very quickly. You can arrange them according to subject, location, or date of shooting.

Except for some bulk-loaded film, most roll and cartridge films have their individual frames prenumbered by the manufacturer. It is also advisable to establish a coding system for each roll of film. A numbering code might include the year, month, day, and roll number; the code "77215-3" would mean roll no. 3 shot on February 15, 1977.

The code numbers should be written on the proof sheet and on the edge of each strip of film, as well as an index in front of your notebook. Use a fine point pen and India ink or Pelican fine drawing ink. It may not be necessary to write the code on more than one strip of negatives per roll, if they are filed in pages with the proofs. But if you anticipate separating the strips, it is a good idea to code each strip. With sheet film, it's best to put your code number on each negative.

Regardless of how you file your negatives, just be sure to do so after every processing session. Otherwise your negatives are bound to get mixed up or damaged.

4

Establishing a Darkroom

As you learned by reading the preceding chapter, processing film doesn't require a photographic darkroom. But the next phase, making prints and enlargements from negatives, calls for a dark space at least big enough for an enlarger, safelight, processing trays, and yourself.

All windows, doors, or vents in your darkroom should be sealed against light. For windows, cover them first with aluminum foil to reflect any heat and block most of the light, then cover an area larger than the window with dark cloth. Vents can be covered with dark cloth, too. Most doors can be sealed with a strip of molding lined with foam insulation, plus a small piece of black cloth tacked to the bottom of the door and allowed to trail on the floor. Although it must be blocked to any outside light, a darkroom does not have to be painted black. In fact, painting a darkroom white allows better vision in the subdued illumination of safelights.

If the room is to be used only for print processing and not for film tank loading or film developing, stray light is less of a consideration. Make this check: If you see no light after 2 minutes in the dark, the room is safe for printing with most papers; if you still cannot see light after five minutes, it is safe for film loading or processing. Your eyes are like a very sensitive light meter, and it is likely that in any darkroom other than a tomb, you will be able to see leaks of light after 30 minutes. But unless you can see the light being cast on another surface, there is little need to be concerned, except if you are using extremely high speed or infrared film, or printing with very sensitive color materials.

When laying out a darkroom, consideration should be given to "wet and dry" areas. Some separation should be provided between the printing (dry) area and the developing (wet) area. In a small room, this can be a problem unless you build a splash barrier between your enlarger and the processing trays. Trays also can be arranged in a tiered fashion to occupy less space.

The *dry area* should have space to include the enlarger, enlarging easel, magnifier, printing paper in a light-tight box or paper safe, timer, paper cutter, negative dusting brush or can of compressed air, burning and dodging tools, and unprinted negatives.

In the *wet area* are processing trays (minimum of three), print tongs, towel, and a sink with running water, if possible. Above the trays should be a

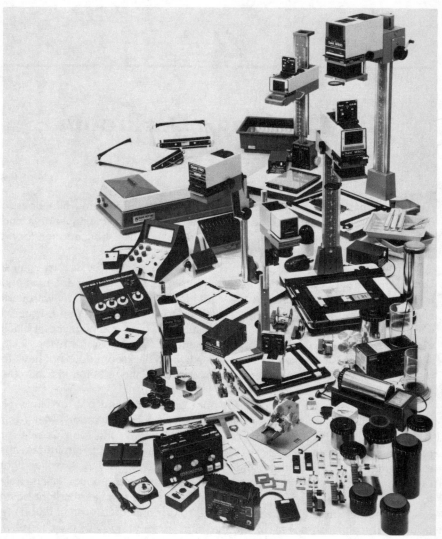

17. *An unbelievable amount of darkroom equipment is available, but it is really the photographer's skill in processing and printing that determines the quality of the final photograph.*

safelight, and a fairly large clock with a sweep second hand that can be read easily in safelight illumination. This will be used to time the print development process (an inexpensive kitchen clock is ideal). For color print processing in a tube, you can use the wet area designated for trays.

Running water in the darkroom itself is not a necessity, but a time-saving convenience. Conventional (not resin-coated) printing paper can be kept briefly in a stand bath of water after fixing, and then transferred to a washing area outside the darkroom. If you use such a *water stand bath* in lieu of

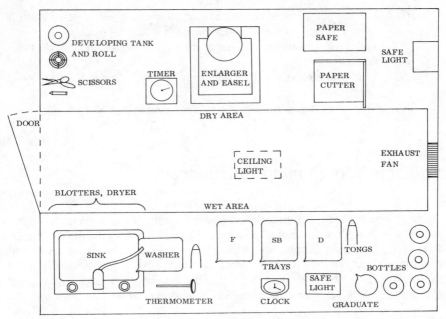

18. *The floor plan of a comfortable darkroom, with dry and wet areas on opposite sides to keep chemical solutions from accidentally harming films, negatives, or print papers.*

immediate washing, be sure to use a deep pan or tray, change the water frequently, and agitate the prints occasionally. Otherwise, the fixer, although diluted by the water, might bleach print images. Ideally, any sink should be large enough to accommodate a print washer or wash tray with a siphon.

If you do have space for a completely equipped darkroom, you should also consider the following conveniences in your plans:

1) A heated print dryer, or a rack for print-drying screens. (Window screens with plastic or fiberglass mesh are excellent for drying prints without marring their surfaces.)
2) A pegboard near the enlarger for hanging enlarging implements like dodging tools, negative carriers, masks, scissors, and tape.
3) A white light or safelight box built into a tabletop for viewing negatives.
4) A white viewing light, with a 40- or 60-watt bulb, directly over the fixer for viewing wet prints.
5) A large sheet of glass over the final wash area on which to squeegee or sponge excess water from prints prior to drying.
6) A drying cabinet, or at least a space for a clothesline to hang wet film (or prints) to dry undisturbed.

7) A water filtration attachment, and perhaps a water temperature control device, especially important for color processing.
8) A ventilation system to remove chemical odors and provide fresh air.
9) A radio or stereo tape machine to make your time in the darkroom more pleasant.
10) A nonshag rug, with padding, to ease your feet; and a tall stool.

Equipment for Printing and Enlarging

More equipment is required for making prints than developing film, although some of the same equipment can be used, such as the thermometer, measuring graduate, funnel, and timer. Here is a complete list of basic and optional equipment for producing black-and-white *and* color prints. Optional items are marked by a #. Descriptions of the equipment follow, and starred (*) items indicate additional details will be found in chapter 12, ''Preparing to Make Color Prints.''

Enlarger*
Enlarger lens*
Enlarger negative carrier
Variable contrast filters
Color printing (CP) filters*
Enlarger color head*#
Voltage regulator/stabilizer*#
Enlarging easel
Enlarging timer*
Enlarging magnifier
Enlarging meter#
Color analyzer*#
Safelight(s)*
Paper cutter
Paper safe#
Anti-static brush, cloth, or can of compressed air
Contact printing frame or glass
Processing trays
Color processing tube*
Thermometer*
Measuring graduate
Stirring rod
Funnel
Storage bottles

Print tongs
Processing timer*
Print washer
Print dryer, blotters, or drying screens
Print squeegee
Tools for dodging and burning-in
Towels
Printing paper
Chemicals

Recently there has been a renewed interest in the darkroom, thanks to the latest processes that make printing color negatives and slides easier, less expensive, and more satisfying than in the past. Equipment manufacturers have seen the potential profits and have begun introducing a greater variety of darkroom equipment, particularly enlargers.

Enlargers

In regard to the purchase of an enlarger, a major investment, an important criterion should be whether you intend making black-and-white or color enlargements, or both. Because filtration is required when exposing color papers, most enlargers have special drawers where square sheets of acetate filters can be placed below the enlarger bulb. But this manual method of preparing filtration is being replaced by permanent filters that are built into the enlarger head's illumination system. Instead of putting filters into a drawer, photographers simply turn knobs on the enlarger to select proper filtration. Enlargers equipped with such *dichroic filter color heads* permit fast and accurate filtration, and make color printing more enjoyable than in the past. They are a wise choice if you are serious about making quick and high quality color prints.

If you're currently unsure about your interest in color work, or unable to afford the color head, consider purchasing an enlarger that can be converted at a later date. These so-called modular enlargers can be fitted with different heads—one has an optical illumination system for black-and-white (i.e. appropriate condensors and enlarger bulb), and another has dichroic filters, quartz halogen lamp, and special ventilation for color work.

There are so many styles, sizes, types, and models of enlargers that even knowledgeable photographers have difficulty choosing the "best" one. Some of the more popular enlarger brands, with models for both professional and home use, are Beseler, Durst, and Omega.

Before purchasing an enlarger, compare them by reading the man-ufacturers' literature and the technical reports published in photo mag-

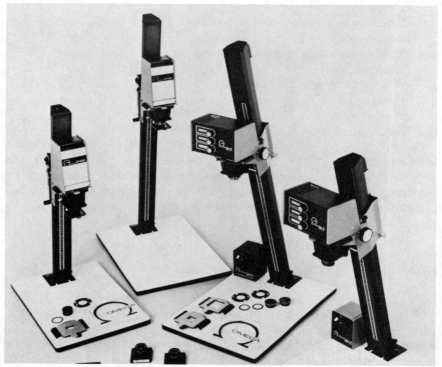

19. Enlargers of modular design can be fitted with various "heads," some with different illumination systems for black-and-white work and others for color printing with dichroic filters.

azines, and by getting personal opinions from people who already have an enlarger. Two important considerations are the size limit of negatives the enlarger will accommodate, and the enlarger's illumination system.

In selecting the best enlarger for your current needs, say 35mm, consider whether someday you might use larger format cameras and film. Although enlargers are designed to accommodate certain sizes of negatives, those that are for larger size negatives usually can be altered to accommodate smaller negatives. This is done by changing the enlarger lens, the condensor lenses, and the negative carrier.

Enlargers are commonly designed for 35mm and Instamatic (126-size) negatives; 120-size films (for 2¼ x 2¼ inches and 2¼ x 2¾ inches or 6 x 7 cm negatives); and 4 x 5-inch sheet films. There are a few models for larger negatives like 5 x 7 inches and 8 x 10 inches.

It's important that your enlarger provides uniform illumination for the size(s) of negatives it is designed to handle. That means light distribution over the total image area of a negative must be even. A frequent problem is that an enlarger gives less exposure at the edges of the print; be certain to check closely the manufacturer's claims concerning negative coverage. Also helpful in determining "corner to corner" illumination of negatives are the technical reports on specific enlargers printed in some photo magazines.

With the popular *condensor* enlargers, light is concentrated by a pair or more of opposing pieces of convex, optical glass condensors. The light source usually is a single tungsten lamp, frosted or clear. A frosted bulb is common, yielding fairly sharp detail and good contrast. A clear bulb gives sharper detail with slightly higher contrast, and requires that the condensors themselves be refocused whenever the enlarger height is changed.

With *diffusion* enlargers, light passes through a piece of frosted (diffusion) glass rather than condensors. A frosted bulb is commonly used as the light source. The lamp housing must be highly reflective and nearly spherical, so that the light is evenly cast onto the diffusion glass. Diffusion enlargers produce soft contrast, and are often used for printing portraits.

Many enlargers are the *condensor-diffusion* type, which use a combination of condensor lenses and frosted diffusion glass to provide excellent image brightness and good contrast. Some enlargers can be altered from condensor to condensor-diffusion by simply inserting special diffusion glass.

The illumination systems used in most color heads with dichroic filters are diffusion types, although some, like Vivitar's Dioptic light source, are a condensor type.

Remember that enlargers using tungsten bulbs require special enlarger lamps, not regular household bulbs which may cause shadows, uneven illumination, or improper colors. Use only the bulb type and wattage designed for your specific enlarger and printing paper.

Diffusion and condensor-diffusion enlargers normally use screw-base 75- or 150-watt tungsten bulbs; those equipped with a dichroic filter color head often feature 75- to 250-watt quartz-halogen lamps for their light source.

There are some *cold-light* enlargers that avoid tungsten bulbs and use a grid work of gas-filled glass tubes mounted in the lamp housing above the diffusion glass. An electrical transformer is required to maintain their steady illumination throughout the exposure. Since the light source is "cold," there is no heat to warp the negative during exposure. This is particularly important with negatives requiring long exposures, as when photo murals are made. Such cold light sources offer uniform distribution of light, minimize grain, and can be adapted to many enlargers currently on the market. They are preferred by many fine print makers.

Some early-model diffusion enlargers have a fluorescent light source, and are also called cold-light enlargers. But these do not work well with modern variable contrast papers for black-and-white, or for color printing papers, because their fluorescent light is bluish and thus not *color balanced* for these papers.

There are a few other enlarger light systems used in special cases: arc light for very high intensity, Xenon-pulsed lamps, mercury-vapor tubes, and even sunlight.

Enlarger lens(es). Very few enlargers, except the least expensive ones, are sold with a lens because there is a great difference in price and quality of such lenses. Focal lengths also will vary, according to the size of the negatives you want to enlarge.

Enlarger lenses are special because they are designed to work with the flat fields of the negative and the print, rather than the curved field for which camera lenses are normally designed. As with camera lenses, most enlarger lenses are coated to reduce flare and improve image contrast.

Also, your enlarger must be able to accommodate the physical size and design of a lens; some small enlargers may not be able to hold some lenses because of their weight or because of recessed or extended mounting threads.

Focal length must be appropriate for the size of negative being enlarged, and the choice also depends on the largest print size you want to make. It should produce at least an 11 x 14-inch print directly on the enlarger's baseboard. The normal enlarger lens focal lengths are:

    25 to 35mm for 110-size or subminiature negatives
    50 or 60mm for 35mm or 126-size negatives
    75 or 80mm for 2¼ x 2¼-inch negatives
    90 or 105mm for 2¼ x 2¾-inch (6 x 7 cm) or 2¼ x 3¼-inch negatives
    135 or 150mm for 4 x 5-inch negatives
    180mm for 5 x 7-inch negatives
    300mm for 8 x 10-inch negatives

Generally, you should not use a focal length lens shorter than normal because some areas of your negative will not be uniformly illuminated. However, there are now some wide angle (i.e. shorter than normal focal length) enlarging lenses on the market that can be used successfully with larger size negatives. The reason that many photographers use *longer* than normal focal length lenses is that they assure complete and more even illumination of the negative. The problem, however, is that a longer lens focal length reduces the size of the projected image. Most enlargers will extend to a height that allows 11 x 14 or 16 x 20-inch prints, when the focal length is normal for the negatives' size (i.e. 50mm lens for 35mm negatives). With a longer lens, the enlarger head must be a greater distance from the paper to produce a large size print. Recently introduced are some zoom-type lenses for enlargers, which have variable focal lengths and allow you to change the image size without changing the enlarger's height.

When choosing a fixed focal length lens that is normal for your negative size, be certain your lens/enlarger combination gives even illumination over the entire negative. This is done by opening the lens to its maximum aperture and visually checking the light projected through the negative carrier. Also, you can make an imageless medium gray print, and then examine its edges and corners to see if there is any variance in the gray. If you find light is coming through unevenly, test the lens at different aperture openings until you find the f/stop beyond which the illumination is uniform. Adopt this f/stop as the *maximum* aperture to use during exposure.

Of course, a small aperture can be a handicap when printing very dense negatives which require long exposures. A temporary way of overcoming the problem of uneven illumination is to burn in the edges of your prints to compensate for the fall-off of light. The only convenient solution, however, is to use a lens of slightly larger focal length.

Another consideration is the speed of the enlarger lens. Most lenses designed for printing are not very "fast" when compared to camera lenses. Enlarger lenses have a maximum f/4.5 or f/3.5 opening, although some are slightly faster with f/2.8 apertures. This is not really a problem unless you make extremely large prints, such as mural size, or if you expect to do rapid printing, and hope to keep exposure time as short as possible. Overheating negatives during very lengthy exposures can cause them to buckle, resulting in an out-of-focus print.

Remember that only the very best enlarger lenses are sharp at extreme aperture openings, so try to avoid using most lenses at their maximum or minimum openings when exposing. Minimum openings are usually f/16 or f/22 on 50mm or 75mm lenses.

A final rule of thumb: the higher the price of an enlarger lens, the better its quality. Buy the best one that will fit in your budget.

Enlarger negative carriers. Important but often overlooked when purchasing an enlarger is its negative carrier. This carrier is a device designed to hold the negative flat and centered within the most uniform area of light

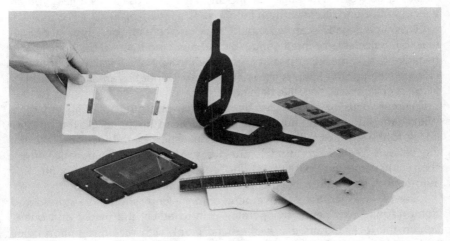

20. *Negative carriers, both glass and glassless, are of various designs and accommodate different sizes of negatives.*

coming from the enlarger head. It also acts as a mask to keep stray light from being projected onto the photo paper. One type is called *glassless* or *dustless,* while the other is a *glass negative carrier.* If a carrier scratches your negative, or allows it to buckle during exposure, the carrier is worthless. Check to make sure the carrier is smooth on all surfaces that come in contact with the negative, and that it holds the negative flat.

Some carriers lock into the enlarger, while others can be rotated or otherwise repositioned so the projected image can be realigned on the baseboard or enlarging easel without touching the negative itself. At least be sure the carrier can be inserted into the enlarger without the negative being touched. Some carriers allow a strip of negatives to be moved back and forth to different frames by using some kind of pressure release device on the enlarger head. This is primarily an aid for fast printing, but not for quality, because you should dust off each individual negative frame before printing.

When considering negative carriers, note that some manufacturers offer both the glass type, which sandwiches the negative as flat as possible, and the one that is glassless, which is less of a problem regarding dust. Using a glass-type carrier is the best way to guarantee that the negative will be in overall focus, particularly when subjected to heat from the enlarger light during long exposures. However, glass carriers present the problems of cleaning and possibly scratching because there are four additional surfaces (besides the negative) through which the light passes.

Another concern with glass-type negative carriers is that they often produce the phenomenon known as "Newton's Rings." These are irregular rainbow-colored rings that are created when two or more smooth surfaces (like two pieces of glass, or glass and a negative) are pressed together with air spaces in between. The rings will appear in the print as circles unless you are very attentive and discover them before making the exposure.

Glass-type negative carriers should be equipped with some type of opaque mask(s), adjustable or interchangeable, so any area beyond the edges of the negative can be masked off to keep stray white light of the enlarger lamp from reaching the photo paper. A glassless negative carrier has an exact opening to fit the specific size of negative being enlarged.

Enlarger focusing. There are both manual and auto-focusing enlargers. With manual focus, you adjust the enlarger head height to get the negative image to the size desired, and then you must sharpen the focus by adjusting the bellows. Auto-focus models are designed to keep the negative image sharp whenever the position of the enlarger is changed, although most auto-focus types require fine focus adjustments anyway.

Ease of enlarger head movement, and locking, should be considered. Some require two hands to operate—one to adjust the height and one to tighten the lock. Others use a one-hand crank with rack-and-pinion gears, and some models feature a one-hand clamp release with a balance weight or spring to afford easy adjustments.

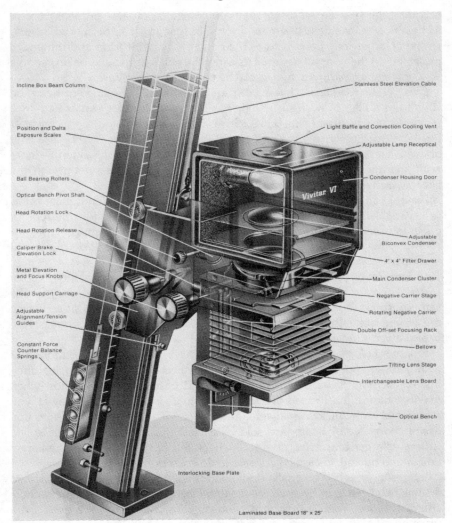

Incline Box Beam Column

Position and Delta Exposure Scales

Ball Bearing Rollers

Optical Bench Pivot Shaft

Head Rotation Lock

Head Rotation Release

Caliper Brake Elevation Lock

Metal Elevation and Focus Knobs

Head Support Carriage

Adjustable Alignment/Tension Guides

Constant Force Counter Balance Springs

Interlocking Base Plate

Stainless Steel Elevation Cable

Light Baffle and Convection Cooling Vent

Adjustable Lamp Receptical

Condenser Housing Door

Vivitar VI

Adjustable Biconvex Condenser

4" x 4" Filter Drawer

Main Condenser Cluster

Negative Carrier Stage

Rotating Negative Carrier

Double Off-set Focusing Rack

Bellows

Tilting Lens Stage

Interchangeable Lens Board

Optical Bench

Laminated Base Board 18" x 25"

21. *Modern enlargers have trim lines and a variety of structural and functional features.*

Enlarger support. Even if well focused, your pictures may appear fuzzy if the enlarger vibrates during exposure. That's why it is important to check the design and sturdiness of the enlarger's support column. Some are simple round posts, while others are shaped like I-beams, T's, or triangles. Some enlargers have double-post design to assure rigidness and avoid vibrations, even when the enlarger is moved to the very top of the support.

Enlarger baseboard. The enlarger's baseboard should be noted, too, to see if it is able to hold the enlarger steady. It also should be big enough to accommodate the largest size of prints you make most often, perhaps 16 x 20 inches. For extra big enlargements, some baseboards can be turned around so the enlarger may be moved to the edge of the work table and the image projected on the floor. Other models allow the enlarger head to be turned to a 90-degree angle so larger images can be projected on the wall.

Enlarger filter drawer. Unless your enlarger has a dichroic color head, be sure it has a filter drawer for holding the filters required for variable contrast papers or for making color prints. Such a drawer is located in the enlarger head, below the light source and above the negative carrier. Without a filter drawer, filters can be used below the enlarging lens, but this often reduces print sharpness because the projected negative image passes through the filters, which may be dirty, scratched, or optically poor.

Variable contrast filters are required when making black-and-white prints with variable contrast papers. These filters make it possible for one type of paper to yield several grades of contrast. With Kodak's Polycontrast paper, for example, such filters will produce contrast grades of 1, 1½, 2, 2½, 3, 3½, and 4. (See more details on page 75.)

Color printing (CP) filters are used to produce correct color balance in color prints. They are placed in the filter drawer in the enlarger head. Used for the same purpose, but less common, are *color compensating (CC) filters* which are placed beneath the enlarger lens because the enlarger does not have a filter drawer. (See more details on page 185.)

Enlarger color head. As mentioned previously, there are newer models of enlargers equipped with a color head, which is a lamp housing featuring built-in *dichroic filters* that permit quick and easy filtration selection when making color prints. Instead of placing filters in an enlarger's filter drawer, you simply dial in the yellow, magenta, and/or cyan filtration at the densities you desire. Some color heads are sold as accessories and can be attached to certain enlarger brands and models. Check this possibility with any enlarger you intend buying, in case you decide to do color printing at a later date.

Interestingly, while originally designed for color work, the dichroic filters in a color head also can be used for making black-and-white prints on variable contrast paper. They will control contrast, thus eliminating the need for a separate set of variable contrast filters. (See also page 75.)

Enlarger voltage regulator/stabilizer. Another item worth considering, particularly for quality color printing, is a voltage regulator/stabilizer. This regulator/stabilizer prevents surges or drops in the electric voltage line from damaging the enlarger bulb or changing its intensity. Such a constant voltage device assures consistent exposures, particularly important when short exposure times are required, or when several prints are being made from the same negative.

22. *Enlarging easels come in many styles, with fixed image sizes or adjustable borders.*

Enlarging Easels

An important printing aid to purchase carefully is an enlarging easel. It holds the photo paper flat so the focused negative remains sharp in the print. Many easels also produce white borders around the edges of prints. The most common and versatile models have *adjustable borders*. These easels are available for papers up to 8 x 10-, 11 x 14-, and 16 x 20-inch sizes. Some have fixed guides on two edges to give ¼-inch borders. More sophisticated easels allow wide border adjustments on all four sides. The best easels have smooth, nonskid bottoms.

Another type is the *single-size easel* that accommodates paper the exact size of the easel—2½ x 3½, 3½ x 5, 4 x 5, 5 x 7, 8 x 10, 11 x 14, or 16 x 20 inches—and makes a ¼- or ⅜-inch white border all around. This type is best used where speed is required in printing, but a disadvantage is that you need a different easel for every size print required. And they cannot be adjusted for cropping negatives to make odd-size enlargements.

Borderless easels give no borders, but hold the paper flat. Some are only for one specific paper size, while the most versatile can be adjusted to various sizes. More expensive *vacuum easels* hold the paper flat wherever you place it, and can be used to make borderless prints of any size.

Multiprint easels allow the printing paper to be moved beneath a light-tight mask so a large sheet of paper can be used to make multiple prints. This is the fastest way of printing small multiple images on a single sheet of paper, such as wallet-size pictures, that are later cut apart.

Enlarging Timer

Besides an enlarger and the related equipment already discussed, a few more items are helpful, if not essential, to the enlarging process. One is a timer which connects to the enlarger's light cord and controls exposure time. Most will operate up to 60 seconds. Some must be reset manually for each exposure, while others return automatically to a preset exposure time. Many have luminescent dials. Some timers can be started by an *accessory foot switch,* leaving the photographer's hands free. The best models will also turn safelights off during focusing, so it's easier to see the projected negative image, and also during exposure, so the photo paper will not be fogged. A few models give an *audible signal* every second, which is especially helpful when you are dodging or burning-in and cannot look at the timer to see how much time has passed—you count the number of clicks (seconds). Newer timers are solid state and some have *digital readouts* instead of moving dials.

Enlarging Magnifier

An enlarging magnifier also is a worthwhile expenditure because it enables the photographer to focus the negative image sharply and easily. The magnifier is placed where the photo paper will be, and the enlarger's focus control is adjusted until the image appears sharply focused in the magnifier.

Enlarging Meter

An enlarging meter can be a time- and paper-saver by helping you determine exposure time without making black-and-white test prints or strips. Like some camera exposure meters, enlarging meters often utilize CdS or silicon cells that make overall (integrated) and/or spot readings.

The density of the projected negative image is read by the meter, which has been set according to the speed and/or contrast grade of your paper. The meter then indicates the length of time for exposure. Before purchasing an enlarging meter, read the instruction sheets of the various brands and models to determine which one, if any, best suits your needs.

Color Analyzer

A color analyzer is a timesaver for determining the proper filtration and exposure for printing color negatives or transparencies. It takes some practice to use effectively, but an analyzer can eliminate the guesswork in color printing. (For the procedure, and more details, see page 195.)

Safelights

Safelights, with low-wattage bulbs and proper filters, can be used to provide illumination in the darkroom. A safelight with an OC (light amber) filter will not affect most black-and-white photo papers, provided the paper is kept at least 4 feet from the light. Bulb wattage varies from 7½ to 15 watts depending on the size of the safelight; do not exceed the manufacturer's recommended wattage, or your paper may be fogged by the safelight. (See also page 194 for details on safelights for color printing papers.)

Paper Cutter

Scissors are inadequate for cutting photo paper or trimming prints, so purchase a paper cutter to use in your darkroom. Some models have a slicing arm, while others feature a rotating disc blade. Buy one large enough to accommodate the largest paper size you intend using. A paper cutter will be a moneysaver because you can buy quantities of large size paper and cut it down under safelight to the other standard sizes you may need. For example, 8 x 10 paper can be cut into two 5 x 7 sheets (with an inch left over), or four 4 x 5 sheets.

Paper Safe

A paper safe, or homemade light-tight paper drawer, is a good, time-saving darkroom accessory because you do not have to keep returning photo paper to its envelope or box when you want to turn on the room lights. Large paper safes or drawers will accommodate several types and sizes of paper.

Dust Remover

Be sure to have an *antistatic brush* or *cloth,* or *can of compressed air,* for dusting negatives.

Contact Printing Device

Often an intermediate step between film processing and enlarging is making a contact proof sheet. This provides positive images which the photographer can study to decide on the best negatives to enlarge. The procedure is simple: negatives are put in contact with photo paper and exposed to light. Most commonly this is done on the enlarger baseboard, with a piece of window glass placed on top of the negatives to keep them flat and in contact with the paper. The enlarger light is used to make the exposure. You can also buy or make a contact printing frame for this purpose, or use a contact printer that has its own source of illumination. (Contact printing devices are discussed in more detail beginning on page 92.)

Processing Trays

Trays are required for processing, and the number and size will vary according to your needs. For black-and-white printing, you'll need trays for the developer, stop bath, and fixer. To speed up washing, a clearing agent (hypo neutralizer or hypo eliminator) can be used, which requires an additional tray. You may want to keep the processed prints in a stand bath—a tray of water—until you're ready for the washing cycle. For washing, a special siphon can be attached to a tray in lieu of using a commercial print washer. Sometimes you may want to bathe your prints in a print flattening solution before drying them, and this will require a tray, too.

Trays should be large enough and deep enough to process more than one print at a time. A convenient size for many photographers is 11 x 14, and the volume of chemical solutions required for such trays is not excessive.

Processing trays are usually plastic or hard rubber, or more expensive stainless steel. Porcelain-covered or enamelware metal trays are safe to use, unless the porcelain or enamel has been chipped and there is danger of the metal contaminating the chemicals.

Label and use the same trays for at least two chemicals, developer and fixer. That way, if the trays are inadequately washed after use, there is little danger of contamination and ruined prints the next time you process.

Tube Processors

Trays also can be used for color print processing, although a color processing tube or drum is the most popular and convenient method. If trays are used, two are adequate for the newer two-step color processes, like Kodak's Ektaprint 2 and Beseler's 2-Step Color Chemistry. Because temperatures for color processing chemicals must be exact, a water bath to maintain those temperatures is often used. Your processing trays can be placed in a sink or in another set of larger processing trays that will hold the water bath.

When a processing tube or drum is used, exposed color paper is loaded into it in the dark and then room lights can be turned on. Chemicals are poured in and out of the tube, sometimes with washes between steps. Final print washing is done in a tray or special print washer. (Read more about equipment for various color print processing methods beginning on page 180.)

Thermometer

An accurate thermometer is a must when mixing chemicals and making sure processing solutions are exactly the required temperatures, especially for color print chemistry. Buy a photographic thermometer that gives readings in both Fahrenheit and Celsius, and at least in divisions of ½°F (0.3°C).

Mixing Aids

Measuring graduates, a stirring rod, funnel, and *chemical storage bottles* are required for print processing, as they are for film processing.

Print Tongs

Tongs are suggested for people who do not like to immerse and agitate prints in the chemical solutions with their fingers. Chemicals can irritate or stain your skin, and they are painful if there are cuts on your hands; read the advice regarding handling that is printed on chemical packages. When print tongs are used, at least two are required in order to avoid contamination of the developer and fixer. Care must be used to avoid scratching the print emulsion with tongs, especially resin-coated papers, which are very susceptible to being marred.

Processing Timer

A timer is vital for making sure your prints are correctly processed. For black-and-white processing, a large clock with a sweep second hand mounted over the processing trays by a safelight will be adequate, but for color print processing, which is more exacting, it's best if your timer can be preset and will signal when time is up. This is especially a requirement if you do color processing in trays, because some of the steps must be done in total darkness. An alternative for occasional use is a wristwatch with illuminated numbers.

Print Washers

There are a number of washers and print washing techniques you can use. Your choice depends on whether you are processing black-and-white or color prints, and using conventional or resin-coated (RC) photo papers.

The RC papers, which include most color papers, require very little washing to remove processing chemicals—usually just 2 to 4 minutes. Many photographers simply run water into a tray, agitate the prints, then keep dumping and refilling the tray with fresh water, plus agitating, until wash time has elapsed. Others use a tray that is equipped with a washing siphon connected to a faucet that keeps circulating fresh water.

With most conventional black-and-white papers, wash time takes from 1 to 2 hours, unless prints are bathed in a clearing agent (hypo neutralizer) before washing. For such papers there are drum-type tumble washers or circular rotating spray washers, both which operate by water pressure. A tray siphon can be used instead.

Print Drying Devices

For drying prints, your choices are equally varied: *blotters, print drying screens,* or *heated print dryers.*

Resin-coated papers require little drying time or special equipment. After squeegeeing or blotting away excess water, prints on RC paper can be laid out on a flat surface, such as a print drying screen, and allowed to air dry at room temperature. To speed the drying process, many photographers use a portable hair dryer to blow hot air over the prints. RC prints also can be dried by clipping them to a clothesline in a dust-free area.

For conventional papers, flat or drum-type dryers shorten drying time. They also should be used to get the best finish on glossy papers that are squeegeed to a *ferrotype plate,* a shiny chrome-covered metal surface. (Glossy-type resin-coated papers do not require ferrotyping.) (Additional information on print drying begins on page 86.)

Print Squeegee

To remove excess water before drying, you can use a roller or blade-type squeegee. Some are specially designed squeegees for resin-coated papers; an auto windshield wiper blade is a popular substitute.

Dodging and Burning-in Tools

Prints can be altered during exposure with tools that can be purchased at camera stores or made at home.

Burning-in involves the addition of light to an area of the print that would otherwise be underexposed. After the regular exposure is made, additional exposure time is given to a selected area. Usually a hole is cut in a piece of cardboard, and the cardboard is held between the lens and photo paper. This holds back the negative image except where it passes through the hole. To keep a circle from showing in the print, the cardboard must be kept moving slightly so the burned-in area blends with the rest of the print. There are commercially made adjustable burning-in devices available, too.

Dodging is just the opposite of burning-in. During the regular exposure, part of the negative image is held back by a dodger, which often is a homemade disc of cardboard taped to the end of a thin but sturdy wire. By holding the dodger between the enlarging lens and photo paper, the selected area is kept from receiving too much exposure and becoming too dark. As with the burning-in device, the dodger must be kept moving slightly during the exposure in order to avoid an outline of the disc or wire in the print. (More details about dodging and burning-in tools begin on page 114.)

Towels

Dry hands are necessary in darkroom work, and many photographers prefer to use lint-free paper towels that are easily discarded. If cloth towels are used, they should be prewashed to avoid lint, and then frequently washed to prevent contamination by chemicals that may dry on them.

Printing Papers

Photo papers vary greatly in many ways. For black-and-white prints, you need to consider brands, sizes, quantities, surfaces, speeds, contrast grades, weights, image tones, tints, and paper bases (conventional or resin-coated). (A detailed discussion begins on page 72.)

Choice of color printing paper requires fewer considerations. Most importantly, the paper type varies according to whether you are printing from color negatives or color transparencies (slides). (Color printing papers are described in detail in chapter 12, "Preparing to Make Color Prints.")

Chemicals

Processing chemistry is different for black-and-white and color print processing, but the key steps are the same—developer, stop bath, fixer. Color print processes sometimes require additional chemicals, like bleach and stabilizer, but these may be combined with the fixer. The specific color print chemistry varies according to the type of color printing paper you use. These chemicals are discussed under descriptions of the various color print processes in chapter 12, "Preparing to Make Color Prints."

For black-and-white printing, the paper developer depends on the type of printing paper you select. In addition, developers come in either powdered or liquid form, and each must be mixed according to instructions packed with the chemicals. Some stock solutions are used full strength, while others are diluted.

An acid stop bath is recommended for black-and-white print processing, rather than just the water rinse many photographers substitute between developer and fixer in film processing.

Fixer for prints can be the same as for films, but dilution is usually different. For volume printing and long lasting results, two separate fixer baths are often suggested for conventional papers (not resin-coated).

Additional but optional chemicals for black-and-white printing include a clearing agent (hypo neutralizer) and print flattening solution, both which can be used for conventional papers but not resin-coated (RC) papers. (Details about chemicals for black-and-white print processing begin on page 82.)

5

Considering Black-and-White Papers and Processing

The previous chapter summarized the equipment and materials needed for making black-and-white and color prints. Before proceeding to make black-and-white contact prints or enlargements, you should consider some materials and other aspects of processing in detail: photo papers, safelights, chemicals, washing and drying prints.

Selecting Photographic Papers

The choice of black-and-white photographic papers is tremendous, although there are only two basic kinds: *contact printing papers,* and *enlarging papers.* Enlarging papers are more sensitive to light, and are used with negatives projected by an enlarger. Contact printing papers, with less sensitive emulsions, are for negatives placed in direct contact with the paper and exposed to a bright light.

While most black-and-white papers are designed for use with black-and-white negatives, a few, like Kodak's Panalure, will produce quality black-and-white prints from color negatives. Others, called *printing-out papers,* will produce black-and-white prints without any chemical processing—but their images eventually fade.

To save money by standardizing papers and processing, most photographers use enlarging papers for making contact proof pictures as well as enlargements. Such *contact proof sheets,* which show positive images the same size as the negatives, can be studied for content and contrast to aid you in selecting the best negatives for enlargement.

Contact printing paper is most often used by photographers who shoot large format films, such as 4 x 5-, 5 x 7-, or 8 x 10-inch, and make contact prints for display instead of just for negative selection.

Whether using contact printing paper or enlarging paper, you have a wide choice of brands, quantities, sizes, surfaces, speeds, contrast grades, weights, image tones, tints, and paper bases. Following is an extensive discussion of these factors so you can better choose the paper(s) best for your purposes.

There are many *brands* of photographic paper, and Kodak has one of the largest selections. Other manufacturers include Ilford, Agfa, and Luminos. Photographers usually refer to papers by brand name, like Medalist (Kodak) and Ilfobrom (Ilford).

You can purchase photo papers in packages and boxes; the larger the *quantity,* the lower the cost per sheet. But don't buy so much paper that it becomes out-of-date before you can use it. Paper packages and boxes have *expiration dates* printed on them, so look for it when purchasing paper. Packaged quantities you can buy range from ten to twenty-five, fifty, one hundred, two hundred-fifty, and even five hundred sheets. Many photographers purchase twenty-five-sheet packages or one hundred-sheet boxes, so photo stores commonly stock those two quantities.

Papers are made in various *sizes,* and the most common are 5 x 7, 8 x 10, 11 x 14, and 16 x 20 inches. If you want to make 5 x 7 prints, or smaller, it's more economical to purchase 8 x 10-inch paper and use a paper cutter in the darkroom to cut it to the required size.

The *surfaces* of paper have two characteristics, texture and brilliance. Kodak describes its surface textures as smooth, fine-grained, tweed, silk, and tapestry. The surface brilliance is described as glossy, lustre, high lustre, or matte. Kodak identifies such surface characteristics by a single letter. For example, F indicates a smooth glossy paper surface, N or A is smooth lustre, Y is silk high lustre.

Each manufacturer has its own paper surface descriptions and codes. Ilford, for instance, uses names identified by numbers, including glossy (1), matt (5), semi-matt (24), velvet stipple (26), velvet lustre (27), and rayon (35).

Speeds of paper vary, just like speeds of film. They indicate the paper's sensitivity to light, and will help you figure exposure. Papers often are described as slow, medium, or fast (or high) speed; numbers sometimes are used to indicate speeds more precisely. Kodak labels its papers with *ANSI Paper Speeds*. These are numbers established by the American National Standards Institute (ANSI), successor to the American Standards Association that had established the film speed numbers now in common use (i.e. ASA film speeds).

The ANSI numbers are a series that indicate the relative paper speed of different papers: 1, 1.2, 1.6, 2, 2.5, 3, 4, 5, 6, 8, 10, 12, 16, 20, 25, 32, 40, 50, 64, 80, 100, 125, 160, 200, 250, 320, 400, 500, 650, 800, and 1000. The higher the number, the faster the paper.

Paper speed does not rank as important a consideration to most photographers as does film speed. They usually choose a photo paper for its contrast, texture, and tone—not because of its speed. Some types of papers come in slow and fast speeds, however, such as Kodak's Polycontrast and Polycontrast Rapid. By comparing the ANSI numbers of those two papers, 160 vs. 320, you can tell that Polycontrast Rapid is twice as fast. That means it requires only half the exposure of regular Polycontrast, and thus Polycontrast

Rapid would be the best choice if you decided to speed up your printing procedure.

Some papers of the same type but of different *contrast grades* also have different speeds, and their ANSI numbers will help you figure changes in exposure when you change to a different contrast grade. For instance, Kodak's Kodabromide comes in five grades, each with a different speed: grade No. 1 = ANSI paper speed of 500; No. 2 = 320; No. 3 = 200; No. 4 = 160; and No. 5 = 125.

Say you were using contrast grade No. 2 (ANSI 320) and decided to switch to a higher contrast, grade No. 4 (ANSI 160). Since No. 4 is only half as fast as No. 2, you would need to double the exposure you used with No. 2 in order to properly expose the same negative on grade No. 4. (You can do this by doubling the enlarger exposure time, *or* by opening up the enlarger lens by one f/stop.)

Knowledge of ANSI paper speeds also helps you determine exposure when you change from one type of photo paper to another. For example, if you switch from Kodabromide to Kodak's Medalist, paper speeds are different even when the same contrast grade is used. Kodabromide No. 3 has a speed of 200, while Medalist No. 3 is slightly slower with a speed of 160. So you need to increase exposure if you switch from Kodabromide No. 3 to Medalist No. 3.

To figure exposure changes, you should know that the *difference between each number in the ANSI Paper Speed series (see* list on page 73) is *1/3* f/stop. Thus, the difference between ANSI 160 and 200 is 1/3 f/stop, between 160 and 250 is 2/3 f/stop and 160 and 320 is a full (3/3) f/stop. This means you can keep your exposure time constant and change the enlarger lens f/stop to adjust for a change in paper speeds.

Alternatively, you can keep the f/stop constant, and change the exposure time to adjust for a change in paper speeds. A simple way to calculate revised *exposure time* is to multiply the known exposure time by the ANSI speed number of the paper you used, then divide the answer by the ANSI speed number of the paper you are going to use. For instance, if you exposed a 200 speed paper for 10 seconds, (200 x 10 = 2000), you would expose a 160 speed paper for 12½ seconds (2000 ÷ 160 = 12.5)—keeping the f/stop the same for both exposures.

You will notice when studying the data sheet packed with photographic papers that some papers have the same speed, regardless of their contrast grade. For instance, Ilford's Ilfospeed paper has the same speed for all its contrast grades, while Kodak's Kodabromide has speeds that vary from grade to grade.

Papers come in various *contrast grades,* which allow you to make prints with good contrast from negatives that vary in contrast. Contrast refers to the relative densities (i.e. range of gray tones, from black to white) that appear in a negative or positive image. A negative of *average* or *normal contrast* has a full range of gray tones and shows detail in both highlights and shadows. To reproduce this full range of tones in the positive print, a paper of normal contrast grade is used.

A negative of *high contrast* shows a limited range of gray tones and emphasizes blacks and whites. To get a print that reveals a more normal range of gray tones, you would use a low contrast grade of paper. A negative of *low contrast* has little differentiation in its range of gray tones. To make blacks and whites more pronounced in order to produce a print with a more normal range of gray tones, you would use a high contrast grade of paper.

Paper contrast grades generally are indicated by numbers, although not all papers are made in a full range of contrast grades. Such grades are Nos. 0, 1, 2, 3, 4, 5, and 6. The higher the number, the higher the contrast produced. No. 2 and No. 3 are considered normal contrast papers, to be used with negatives of normal contrast. Nos. 0 and 1 are called low-contrast papers, to be used with high contrast negatives to produce prints of normal contrast. Higher contrast papers are Nos. 4, 5, 6, to be used with negatives of less than normal contrast to produce prints of normal contrast.

Keep in mind that contrast grade numbers are relative to the paper manufacturer. Even using the same negative, a No. 3 grade of paper from Kodak may produce a print of different contrast than a print on a No. 3 paper made by Ilford. You must judge the contrast result yourself.

The contrast grades of a few papers are indicated by words instead of numbers. The various contrasts of Kodak's Kodabrome RC paper, for example, are described as soft, medium, hard, extra hard, and ultra hard.

Some photographers choose a contrast grade that will purposely produce a print of non-normal contrast. To diminish or eliminate the middle gray tones in a print, for example, they will print a high contrast negative on a high contrast paper (Nos. 5 or 6).

There are some papers of *variable contrast,* and these require filtration during enlarging to change contrast. Kodak's most popular papers of this type are Polycontrast and Polycontrast Rapid. By placing Polycontrast filters in the enlarger head's filter drawer, or beneath the enlarger lens, print contrast can be altered on the same paper in a range from Grade No. 1 through Grade No. 4.

The filters are made in half-grades, so contrast can be controlled more precisely than with graded papers, except in extreme low or high contrast cases. Polycontrast filters are numbered 1, 1½, 2, 2½, 3, 3½, and 4. *When a variable contrast paper is used without any filters, its contrast grade is considered No. 2.* (Without the filter, the paper speed of Polycontrast is two-thirds faster than when a No. 2 filter is used.)

Variable contrast papers are popular because you need to have only one paper on hand, instead of several grades, in order to print negatives of different contrasts.

Photo papers are made in various *weights,* but not all types of papers are manufactured in all weights. Paper weights, including those of Kodak's, often are indicated by abbreviations: LW = light-weight, SW = single-weight, MW = medium-weight, and DW = double-weight. Other companies use different designations, like Ilford, which indicates its single-weight papers with a P, and double-weight papers with a K. Most common weights of conventional papers are single weights for prints up to 8 x 10 inches, except portraits, and double-weight for prints 11 x 14 inches and larger, as well as for portraits of any size. Resin-coated papers are medium-weight, regardless of size.

Image tone and *image color* are other terms used to describe photographic papers. They refer to the color of the silver image (i.e. everything but white areas) produced on the paper. Such tones are generally described as cold, neutral, or warm, and are combined with a specific color: blue, black, or brown. Papers of warm-brown tones are popular for portraits, while neutral-black or warm-black papers are preferred for general photography. Print tones also can be changed to some degree by changing the paper developer (see page 82). And toning chemicals can be used after processing to alter a print's tone (see page 85).

Tint refers to the color of the paper itself. Paper stock used by Kodak is

Different grades of paper alter contrast in a photograph. The same negative was printed on all six grades of Ilford's Ilfospeed paper.

23. *Grade No. 0—lowest contrast.*   24. *Grade No. 1—low contrast.*

25. *Grade No. 2—normal contrast.*   26. *Grade No. 3—normal to high contrast.*

27. *Grade No. 4—higher contrast.*   28. *Grade No. 5—highest contrast.*

described as white, warm-white, and cream-white. Warm-white and cream-white papers are popular choices for printing portraits.

The *base* of photo papers is another consideration. *Conventional papers* are of an ordinary fiber base that absorbs water and chemical solutions, while *resin-coated (RC) papers* have a water-resistant base. Because absorption is reduced, processing and washing times also are reduced with the use of RC papers. (RC, by the way, was a trademark of Eastman Kodak Co. to indicate its resin-coated papers, but this abbreviation is now commonly used to identify any manufacturer's water-resistant photo paper, whether with a resin-coated, plastic-coated, or polyethylene-coated base.)

Resin-coated photo papers, both black-and-white and color, have been a boon to rapid processing and helped spark renewed interest in home darkrooms. As these print materials continue to improve, they will be used more and more for fine photographic printing. Currently, however, they are relatively new and untested as to their permanence from an archival standpoint. Will black-and-white RC prints made today be as good after ten years, or fifty years?

The two leading manufacturers of black-and-white resin-coated papers are Kodak and Ilford. Each makes variable contrast RC (Kodak Polycontrast Rapid RC and Ilford Ilfospeed Multigrade), as well as papers of separate contrast grades (Kodabrome RC and Ilfospeed). Instead of identifying them with traditional numbers (1, 2, 3, 4, 5, 6), Kodak describes its RC contrasts as soft, medium, hard, extra hard, and ultra-hard grades.

Ilford's resin-coated paper, Ilfospeed, has contrast grades indicated by numbers (0, 1, 2, 3, 4, 5). The company's variable contrast RC paper, Ilfospeed Multigrade, produces grades 0 through 4 in seven contrast steps, through the use of Ilford's variable contrast filters, Nos. 1, 2, 3, 4, 5, 6, 7.

Many photographers judge Ilfospeed and Multigrade superior to Kodak's RC papers because Kodak's Kodabrome RC and Polycontrast Rapid RC seem to dry with a slight veiling, or graying, in the black areas of the image; the Kodak prints do not seem to have as much brilliance as prints on Ilfospeed or Multigrade paper. Kodak is experimenting overseas with RC papers, hoping to clear up that problem and then introduce improved RC papers to the U.S. market.

Special mention should be made of Kodak's *Panalure* paper, designed for making black-and-white prints from color negatives. While other black-and-white photo papers will produce images from color negatives, they are not sensitive to all colors. This means some colors of the subject will print too dark or too light. Panalure, however, is sensitive to all colors and thus will render colors of the subject in gray tones that are more realistic. Panalure paper is available in two varieties. Type F is white, glossy and single-weight, while type E is white, fine-grained, lustre and double-weight, and best suited for portraits. Note that Panalure paper will fog if used under safelights designed for normal black-and-white papers; use a dark amber (No. 10) safelight with 7½-watt bulb instead. (See also page 263.)

With so many considerations concerning selection of a photo paper— brand, surface, speed, contrast grade, weight, image tone, tint, and base—it will take some experimenting before you find the papers suited to the images you capture on film, and for the print purpose you have in mind. A portrait for wall display might be printed on 11 x 14-inch, double-weight, cream white, brown tone, fine-grained lustre paper, while an animal's photo to be reproduced in a newspaper probably would be printed on 8 x 10-inch, single-weight, white, neutral-black, smooth glossy paper.

Sooner or later you should have reliable combinations of certain films and papers and developers that lead to high quality prints, without guesswork. Test carefully, and don't assume, for instance, that switching to different photo paper will produce results that match or surpass your previous prints; you may have to switch developer at the same time. Read a photo paper's data sheet to learn the characteristics of that paper and the manufacturer's processing recommendations.

Following is a list of some current brands of black-and-white photographic papers, including their manufacturers, contrast grades, image tones, and weights. Paper base is conventional unless indicated RC (resin-coated). Papers designed solely for contact printing are listed separately. Surfaces types are too varied to summarize in the lists; see samples available at camera stores.

BLACK-AND-WHITE CONTACT PRINTING PAPERS

MANUFACTURER AND PAPER NAME (RC = resin-coated)	CONTRAST GRADE (0, 1, 2, 3, 4, 5)	IMAGE TONE C = Cold tone N = Neutral tone W = Warm tone	PAPER WEIGHT SW = single wt. DW = double wt. LW = light wt.
KODAK			
Azo	0-5	N	SW
Velox	1-4	C	SW
Resisto (RC)	2-3	N	SW
Ad-Type	1-4	N	LW
Studio Proof	POP*	reddish brown	SW
ILFORD			
Industrial Contact	1-5	N	SW, DW

*Printing-out paper.

BLACK-AND-WHITE ENLARGING PAPERS

MANUFACTURER AND PAPER NAME (RC = resin-coated)	CONTRAST GRADE (0,1,2,3,4,5,6)* VC = variable contrast	IMAGE TONE C = Cold tone N = Neutral tone W = Warm tone B = Brown tone	PAPER WEIGHT SW = single wt. DW = double wt. MW = medium wt. LW = light wt.
KODAK			
Kodabromide	1-5	N	SW, DW, LW
Medalist	1-4	W	SW, DW
Kodabrome II RC	1-5†	N	MW
Polycontrast	VC	W	SW, DW, LW
Polycontrast Rapid	VC	W	SW, DW
Polycontrast Rapid II RC	VC	W	MW
Ektalure	single	W	DW
Portralure	VC	W	DW
Panalure	single**	W	SW
Panalure Portrait	single**	B	DW
Panalure II RC	single**	W	MW
Mural	2-3	W	SW
ILFORD			
Ilfobrom	0-5	N	SW,DW
Ilfospeed (RC)	0-5	N	MW
Ilfospeed Multigrade (RC)	VC	N	MW
Ilfobrom Galerie	1-3	N	DW
LUMINOS			
Bromide ZF	0-5	C	SW
Bromide RD (RC)	1-4	N	MW
Bromide	2-4	N	DW
Charcoal R	single	W	DW
DeLuxe Rapid Portrait	2-3	W	DW
Portrait Proof	single	W	MW
Mural	2-3	W	SW,MW
AGFA			
Brovira	1-6	N	SW,DW
Portriga Rapid	2-4	W	DW
Brovira Speed 310 RC	1-6	N	MW
Brovira Speed 312 RC	1-6	N	MW

*0—1 indicate low contrast papers (for negatives of high contrast); 2—3 indicate normal contrast papers (for negatives of average contrast); 4—6 indicate high contrast papers (for negatives of low contrast).

†Contrast grades are called: soft, medium, hard, extra hard, ultra hard.

**Special paper for making black and white enlargements from color negatives.

Considering Safelights

Safelights allow you to have some illumination in the darkroom while making black-and-white prints, especially to inspect the prints as they develop. The type of safelight suitable for a specific paper is listed on the data sheet packed with the paper.

In general, a *light amber* safelight is recommended for most black-and-white contact and enlarging papers. Kodak identifies light amber as an OC safelight or safelight filter. Other manufacturers use other terms for similar safelights, such as Ilford's 902. Better quality safelights usually allow filters to be interchanged. This is necessary if you do color printing as well as black-and-white, because some color papers should be used only with a *dark amber* (No. 10) safelight, as should Panalure paper.

Safelights may fog photo papers if used too close to the paper, at too intense an illumination, or for prolonged periods of time. After selecting the safelight or safelight filter recommended for the paper you're using, be certain to use the proper wattage bulb (maximum is usually 15 watts, but sometimes 7½ watts for color paper), and keep the safelight the recommended distance from the enlarging and developing areas (usually no less than 4 feet). Also note that variable-contrast papers should not be exposed to them for more than a total of three minutes.

To be certain your darkroom safelights will not fog photo papers, conduct a test. First, make a control print for comparison, exposing and processing under safelights as you normally would. Next, expose a second print for the same length of time, but turn off the safelights before removing the paper from its light-tight box and putting it in the easel. After exposure with the enlarger, cover up one-quarter of the paper with a piece of cardboard, and turn on the safelights. Once every minute, move the cardboard to cover up a larger portion of the photo paper each time. Do this for a total of 5 minutes (3 minutes with variable-contrast papers), then turn out the safelights and develop this second print for the same time as the first print.

After both are dry, check for safelight fog by comparing the prints' density and contrast. Look for added density in the highlight areas. Especially note if the first print, made under safelights in your usual manner, seems dull or flat when compared to the portion of the second print that was always covered by cardboard when the safelights were on. That's because safelight fog reduces the overall brilliance of a print.

Remember that safelight fog will not occur in unexposed parts of the print (including the white borders). This means you cannot simply expose photo paper to safelight to detect such fog; it must have some previous white light exposure to affect the silver halides in its emulsion, as when a negative is projected on the paper by an enlarger.

If neither print shows signs of fog, you can assume your safelights are indeed "safe." If, however, there is any fogging, compare the various exposed portions to determine how many "safe" minutes you have before fogging occurs. Better yet, reduce the wattage of the bulb or move the safelights farther away from the working area and conduct the test again.

Of course, it is always best to limit the time photo paper is exposed to safelights. When it is not protected by the light-tight box or envelope, the paper should be turned emulsion side down in the darkroom.

Some enlarging timers turn the safelights off when the enlarger is turned on. This makes it easier to focus the negative's image prior to inserting the photo paper in the enlarging easel, and it means the paper will not be affected by safelights during the time of exposure. Many photographers also keep prints facedown during most of the time in the developer, in order to avoid overexposure to safelights.

One other caution: be careful that undeveloped paper out of its light-tight box is protected from stray light that may come from the enlarger prior to actual exposure, as during focusing or easel alignment.

Choosing Chemicals

The chemicals for processing black-and-white prints should be familiar ones: developer, stop bath, and fixer. The major consideration is in the selection of a developer. It must be appropriate for the type of paper you are using. Data sheets packed with photo papers recommend specific brands of developers, and dilutions.

Developer. The black or brown image tones of photo papers are affected by paper developers, so they are described as either *cold, neutral,* or *warm tone developers.*

Other considerations regarding a developer include whether it is strictly a paper developer for prints or a universal type that will develop both prints and films.

You should also be aware of a developer's rate of development, its capacity (the number of prints it will process), and its keeping properties (how long it can be stored in a full, tightly capped bottle).

The choice of a developer includes whether it is packaged as a powder or liquid concentrate. And certain developers are best used for papers that are to be chemically toned.

Following is a list of popular paper developers, including manufacturer, brand, tone, and packaging.

BLACK-AND-WHITE PAPER DEVELOPERS

MANUFACTURER AND DEVELOPER NAME	DEVELOPER TONE C = Cold tone N = Neutral tone W = Warm tone	PACKAGED AS: Powder (P)	Liquid (L)
KODAK			
Dektol	C-N	P	
Ektaflo, Type 1	C		L
Selectol	W	P	
Selectol Soft	W	P	
Ektonol	W	P	
Versatol*	C		L
ILFORD			
Bromophen	N	P	
Ilfospeed II	N		L
Ilfospeed Multigrade	N		L
ETHOL			
LPD	C-N-W†	P	L
EDWAL			
TST	C-W†		L
Platinum	N		L
Super III	N		L

*Universal-type developer; also can be used for developing films.
†Tone controlled by dilution.

It is always best to choose a developer that is appropriate for the type of photo paper you are using, so read the paper's data sheet for developers recommended by the paper's manufacturer. A popular general-purpose developer is Kodak's Dektol, designed specifically for cold and neutral tone papers.

Dektol is packaged in powder form. You can mix a gallon of stock solution to have plenty on hand. In a full, tightly capped storage bottle, stock Dektol will keep up to six months (two months in a bottle half full). It is diluted one part Dektol to two parts water (1:2) for a working solution, and one gallon of working solution will make up to one hundred and twenty 8 x 10-inch prints before becoming exhausted.

For warm tone papers, Kodak's Selectol is a good choice. (For even less contrast, use Kodak's Selectol Soft developer.) A gallon of stock Selectol will keep up to four months in a full, tightly capped storage bottle (six weeks if the bottle is half full). It is diluted one part Selectol to one part water (1:1) for a working solution, a gallon of which will make up to eighty 8 x 10-inch prints before exhaustion.

Developers must be mixed carefully according to their package instructions;

especially adhere to the proper mixing temperature, or some of the chemicals may not dissolve properly. Be certain to mark the date of mixing on the stock solution bottle.

To make sure they get the best possible print results, most photographers do not save developer working solutions between printing sessions. They discard the used developer from the tray and begin every session with freshly mixed developer. Besides, most paper developers will keep only one working day (up to 12 hours) in an open tray.

Stop bath. Despite the trend in film processing to use a water bath between developer and fixer steps, an acid stop bath should always be used when making prints. This will quickly stop the developing action, and also prolong the effectiveness of the fixer.

An easy and inexpensive stop bath is to use acetic acid. Start with a small bottle of glacial (99 percent) acetic acid, and mix three parts acid to eight parts water. This will become your stock 28 percent acetic acid solution, which is then rediluted one-and-a-half parts to thirty-two parts water for a working stop bath.

One important warning when mixing the concentrated glacial acid: always pour the acid into the water. If water is poured into the acid, it may boil and spatter, causing severe skin burns.

A stock acetic stop bath will keep almost indefinitely in a tightly capped storage bottle, and a working solution will keep up to three days in an open tray. Up to twenty-two 8 x 10-inch prints can be processed per quart (or liter) of acetic acid stop bath in working solution before it should be discarded and replaced.

There are some prepared stop bath solutions, like Kodak's Indicator Stop Bath, that signal when they are exhausted by changing color.

Fixer. As you recall, a fixer dissolves the remaining silver halides in the emulsion that was not used in forming the image, and thus makes the image permanent. If the unused silver halides remain, they can be affected by light over a period of time, and therefore ruin your print. This can occur because of faulty fixer or fixing technique.

Fixers must be fresh, and prints must be agitated correctly. Overfixing is not an alternative; it only creates another problem because overfixing can eventually bleach the image and ruin your print. Proper fixing also is important if you intend to tone the prints.

Remember to keep the fixer at suggested fixing temperatures, usually 65° to 70°F (18.5° to 21°C). If you don't, overfixing will result, even if you fix for the recommended time. That's because the fixing action occurs more rapidly at higher temperatures.

For the most effective fixing of conventional papers (not resin-coated), *two fixer baths* are suggested. The first bath does most of the work removing the unused silver halides, and the second bath finishes the job. Fixing time in a single fixer bath is 5 to 10 minutes; with two-bath fixing, you should fix prints 3 to 5 minutes in each bath.

Regarding resin-coated papers, Kodak recommends 2 minutes in the fixer for its RC papers (followed by a 4-minute wash), while Ilford recommends 30 seconds for its RC papers in Ilford fixer (and then a 2-minute wash).

Fixers keep up to two months in tightly capped storage bottles. Working solutions will keep one week in an open tray. You can process about twenty-five 8 x 10-inch prints per quart (or liter) of fixer mixed for a working solution (some fixers must be diluted). With a two-bath fixer set-up, discard the first bath after fixing fifty 8 x 10 prints per quart (or liter), and replace it with the second bath. Then use fresh fixer to replace the second bath. There are some simple tests, with solutions like Hypo-Check, which will indicate if the fixer is exhausted; if a drop or two of Hypo-Check turns cloudy in the fixer, discard the fixer.

Clearing agent. Optional chemicals for print processing include a clearing agent, if you want to save time and water. This hypo neutralizer or hypo eliminator solution helps rid the prints of fixer, thus allowing shorter washing times for conventional photo papers. (Resin-coated papers inherently have brief wash times, 2 to 4 minutes, and should not be bathed in clearing agents.)

With Kodak's Hypo Clearing Agent, single-weight papers get a 2-minute treatment, and double-weight papers 3 minutes—both with agitation. Wash time is then reduced from one hour (the time required for papers not treated in clearing agent) to 10 minutes for single-weight papers, and to 20 minutes for double-weight papers.

Hypo Clearing Agent will keep one day in an open tray and up to three months in a tightly capped storage bottle. It can be used to process fifty 8 x 10-inch prints per quart (or liter) if a *water prerinse* is given after the fixer, or twenty 8 x 10-inch prints per quart if the prerinse is eliminated.

Print flattener. If you have difficulty with prints curling after you dry them, you can treat prints (except those on resin-coated papers) in Kodak's Print Flattening Solution. This keeps the paper and emulsion layer from becoming too dry, a common occurrence in heated buildings during winter. Average working solution is one part flattening solution to ten parts water (1:10), but dilution should vary according to conditions: 1:5 if the air is very dry; 1:20 if the air is moist. Treatment is for 5 minutes at 68°F (20°C), after prints have been washed. An alternative way to uncurl prints is simply to dampen their backs (not the emulsion side) with water, then place them between blotters and under a heavy weight while they re-dry.

Toners. There are chemical toners that change the mood of your black-and-white prints by coloring the images to increase the realism of your photographs. The most common toners yield shades of brown, and often are used with portraits and landscapes. Blue toners are popularly used with snow scenes, while red tones give extra interest to sunset and fire photographs.

Many toners are premixed (requiring only dilution), easy to use, and keep well over long periods of time. (A discussion of toning appears in chapter 8.)

Washing Prints

Proper print washing is important to remove all chemicals and insure the stability of the images, especially against fading or staining. Running water is best, with frequent agitation, and prints should have a change of fresh water every 5 minutes during the wash cycle. Wash time for conventional single-weight papers is normally one hour, but prior use of a clearing agent cuts the wash time to 10 minutes. For double-weight papers, the regular one-hour wash is reduced to 20 minutes.

Resin-coated papers, most all of which are medium-weight, require only a 2- to 4-minute wash (a clearing agent is neither required nor recommended). Wash water temperature can range from 65° to 75°F (18.5° to 24°C); colder temperatures prolong wash time, and higher temperatures may damage the paper's emulsion.

Keep in mind that *wash time is figured from the time the last print goes into the wash water*. If you occasionally transfer prints from the fixer into the wash water, they will contaminate any previous prints that are washing. Use a *water stand bath* instead, and then wash your prints in well-timed batches. Remember, however, that RC prints should not be allowed to soak because moisture will seep in along the edges and cause curl to the paper.

Drying Prints

There are a number of techniques for drying your prints, depending on the paper's surface.

Blotters. Using clean blotters is one of the most basic and least expensive ways to dry conventional print papers, but not resin-coated (RC) papers. As with most of the other print-drying procedures, the first step is to sponge or squeegee all excess water off the front and back of the prints. Do this on a piece of heavy plate glass placed at an angle over your washing area or some place where the water can drain. Before using, clean the glass thoroughly. Make sure your sponge or squeegee is free of anything that may scratch the delicate wet print emulsion. Don't apply too much pressure or you might damage the print surface or wrinkle the paper; single-weight papers require more caution than double-weight papers.

Use two sets of lint-free blotters, and only those specifically made for photographic purposes. Alternately stack prints and blotters, then press down on them to guarantee contact. After a few minutes, transfer the prints to the second set of dry blotters. It's best to use two blotters between each print. You can shorten the drying time by adding sheets of corrugated cardboard between each pair of blotters to allow air to circulate. Some photographers later transfer the prints to a third set of dry blotters to speed up absorption of the remaining moisture. Cover the stack with a flat board or piece of Masonite at least as large as the blotters, and weigh it down to make sure the prints dry flat. All wet blotters can be hung up to dry.

Prints, too, can be hung on a clothesline to dry. Use at least two clothespins on top, and several on the bottom to minimize curling. Prints dry more quickly this way than with blotters, but you may need to flatten them after drying by using weights. There are blotter rolls sold in photo stores, but these are more clumsy to use than individual flat blotters, and they also cause prints to curl. One important caution: Blotters eventually become contaminated or stained, so discard them when they do. Otherwise, the contaminates or stains may be transferred to your prints during the drying process.

Print drying screens. One of the safest, fastest, inexpensive, and most satisfactory methods for drying prints is by using drying screens, especially for resin-coated papers, which must be air dried. These are commercially available, or you can make them easily with plastic or fiberglass window screen material and either aluminum or wood molding for a frame. Such screening will not react to water or chemicals; never use wire window screen. Buy or make the screens at least as large as your biggest prints. A good size is 18 x 24 inches, which will handle one 16 x 20-, two 11 x 14-, or four 8 x 10-inch prints.

To use the screen with conventional papers, place sponged or squeegeed prints facedown on one of the framed screens, then place a second frame of screen on top to keep the prints from curling. More prints can be placed on this second screen, facedown, and covered with another framed screen. The frame moldings should be thick enough to allow air to circulate between the screens. Resin-coated papers dry flat and do not need a covering screen; place them faceup on the screen.

A stack of screens and prints can be placed in a warm area, or into a drying cabinet. With screens in a forced air cabinet, prints on conventional paper may be dry in less than an hour; with screens in room air circulation only, 4 to 8 hours; and with blotters, 24 hours or at least overnight. Resin-coated (RC) papers dry in room air within a half-hour if squeegeed before being placed on the screen.

Heated print dryers. Heated print dryers are another choice for drying conventional print papers. The smallest and most common styles use a cloth apron to hold the prints in contact with a heated surface. Some are "flip-flop" models that have drying surfaces on two sides. Heated dryers are popular for drying papers with a glossy surface (except resin-coated papers). This is accomplished by squeegeeing "F" surface (glossy) papers facedown on a chromium-mirrored metal plate called a *ferrotype tin*. This shiny plate is placed on the dryer's heated surface, covered with a blotter, and held down by the dryer's apron.

Problems occur when the dryer is too hot and the paper dries with tiny cracks or circular ripples called "oyster shell" marks that are evident on the glossy surface. Also, if the print is insufficiently washed, or the ferrotype plate is dirty, the glossy surface may stick and ruin the print, or it may have unglossed spots that make the finished print unsatisfactory. You can purchase a solution that will clean and polish dirty ferrotype surfaces, and bathing the prints in a hypo clearing agent is also recommended.

Glossy-surfaced resin-coated papers do not require a ferrotype tin to achieve a gloss, so many photographers have switched to RC paper to avoid the problems of drying conventional glossy printing papers (see below). Also, prints dried at high heat often emerge from the dryer with a considerable curl, or wrinkles. If they do not flatten out after several hours, these should be rewashed, and redried at a lower temperature.

Matte finish prints are dried faceup and covered with a photographic blotter, so any stain or residue in the dryer's apron will not be transferred to the print's surface. Attending a small heat dryer takes quite a bit of time. Most photographers find that print drying screens, although slower, are less of a hassle and free you to do less tedious things than manning a hot print dryer.

Another problem with heat dryers is that they can change the contrast or color of a print significantly. Particularly avoid them with prints that have been toned, since heat drying can slightly increase contrast and darken prints, as well as alter the toning color. For instance, a sepia-toned print may redden. If you have a heated print dryer, use it carefully in order not to change or ruin your prints.

Precautions for Drying Resin-Coated (RC) Papers

A normal heated print dryer may damage the surface of resin-coated prints, if they are held in contact with the hot surface. However, RC prints may be laid faceup on such a dryer, if protected underneath by the dryer's apron or a blotter. Forced air heat is better for drying RC prints than placing them on a hot surface; a household hair dryer will dry them very quickly. Drying screens work well, too.

Speed the drying process by removing excess water with a sponge or squeegee. Or you can blot the prints with a paper towel or photo print blotter.

Then they can be laid upon any flat surface for drying by regular room air circulation.

Some special dryers for resin-coated papers employ a series of rubber or sponge rollers to remove excess water and transport the prints through forced hot air. Nonheating RC dryers include the water-removing rollers and racks to separate prints for room air drying.

6

Making Black-and-White Contact Prints Step by Step

A logical step after developing film is to make enlargements from the negatives. But contact printing each roll of negatives onto a sheet of photo paper is the first thing many photographers do. The resulting print is often referred to as a *proof sheet*.

The procedures for processing contact prints are the same as for processing enlargements, so read this chapter to learn basic print processing techniques.

A proof sheet provides the first positive view of your negatives. Since all the images from one roll of 35mm film (twenty or thirty-six exposures) or one roll of 120-size film can be contact printed onto one piece of 8 x 10-inch photo paper, you can conveniently study an entire roll of film by looking at a single proof sheet. This makes it easier to select negatives for enlarging.

Also important is that proof sheets help you file, retrieve, and protect those negatives. The 8 x 10-inch sheets can be kept with their corresponding negatives in a notebook or file folders. And when you want to locate a certain negative, by searching proof sheets for the wanted image instead of looking through the negatives themselves, your negatives are protected from constant or careless handling.

After proofing a number of rolls of film, you learn to tell which exposures produce the best results. If a record of shutter speeds and f/stops is kept, and then marked on the proof sheets, this should help improve your camera work in the future.

Also, if you exposed a particular subject at different f/stops or shutter speeds (called bracketing), you can easily spot the best exposure by looking at the proof sheet. And if your proofing procedures are standardized, any problems with processing techniques, chemicals, or even "bad" film should be apparent when you study the proofs.

For these varied reasons, it is recommended you *always* proof your negatives, even if none of the images on a particular roll seem important enough to bother. Those "poor" shots may be useful later, perhaps when combined with other images in a collage, or in a multiply-exposed or superimposed print.

Because a proof sheet is made by putting negatives in direct contact with a piece of printing paper, there is nothing between the negative and the

29. *Contact printing negatives produces positive images of the same size, and a proof sheet of each roll can be very useful (see text).*

photographic paper emulsion to distort the image. Thus, a contact print has the potential to be the best possible print that can be obtained from any negative, yielding its maximum detail and greatest sharpness.

No wonder many great photographers—like Ansel Adams, Edward Weston, and Wynn Bullock—have shot large-format film, often 8 x 10-inch or larger, and contact printed the negatives to make the final prints. When done properly, the contact print represents, technically, the highest form of photographic printing. The negative must be carefully composed, exposed, and processed because most of the printing controls, like dodging and burning-in, are not easily done when making a contact print.

Preparing for Contact Printing

Proof print, proof sheet, contact print, and contact sheet are terms often used interchangeably, although they do not strictly mean the same thing. *Proof sheet* or proof print may apply to any print, whether enlarged or not. A *contact sheet* or contact print results only when the negative is in direct contact with the printing paper. Since a proof sheet is generally made by the contact method, photographers casually use the terms proof sheet and contact sheet to mean the same thing.

There are a number of ways to make contact or proof sheets. The simplest requires neither a darkroom nor chemicals; all you need are the negatives, a smooth board, a clean piece of glass larger than the paper size, and some *printing-out paper*. The negatives are placed on this paper, with the glass and board sandwiching them in place. The paper is exposed to a very strong light source until an image appears; no wet chemical processing is required.

This was a very early and common form of proof printing, primarily used by commercial portrait studios to show customers the choice of poses. These proofs were easy to make, inexpensive, and the image eventually faded completely (unless bathed in fixer), leaving a dark reddish piece of paper. This discouraged the customer from keeping the proofs and not ordering a finished print. Printing-out proofs have lost their popularity, although the paper is still available, such as Kodak's Studio Proof.

Most proof sheets today are done with normal photographic printing methods, utilizing a darkroom and chemicals. Under safelights, either contact printing paper or enlarging paper is placed emulsion side up on a smooth surface. Negatives are positioned emulsion side down on the paper, and clean glass is placed over them. The paper is exposed to a source of light, often an enlarger, and then the print is processed as usual in developer, stop bath, and fixer.

There are some special *contact printers* available, built like boxes with a glass and a cover on top, and a light bulb inside. In a darkroom, under safelights, negatives are placed emulsion side up on the glass, then the photographic paper is aligned emulsion side down. The cover, a pressure plate, is brought down to assure contact. The white light in the box is turned on to make the exposure.

Instructions with the contact printer recommend the proper wattage of light bulbs, and exposure times. Data sheets packed with contact printing papers also indicate the paper's speed to help you figure exposure. Some contact printing devices are equipped with rheostats for controlling the intensity of the light, as well as timers for making exact exposures. The most sophisticated have multiple lights to control the exposures to individual negative frames or strips.

While some photographers buy or construct contact printing boxes, most use an enlarger to make proof sheets. You may want to purchase a *contact printing frame* to hold the negatives and paper in place beneath the beam of the enlarger's light. These frames have tension backs that force negatives and paper against a front glass. Some models hold the negatives securely in position while the paper is being inserted. Their primary advantage is that duplicate proofs can be made without having to remove or realign the negatives between exposures. However, for general proofing, you need only a piece of moderately heavy plate glass to hold negatives and paper in contact. It should be about 9 x 12 inches, with sanded or taped edges.

30. *Proof sheets can be made by placing negatives and print paper together in a contact printing frame and exposing them to light from an enlarger.*

31. *More commonly, negatives and print paper are kept in contact during exposure by covering them with a piece of glass.*

When making an exposure with the enlarger light, place the printing paper on the enlarger's baseboard, then the negatives, and cover with the glass. The paper's emulsion side should be up, the negative's emulsion side down. A thin piece of foam rubber placed under the paper will guarantee uniform contact between the paper and the negatives.

If your negatives have too much curl to them, cover with heavier glass, or gently push the glass down with your fingers during the exposure. If the glass you use for making contact proofs with your enlarger gets scratched or broken, it is easy and inexpensive to replace. And, if used carefully, it offers little risk of damage to your negatives.

Another consideration is the choice of photographic paper for making proof sheets and contact prints. There are special contact printing papers, like Kodak's Azo or Velox, with emulsions that are considerably "slower" in speed than those of enlarging papers. That's because contact printing papers are designed for use with the close, bright lights of contact printing boxes.

Such papers have wide latitude to provide good results with negatives that have considerable variation in density.

But if you're like most photographers, you'll use an enlarger and enlarging paper to make proof sheets. Besides convenience, an advantage to using your regular enlarging paper is that the proofs will exhibit contrast similar to what you'll get in the final enlargement.

If your proofs are only for negative selection and filing purposes, they can be quickly made by using a resin-coated (RC) paper. With such papers, time for developing, fixing, washing, and drying is cut to a minimum. Whether using RC or conventional papers, don't use one with a textured surface like silk or tweed, because it will interfere with appraising the proof for image details and flaws in the negatives.

The contrast grade of the paper you use for proofing should be normal, grade No. 2. Of course, due to the variance in manufacturers' grading standards, some brands of paper may be marked grade No. 1 or No. 3 and still give normal contrast. But if your proofing requires a contrast grade softer or harder than Nos. 1, 2, or 3, something was wrong with your film, exposure, or processing.

Get the "dry" area of your darkroom ready first. If using an enlarger, turn it on, and move the enlarger head up to a height where its light will be broad enough to cover the contact printing frame or contact cover glass. With the negative carrier in place, focus until the carrier's edges are projected sharply on the baseboard. Do not focus on an enlarger's condensors, because specks of dust may be projected onto the photo paper and mistakenly appear as flaws in the negatives.

If you are proofing with an enlarger but using Kodak's Velox or Azo or similar contact printing paper of slow speed, it's a good idea to remove the enlarging lens to increase the light intensity and thus shorten the exposure. In this case, examine the pattern of light the enlarger produces and raise or lower the enlarger until uniform illumination appears over the proofing area on the baseboard.

Once you know the enlarger height required to cover your proofing paper with light, mark it for the future. Either measure the distance from the baseboard, or paint a line on the enlarger's support column at the appropriate point. Some enlargers incorporate a measuring tape on the support column, with a pointer attached to the enlarger head.

When the proper enlarger height has been set, stop down the enlarger lens (if you are using a lens). With normal grade No. 2 paper, stop down from the widest aperture opening at least two or more f/stops, usually to f/5.6 or f/8 with a 50mm lens. This gives you more control of exposure time; it's not advisable to expose proof sheets less than 4 seconds unless your enlarger is equipped with a very accurate solid-state electronic timer. Also, with very short exposure times, fluctuations in the household electric voltage may cause inconsistent results, unless you have a voltage regulator/stabilizer.

Whether your proofing device is simply glass, a contact printing frame, or a self-contained contact printer, clean the glass to make sure it is free of dust and fingerprints.

If you have washed and dried your negatives properly, there should be no reason to clean them, particularly if they were cut in strips and placed into protective sleeves as soon as dry. If not, you may want to run a soft antistatic or lint-free cloth over them, but be very careful to handle the negatives by their edges, and don't press too hard. To avoid risking scratches, some photographers never clean their negatives for proofing, but only when making a final print or enlargement.

Next, set up the "wet" area of your darkroom. Use three trays big enough for your proofing paper, and pour in developer, stop bath, and fixer. With 8 x 10-inch size trays, fill each with about 32 ounces, or one liter, of chemical. Lesser quantities can be used if only a few sheets of paper are to be processed, but the solutions must cover all prints completely. Chemical temperatures should be 68° to 70°F (20° to 21°C); there will be a loss in contrast if developer temperature is less than 68°F. (Read details about various chemicals and other considerations for making black-and-white prints in chapter 5, "Considering Black-and-White Papers and Processing.") Here's a summary of suggested chemicals to use, if you have no personal preferences as yet.

Developer. Kodak's Dektol, diluted one part stock solution to two parts water (1:2), is an excellent print developer, packed in powder form. If you prefer a liquid concentrate, try Kodak's Ektaflo, Type 1, diluted 1:9.

Stop bath. For a stop bath, dilute a 28 percent acetic acid stock solution 1.5:32, one and a half parts stock solution to thirty-two parts water (stock solution is prepared by mixing three parts glacial acetic acid with eight parts water). Also available are stop baths that change color to indicate when they are exhausted and should be replaced. Two such types, both liquid concentrates that must be diluted for use, are Kodak's Indicator Stop Bath and Ektaflo Stop Bath. When they turn from yellow to purplish blue, discard them.

Fixer. Popular ones are Kodak's Fixer, in powder form, as well as Rapid Fixer and Ektaflo Fixer, both liquid concentrates, which require dilution with water to make working solutions.

Optionally, you can prepare another chemical solution for your prints, a *clearing agent,* which helps eliminate the fixer and allow prints to be washed in a short time. Use this solution, like Kodak's Hypo Clearing Agent, with conventional papers, not resin-coated.

Facilities for print washing also should be made ready. If you plan to make a considerable number of prints with conventional photo papers, a stand bath (a tray of tap water) can be set up to hold the prints after fixing. Then you can easily and adequately clear and wash prints in batches.

Turn on the safelight(s) in your darkroom's "wet" area, and check that

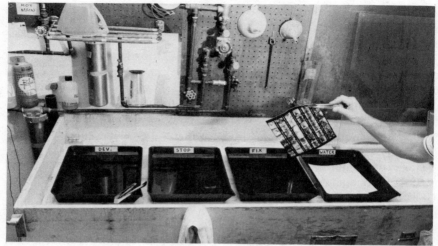

32. *Marking trays avoids the possibility of putting prints in the wrong solutions. The usual order is developer, stop bath, and fixer; an optional stand bath of water can be used to hold prints before washing them.*

your processing clock or timer is plugged in and working. Place print tongs at their appropriate trays, and be sure clean towels are handy.

Determining a Standard Exposure and Contrast Grade for Proofs

In order to make contact proofs as quickly as possible, and avoid remakes, you should establish a standard procedure for each type of film you shoot. Then by using the same enlarger height, f/stop, exposure time, printing paper and developer you'll get a good proof every time.

For initial testing to determine a *standard exposure,* select a strip of negatives which appears to have good contrast. Place this negative strip with a sheet of photo paper for contact printing, making sure they are placed emulsion to emulsion (see page 98).

Next, cover two-thirds of the negative strip with black cardboard (use the piece packed with the photo paper). With your enlarger's lens set at f/5.6, expose for 4 seconds. Then uncover another one-third of the paper, and make another 4-second exposure. Finally, remove the cardboard completely, and make a final exposure of 4 seconds. Thus, one-third of the paper is exposed for 4 seconds, another one-third for 8 seconds, and the other one-third for 12 seconds.

Mark the exposed paper by bending a corner and return it to the light-tight paper package. Then take a small piece of photo paper and expose it (without the negatives) to the enlarger's light for 12 seconds, with the enlarger's lens wide open. Now take this paper, as well as the piece previously exposed with negatives, plus an *unexposed* blank piece of paper, and develop all three at the same time.

Once through the fixer, examine the test print. If none of the exposures has produced images with good contrast (all too light or too dark), repeat the test with a different set of exposures. If all are too dark, you'll need to shorten the exposure time.

If exposure time is less than 4 seconds, exact timing may be impossible if your enlarger timer is not precise enough for short exposures. In such cases, decrease exposure by stopping down the enlarger lens. Stopping down one full f/stop cuts exposure in half. That means if you require a 2-second exposure at f/5.6, but don't trust your timer for such a short exposure time, you will get the same results by making a 4-second exposure at f/8. (Stopping down from f/5.6 to f/8 cuts the exposure in half, but doubling the time from 2 seconds to 4 seconds without changing the f/stop makes the identical exposure.)

In judging the test print, first determine the *minimum* exposure required to produce the *maximum black* in the paper. This is easily done by comparing it with the piece of blank paper which was exposed 12 seconds to the enlarger's full light (without any negative). This paper has developed to the maximum black possible, so compare it to the three exposures of the negative strip. Match the all-black piece to the black seen in the edges of the printed negatives, and choose the shortest exposure of the three that gives the maximum black.

Next, to determine a *standard contrast grade* for proofs, you should compare the all-white piece of developed (but unexposed) paper with the brightest highlight areas of the printed negatives. The highlight areas to compare must be ones that give the *maximum white* you would desire in a final print.

If any areas of the test print where you expect some image detail match the white test piece, you need to *decrease* the contrast grade of your paper to a softer grade (i.e. to a lower number, such as No. 3 to No. 2, or No. 2 to No. 1). If there are any areas of the test print where you expect white but get a gray, you need to *increase* the contrast grade of your paper to a harder grade (i.e. to a higher number, such as No. 2 to No. 3, or No. 3 to No. 4).

If a change in paper contrast grade is indicated, make another set of test prints with the different grade paper—expose maximum black and maximum white pieces, as well as a strip of negatives. (If you ever find it necessary to use a grade No. 0 or No. 5 paper to achieve the proper contrast in a proof print, it indicates there was probably something wrong with your film's exposure or processing.)

Once proof print results are satisfactory, you can standardize your exposure and paper grade for the future. Proofing will then be simple and fast, and produce the best contact prints. But you must keep everything the same: film, film developer, photo paper and contrast grade, enlarger height, printing exposure, paper developer, and processing technique.

Exposing Contact Prints

Arrange the negatives in a nearby clean space in the order in which they are to be proofed. Turn off the room light, and under safelights (at least 4 feet away), center a sheet of photo paper on the enlarger baseboard. You'll recall an 8 x 10-inch sheet will accommodate a cut-up thirty-six exposure roll of 35mm film or a twelve-exposure 120-size roll. The paper's emulsion (shiny side) should be face up. Lay the negatives on top, emulsion (dull side) down, and cover with the piece of glass.

If using a contact printing box, the negatives should be positioned on the glass emulsion side up, then covered with the print paper, emulsion side down.

Determining which are the emulsion sides of negatives and papers may not be easy in dim safelight, but remember that the edges of most photographic films and papers tend to curl *toward* the emulsion side. To be sure the images will appear as you shot them (not backward), the negative emulsion should always face the print paper emulsion. Just think "emulsion to emulsion."

Developing Prints

Make your exposure according to the predetermined time, then lift the glass or contact printer pressure plate and carefully remove the paper. Start the processing timer or notice the clock, and insert the paper into the developer, face up, using your fingers or a print tong. Do this quickly and smoothly so the developing process will be uniform.

Developing times vary according to paper type and developer. There is a *minimum-maximum time range* in which the print will develop correctly.

For instance, with Kodak's Polycontrast paper in Dektol developer (diluted 1:2), recommended development time is 1½ minutes; the minimum time in which a Polycontrast print can correctly develop is 1 minute, and the maximum time is 3 minutes.

Another example is Kodak's Velox contact printing paper. In Dektol (diluted 1:2), the recommended development time is 1 minute, while the useful development range is 45 seconds to 2 minutes.

Always allow a print to develop for at least the minimum time, even if it is obviously developing too fast, because this will help you refigure exposure time when remaking the print. Some photographers "save" a print by pulling the paper out sooner than the minimum time, but the print's quality will be nowhere near its potential. By cutting the developing time, you are preventing the paper from developing to its maximum black and contrast is reduced. Such underdeveloping may also create *mottling* in the print (see page 113).

If the print does not develop adequately within the maximum development time, it's best to remake the print. That's because overdevelopment can produce excessive fog, which will dull the highlights from white to gray.

A good habit is to be consistent with your developing time for a particular paper in order to obtain the best quality print that your paper and developer can produce.

The contrast of some papers, as you are advised in their data sheets, can be adjusted by manipulating exposure and development. With Kodak's Medalist enlarging paper, for instance, more exposure and less development will decrease contrast, while less exposure and more development will increase contrast. Of course, extreme under- or overdevelopment can cause mottling or fogging.

Agitating Prints

As with films, it is necessary to agitate prints in the developer and the other processing steps. This is accomplished by gently rocking the tray throughout the development period. Lift up one corner of the tray several times to create motion with the chemicals, and when the action subsides, rock another corner. Alternating corners prevents a pattern in the developing action, and the creation of *surge marks* (see page 45). If part of the paper rises to the surface, poke it down with a print tong—or your fingers—but be careful not to scrape the emulsion.

Reserve one pair of tongs for use in the developer tray, and one or two for the stop bath and fixer, and thus avoid contaminating the developer with tongs that have been in the stop bath or fixer. Also, if your fingers have been in the stop bath or fixer, rinse them thoroughly before putting them back in the developer. Some photographers use one hand exclusively in the developer, the other hand in stop bath and fixer. After a while, precautions against contamination become second nature to you and help avoid darkroom problems.

Stopping Development and Fixing Prints

When near the end of the development time, pull the print out of the developer by one corner and allow it to drain over the tray for the final 10 seconds.

Slide the print into the *stop bath* when development time is up, being careful to keep the developer tongs out of the stop bath. Agitate as before, keeping the submerged print in the stop bath for 5 seconds with resin-coated papers and 5 to 10 seconds with conventional papers. With a different set of tongs, drain the print over the stop bath, then slide it into the *fixer*. After at least 60 seconds of continuous agitation (or 30 seconds with resin-coated paper), you can turn the room lights on to examine your print.

First make certain all unexposed photographic paper is covered up in its light-tight envelope or box before turning on the lights, or you might expose and ruin the paper. The habit of checking to be sure the paper is protected before turning on a white light will quickly become an automatic reflex.

If the fixer is not fresh, it is advisable to allow as long as 2 minutes' fixing time before turning on a white light. This is to avoid eventual staining in white areas of the print because unexposed silver in the paper's emulsion is still sensitive to light until it is adequately dissolved by the fixer.

Viewing Wet Prints

An exciting moment is the first look at any print, even a contact proof sheet. To view a print during the fixing stage, it is usually necessary to lift it from the fixer tray and hold it at an angle to your viewing light in order to eliminate reflections from the print's chemical-covered surface. Some photographers include a flat drainboard in their darkrooms for viewing wet prints. Be certain to rinse the print briefly in fresh water before placing it on the board, and you can squeegee excess water off the paper to make viewing even better.

Practice teaches you the best way to judge wet prints or enlargements. For one thing, most photo papers have a *dry-down factor* which makes them seem darker once they are completely dry (see page 113).

As for proof sheets, your most immediate concern is contrast. If a wet proof seems too contrasty (no gray tones) or too gray (no strong blacks or whites), make another proof at a different exposure. If the first proof is satisfactory, return it to the fixer for the remaining time required.

Washing and Drying Prints

Remember to agitate the print in the fixer, and drain the print before transferring it to the wash water. Resin-coated papers can be washed immediately for 2 to 4 minutes.

If additional prints are to be made with conventional photo papers, you can put fixed prints into a water stand bath until you're ready to wash all the prints at once. Washing requires at least 1 hour, with a change of water every 5 minutes.

To speed washing of conventional papers, bathe them first in a clearing agent solution, with agitation. Kodak's Hypo Clearing Agent requires a 2-minute treatment for single-weight (SW) papers, and 3 minutes for double-weight (DW) papers. Afterward, single-weight papers should be washed for 10 minutes, and double-weight papers for 20 minutes. Be sure to agitate and separate the prints during the wash cycle. There are some clearing agents, like Permawash, that work faster than Kodak's. Regardless, mix only the quantity of clearing agent required to clear the number of prints you've made, because the solution does not keep longer than 24 hours. Do use a clearing agent with RC prints.

A good time to clean up your darkroom is while your prints are washing. Pour all reusable chemicals back into storage bottles, and mark down the quantity of paper run through them. If using a funnel, remember to wash it off after use with each solution in order to avoid chemical contamination. Also, wash the trays in hot water, and sponge them to remove any chemical residue.

(Methods for drying prints are discussed in detail in the previous chapter, beginning on page 86).

Enlarging Proof Sheets

Sometimes it is useful to have proof images larger than contact size, because they can be studied without using a magnifier. With a 4 x 5-inch enlarger, you can make bigger images, printing as many as six to nine 35mm negatives at the same time. Use a glass negative carrier to hold the strips of negatives flat. Adjust the enlarger so all the projected images fit onto your proof paper.

If you want to get a uniform proof print from over- or underexposed negatives, group negatives of similar density together and adjust your printing exposure and paper contrast grade accordingly. Follow procedures for making enlargements, described in the following chapter.

Processing Prints by Batch

Processing prints in batches (sometimes called *gang processing*) is a time-saving technique, especially when making contact proof sheets or a number of prints from the same negative. You will need a light-tight storage box or paper safe to hold the exposed prints (or proof sheets) until you are ready to process them. An empty one hundred-sheet size photographic paper box works well. Tape one end of the box to act as a hinge, so the lid will open and close easily.

After exposing a sheet of paper, stack it in the storage box and always place subsequent sheets in the same direction. When ready to process, take several sheets and leaf them, as a bank teller does when counting currency, so one end sticks out over the other. If arranged in this manner, one sheet at a time can easily be taken off the top of the stack with one hand.

For batch processing, use your hands, not tongs. One hand gets wet in the developer, and the other hand stays dry to pick up each sheet of exposed paper. There are two different procedures, depending whether you are processing conventional papers or resin-coated papers. The following technique is for *conventional papers*.

Place your stack of prints in a dry spot near the developer tray. Wait until the second hand of your timing clock is approaching some convenient marking point, say the hour or half-hour, and *drop* the print face down in the developer. Be careful not to splatter the developer, or get your dry hand wet. With your wet hand, gently push the print down at the center and move it around to allow any air bubbles to escape. Prints are dropped facedown so there is no risk of damaging the emulsion with your fingers. Drop the second print on top when the clock's second hand marks 10 seconds and follow with subsequent prints every 10 seconds.

Continue to agitate the prints throughout the developing time, by interleafing with both hands. Do this by switching the bottom print to the top of the tray, and turning it *faceup*. Follow in order with the other prints, bottom to top, turning them faceup. This provides adequate agitation, if you also rock the tray and slide each print around in the developer as you place it on top.

The image direction of the *first* print should be turned in the *opposite* direction of all the other prints, so you know which print to remove first. Toward the end of the developer time, adjust your pace of interleafing so the first print is back on the bottom.

At the final 10 seconds of developing time, pull this bottom print from the developer and allow it to drain over the tray. When time is up, drop it facedown into the stop bath tray, pushing it down with the other hand to begin agitation. Use the hand still wet with developer to pull the next print from the bottom of the developer tray, drain it 10 seconds, and drop it into the stop bath. Continue in order from the bottom, so each print will have an equal amount of time in the developer.

Accomplished printers can easily batch process as many as twenty-five sheets of conventional photo paper in a 3-minute developer time, with no processing flaws. In the beginning, practice with three or four sheets at a time. The maximum number you can process at once depends on the developer time, print size, and your agility.

Because developer time for *resin-coated papers* is so short (60 seconds is recommended for Kodak's Polycontrast Rapid II RC), the number of RC prints you can process at one time is especially limited, and a different agitation technique is required. One reason is that the emulsion surface of resin-coated papers is somewhat more delicate than conventional photographic papers. Scratches from fingernails or the edges of another piece of photo paper will show up as gray or black marks when the paper is fixed.

If the scratches occur in the developer stage, there is very little you can do except remake the print. But if the marks are created in the fixer stage, sometimes they can be gently rubbed out with your fingertips.

Because of their resin-coating, RC papers drain quicker, so they can be placed in the developer every 5 seconds (instead of 10). At that rate, six prints will all be in the developer within ½ minute. With just 30 seconds of developer time left, it is necessary to agitate all the prints at once. This is different than agitating conventional papers, because RC prints cannot be easily interleafed without risking surface scratches.

After the resin-coated prints have been dropped in the developer, one by one (every 5 seconds), facedown, use both hands and push the prints in from all sides until they are stacked together in the center of the tray. Be careful when doing this not to actually pick the prints up from the developer, since this will force them in contact with each other and impede the flow of fresh developer between each sheet. Agitate the stack from their corners, using your thumb and forefingers to gently twist the stack from side to side and end to end. If done properly, the prints will move freely, allowing fresh developer to be continually brought in contact with the emulsion.

As you near the end of the development time, drain the first print (it should be on the bottom of the stack) for 5 seconds, and drop it facedown in the stop bath. Continue transferring the remaining prints at the same rate. Once all the prints are in the stop bath, pushing them down as each successive print is inserted, immediately drain and place them into the fixer one by one. Continue group agitation in the fixer until fixer time is up (usually 2 minutes), then wash them. Washing resin-coated papers is much faster than conventional papers and requires special consideration.

To avoid damage to their emulsion, most resin-coated papers should not be washed longer than 4 minutes; normally, a 2-minute wash is recommended. A simple print washer of the flow-through type is the best style for RC papers. Water enters through small holes at one end of the washing tray, passes over the prints, and drains out the other end. The rate of water exchange is controlled by water pressure from the faucet. Tumbling-style drum washers are not adequate because of their slow rate of water exchange and the tumbling action which may scratch print surfaces.

Because of the slick surface of resin-coated papers, the prints will not bunch up or stick together unless you try to wash too many for the size of the tray, or unless the prints' surfaces are not all facing in the same direction, whether up or down.

If you have only a few resin-coated prints, you can easily and efficiently wash them in a regular tray tilted at a slight angle under a running faucet. Dump the tray water two or three times, and interleaf the prints carefully during the short wash time required.

Do not allow RC prints to wash more than the recommended time, or to soak before washing, because moisture can get into the paper along its edges and cause the print to curl.

7

Making Black-and-White Enlargements Step by Step

After reading chapters 4, 5, and 6, you should be ready to make black-and-white enlargements.

Preparing the Darkroom

The first step in enlarging is to get everything ready in the *dry area* of your darkroom. Start by checking over the enlarger. Periodic cleaning of the enlarger lens, condensors, and lamp housing is necessary in order to avoid dust—always a curse in the darkroom. Use a lint-free cloth or a dry photo chamois, but only clean enlarger lenses with photographic lens cleaning tissue.

A dirty lens will reduce image sharpness and contrast, so keep it free of dust and fingerprints. Use a *lens cap* between printing sessions to protect the lens. Before printing, look through the lens with the enlarger light on to see if the lens is dirty on the other side; if so, remove the lens to clean it. Use *liquid lens cleaner,* if necessary.

The enlarger's support column may require occasional lubrication for smooth up and down movement. Check this, too, now and then.

Make sure safelights, enlarger timer, and enlarger are plugged in and working. Set up the enlarging easel, adjusting the border masks for the size of prints you intend to make first. Clean the enlarging magnifier for sharp focusing. If needed, have variable contrast filters clean and ready. Be sure your enlarging paper is handy, and sufficient for the printing job ahead, as well as your dodging and burning-in tools. And don't forget to arrange the negatives in the order you intend printing.

Now prepare the *wet area* of your darkroom, setting up three processing trays and pouring in premixed solutions of developer, stop bath, and fixer. If you do not already have a favorite set of chemicals, try these: developer—Kodak's Dektol, when diluted 1:2 (one part stock developer to two parts water) is suitable for many photo papers; stop bath—Kodak's 28 percent Acetic Acid, which is diluted 1.5:32 for a working solution; and Kodak's Fixer or Rapid Fixer, diluted according to instructions on their packages. (Also, read more about print processing chemicals, beginning on page 82.)

Optionally, you can set up two more trays—for a water stand bath and clearing agent—unless you are processing resin-coated papers. For the stand bath, where prints remain before washing, use regular water from the faucet. For the clearing solution, which neutralizes the fixer and thus reduces wash time by two-thirds, try Kodak's Hypo Clearing Agent, or Orbitbath or Permawash. (Never use the clearing agent as a stand bath.)

Arrange the trays in the sequence of processing, usually left to right for right-handed persons. When mixing chemicals, or diluting them for working solutions, do so in the order of processing. This helps avoid chemical contamination, even though measuring graduates, mixing containers, stirring rod, funnel, and thermometer should always be thoroughly washed before preparing each solution.

Normal processing temperatures range between 68° and 75°F (20° and 24°C) for all black-and-white print chemicals, but read the directions packed with the chemicals for specific temperature recommendations. Use hot or cold water baths to warm or cool chemicals, as necessary. Keeping them stored at working temperature eliminates the need for a water bath.

The trays should be filled with enough solution to completely cover the prints. Generally, at least one quart (about one liter) should be poured in 8 x 10-inch size trays, and two quarts in 11 x 14-inch trays. Don't be stingy with the chemicals, or mottled and stained prints may result. The fixer tray usually is filled with maximum solution because most often it will contain several prints at the same time.

Set out print tongs, one at the developing tray, another at the stop bath tray, and a third at the fixer tray. Some photographers use just one pair of print tongs between the stop bath and fixer trays, but this reduces the life of the stop bath because fixer will be carried back to it by the tongs. Regardless, mark one pair of tongs for use only in the developer and never in the other chemicals. Mark these developer tongs in some manner that will make them easy to identify under safelight illumination.

Finally, make sure the safelight near your processing trays is on, the processing timer or clock is working, wash water is running at the proper temperature, and towels are handy.

Selecting and Cleaning Negatives

If you have established a standardized proofing procedure (see page 96), choosing the "best" negatives to print will be quite easy—at least in regard to exposure and contrast. Content and composition are other considerations, and close inspection of the proof sheet is necessary. Because 35mm images are so small, you should use some sort of magnifier to study them. Photo stores carry special magnifiers for this purpose; an excellent and inexpensive one is Agfa's Lupe 8X (pronounced "loop"), which covers one 35mm frame.

Besides content, carefully examine the images for any physical defects, such as mottle, scratches, or spots. If these are noticed in the proof, inspect the negatives themselves to see if perhaps some of the flaws are simply the result of careless proofing, instead of damaged or dirty negatives.

Each negative you select for printing should be cleaned prior to putting it in the enlarger. This can be done with air, blowing it at both sides of the negative. A can of compressed, inert air can be used for this purpose. Omit and Dustoff are two popular brands. A less effective substitute is a small hand-squeezed rubber blower available at most camera stores; some even have a soft brush attached to help remove dust particles.

An excellent dusting device is an *antistatic brush* that neutralizes static electricity on the negative so the dust will brush away—instead of just being pushed around on the negative. Antistatic dusting cloths also are available for cleaning negatives. Protect any such cloth or brush when not in use so that grit or other substances will not become imbedded in them and possibly scratch your negatives.

Occasionally, impurities accidentally dry on the film. The safest way to remove these is to rewash the film in water, and dry it again. If a negative is smudged with fingerprints, carefully wipe it with a soft, lint-free cloth dampened with *liquid film cleaner.*

Sometimes you can remove smudges or other residue, or fill in light scratches on negatives, by using your finger to rub some of the skin oil normally found at the sides of your nose, and transferring it to the negative. Spread it evenly in the same direction. Vaseline also can be used, moderately and cautiously, to fill in negative scratches. Practice first on an unimportant scratched negative to see the result and make sure your application technique is correct. Expose Vaseline-treated negatives in a glassless negative carrier.

To avoid fingerprints, handle all negatives by their edges, or with *clean cotton gloves.* Check for dust on both sides of a negative by holding it at an angle to the enlarger light. Do this before and after putting the negative in the negative carrier.

Loading the Negative Carrier

Carriers that have glass to hold the negative flat and in place should be cleaned and checked for dust regularly. (Clean the glass with water, never with a commercial window cleaner, like Windex, which may leave a chemical film that will affect your negative and thus the print.) A glassless negative carrier should be checked frequently for burrs or nicks, and wiped or polished clean to prevent scratches on your negatives. Most glassless carriers are two plates of metal or hard plastic, either hinged together or kept in alignment by registration pins. They require pressure to hold the negative flat and in position.

Always position the desired negative correctly in the carrier opening before bringing the carrier's top and bottom plates together. Once pressure is applied, never try to reposition the negative or move from one frame to another without reopening the carrier. With carriers that have registration pins to align the top and bottom plates, be careful negatives do not slide onto the top of the pins when the carrier is being placed in the enlarger. Otherwise, the negatives may be creased and their images damaged.

Some enlargers have lamp housings that raise up to allow the carrier to be inserted, then come down to rest on the carrier and provide the pressure to keep the negatives flat and in position. Never leave such a housing raised when not in use, because dust may settle inside on the enlarger lens and condensors.

Negatives should be placed in the carrier emulsion (dull) side down, unless you purposely want to print the image in reverse. Turn the negative around bottom-to-top so the image will be projected top side up on your easel.

Making Final Adjustments

Be sure the enlarging easel is adjusted for the print size you desire. The portions of photo paper that are covered by the easel's frame and masking strips will become white borders around the print.

Turn the room lights off and switch the enlarger on. The lens aperture should be wide open to provide the brightest image and easiest focusing. Raise or lower the enlarger until the negative is projected in the image size desired, then adjust for fine focus. If your easel or baseboard is dark, cover it with a piece of white paper for easier composition and focusing.

Because focusing is so critical, an enlarging magnifier will be a great help. This is placed on the easel or baseboard, where a portion of the projected image is viewed through the magnifier eyepiece.

Do not leave the enlarger turned on any longer than necessary, because heat from the lamp can buckle the negative in a glassless carrier and put it out of focus.

Figuring Exposure by Making a Test Print

Now you're ready for the actual exposure, but this can be guesswork until you gain experience. Unless you use an enlarging meter (see page 64), the best idea is to make a test print, or test strips, to determine the correct exposure, and therefore avoid wasting time and paper. For your initial test print, use a negative of normal contrast with a normal contrast paper, grade No. 2 (or a No. 2 filter if you're using a variable contrast paper).

Exposure, as you know, is controlled by the f/stop of the enlarger's lens and the length of time the enlarger lamp is turned on..After focusing, stop down the lens aperture to f/8 or f/11 for good depth of focus. With the enlarger turned off, remove a sheet of photo paper from its light-tight box and place it in the easel.

Now expose sections of this paper for different amounts of time. First, expose the paper for 5 seconds, then cover up an inch or two with a piece of cardboard, and expose again for 5 more seconds. Continue covering more of the paper and making additional exposures in equal increments. When finished, you should have a print exposed variously for 5, 10, 15, 20, and perhaps 25 seconds.

Process the test print, then study it under room light to pick the section (and thus the exposure) that gave you the best results. If none of the exposures produced an acceptable image, make another test print. If your first images were all too dark, shorten the exposure times; if all of them were too light, increase the exposure times.

Remember that exposure also can be altered by changing the enlarger lens f/stop. A change of one full f/stop is equal to doubling or halving the exposure time. For instance, if you're going to double an exposure of 10 seconds at f/8, instead of increasing the time to 20 seconds at f/8, keep the time at 10 seconds and open the lens to f/5.6.

Likewise, if you're going to halve an exposure of 10 seconds at f/8, instead of cutting the time to 5 seconds at f/8, you keep the time at 10 seconds and close the lens down to f/11.

When a test print yields a section you determine to be of correct exposure, study the images more carefully in regard to contrast. Perhaps the grade of paper (or contrast filter) you chose to use with the negative is not the best choice. If the blacks are not as black as they should be, but increasing the exposure makes the whites go gray, you need to use a paper of higher contrast, say grade No. 3 or greater. On the other hand, if the blacks are good, but the whites are so bright that details are lost, you need to change to a

33. Study the test print to see which exposure gives the image you like best. The exposures here were in 5-second increments, at f/11; the lightest section was exposed for 5 seconds, the darkest for 25 seconds.

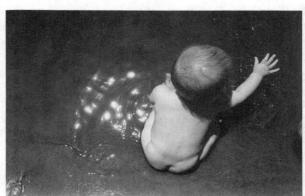

34. The final print, with an exposure of 20 seconds, at f/11.

lower contrast grade, like No. 1. Of course, with variable contrast papers, you change to a filter of a higher or lower number in order to alter contrast.

Whenever you change to a different contrast grade (or filter), check the paper's data sheet as to the ANSI paper speed to see if a change in exposure also is needed. Instead of making another test print to determine exposure, the ANSI speed can be used to refigure exposure (see page 73).

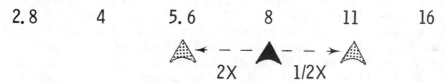

35. Light-admitting relationships of f/stops: opening up to the next wider f/stop (such as f/8 to f/5.6) doubles the amount of light transmitted by the lens, while closing down to the next smaller f/stop (such as f/8 to f/11) cuts the amount of light in half.

36. *The grade of paper affects contrast, and thus the outcome of a print. This print was made on No. 2 normal contrast paper.*

37. *The same negative printed on a No. 6 high contrast paper; notice the change in gray tones. For other examples, see Illustrations 23—28 in chapter 5.*

Changes in the magnification of the negative image will also alter exposure time. For a larger image, the enlarger head must be raised, and the greater the distance the light source is from the paper, the longer the exposure required. As a practical guideline, every time you double the distance between the lens and photo paper, increase exposure four times. For example, the enlarging lens is 12 inches from the paper and produces a good print at f/8 with 10 seconds' exposure. If the enlarger head is raised so the lens is now 24 inches from the paper (twice the original distance), exposure time will be about 40 seconds (at f/8) to get a good print. To avoid such a long exposure time, you can open up the f/stop instead. To increase exposure four times, open to f/4 (at 10 seconds).

If you raised the lens one and a half times the original distance from the paper, increase exposure two times. Thus, using the example above, increasing the lens-to-paper distance from 12 inches to 18 inches will increase exposure time from 10 seconds to 20 seconds at f/8 (or keep the exposure time at 10 seconds and open up the lens to f/5.6).

After you finally establish exposure (f/stop and time), and contrast grade, you may want to make a final test with a single strip of paper to check for print density and contrast. In this way, in case you've misjudged anything, you don't waste a full sheet of paper. Be sure to position the strip where the projected image has a variety of tones, from dark to light.

With experience, you can establish basic guidelines for figuring exposure and contrast grades without tedious test printing. A simple test strip may be all you need to make before exposing a full sheet of paper to produce the final print.

Appraising the Final Enlargement

After the final enlargement is developed and in the fixer or wash, you can inspect it by room light. Be sure any unexposed or undeveloped paper is in a light-tight box or paper safe before turning on the light. Study the print carefully, not only for exposure and contrast but for composition and technical mistakes.

If the easel was accidentally moved, your subject may be ill-composed, or the horizon could be tilted. If either the enlarger or easel was jarred during exposure, the image may be blurred. If paper was improperly positioned in the easel, the print borders may be crooked, or too thick or too thin.

Look for excessive dust spots, and scratches made by print tongs or your fingernails during processing. And check for stains. By noticing errors at this stage (before drying), you still have everything set up and can easily make another print.

38. A problem called mottling can occur when an overexposed print is pulled from the developer before developing action is complete. Streaked or blotchy development and low contrast will be evident.

39. A properly exposed and developed print, with good contrast.

Figuring the Dry-Down Factor

Another thing to consider when judging a wet print is what can be called a *dry-down factor;* prints that are wet appear lighter than when they are dry. They "dry down" darker than you might expect, sometimes as much as the equivalent of one-half f/stop in exposure. However, this increase in density varies considerably for each brand, grade, and surface of paper. You can make a test that reveals this, as well as provide yourself a "perfect" sample print for comparison with wet prints in the future.

Expose and process a print that looks good when inspected wet under lights you normally use for studying prints at that stage. Then make five more prints, each at 10 percent *less exposure* than the previous one. Mark the total percentage of reduced exposure on the back of each print, using a grease or lead pencil so it won't wash off. Process and dry all the prints as you normally do.

If this is the first time you have printed, or even if you have been printing for some time, this test will surprise you as to how much difference drying really makes. View the prints all together, as well as separated, under lighting conditions similar to those where the prints normally will be viewed.

Pick the print you like best, then use the percentage of exposure reduction marked on its back to determine exposure for future prints. If the print of 10 percent exposure reduction looks best, expose subsequent prints 10 percent less than you normally would. Those prints will seem light when viewed wet, but they will dry down to the density you like.

You also can use a proportionately lighter print to put up dry in the darkroom for matching with wet prints. For example, if you've determined that a 10 percent reduction is best, a dry print of 20 percent exposure reduction will be the print to post for viewing in the darkroom. Your wet prints should match its density, so they will dry down to the final density you prefer. (If you liked the print of 20 percent exposure reduction best, post the print of 40 percent exposure reduction for matching wet prints viewed in the darkroom.)

For every type of paper you use that's of a different brand, grade or surface, record its dry-down information, including the percentage of exposure reduction, as well as the developer and developer time. Caution: if you ever change your darkroom viewing light wattage or style, it will be necessary to redo the dry-down tests because illumination of the wet print will change and so will your evaluation of its density. (For details about washing and drying enlargements and other black-and-white prints, read the information previously given in chapters 5 and 6.)

Improving the Print

There are several things you can do during the exposure or processing of a print that will enhance the result. Because "straight" printing may not give you the best print possible, some clever yet common manipulation often makes the difference between a poor print and a good print.

Two things can be done during the print exposure stage, *dodging* and *burning-in.* By dodging, you prevent full exposure of certain areas in the print, thus improving detail where the image would otherwise develop too dark. By burning-in, you add additional exposure to certain areas of the print, thus improving detail where the image would otherwise develop too light.

Dodging tools are usually homemade, and resemble a wand with a disc at one end. You can cut various circles and other shapes from black posterboard, opaque plastic, or other dark material, then fasten each with tape or glue to a piece of wire, such as a thin black coat hanger. The disc must not transmit light, nor be of a color or material that will reflect light from the photo paper back onto the photo paper. The support wire must be firm yet thin, so it will not cast a shadow on the print.

A burning-in tool is an opaque board with a hole in it. You can make it from dark, nonreflective posterboard, plastic, or other material. When held midway

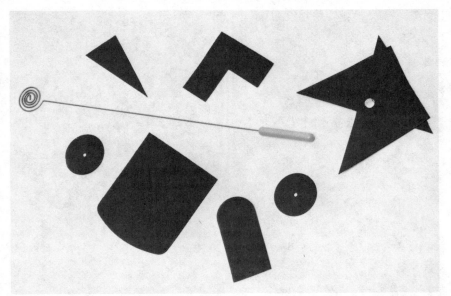

40. *Commercial or homemade dodging tools of various shapes are used during exposure with an enlarger to lighten areas in a print.*

between the enlarger lens and baseboard, it must be big enough to block all the enlarger light. You can buy or make a burning-in device that features a rotating wheel with holes of various shapes and sizes, or adjustable with flexible leaves like a lens aperture.

Also consider your hands as effective burning-in and dodging devices. You can hold them together so light will shine only between your thumb and forefingers for burning-in, or shape your fist or fingers to dodge areas near the edge of a print.

Always select the appropriate tools and practice your technique for the specific negative being printed before placing photo paper in the enlarging easel.

Dodging is accomplished by moving your dodger—the wandlike device or your hand—into the projected beam of enlarger light and over the area of the print you wish to lighten. The basic exposure time must be long enough to allow time for dodging. If exposure time is too short, especially if you have two or more areas to dodge, decrease the enlarger lens opening by one or two f/stops so you can increase the exposure time (see page 109). Beware of excessive exposure times, particularly if using a glassless negative carrier, because your negative may buckle from enlarger lamp heat and thus change focus. Initially, until you become confident about dodging, you may want to practice dodging with test strips in order to judge exposure and save photo paper.

41. In this backlighted photograph, the photographer decided the dog was too dark in the print.

42. To lighten up the dog, he used a dodger during part of the exposure to keep the dog's image from striking the paper.

When dodging, keep the dodging tool moving so its shape, or support wire, won't show up in the print. The dodger can be moved either laterally or up and down. The dodger is often a circle or oblong disc, but you may want to make one that is the general shape of the area to be lightened. Make it small enough so that it can be moved around enough without inadvertently lightening surrounding areas.

You may want to record dodging data on the proof sheet, in case you make additional prints later. Along with other basic information, indicate the dodged area and time. For example "dodge face for 5 seconds."

Burning-in, unlike dodging, is done after the basic exposure rather than during it. Keep the opening in the burning-in tool moving around the area to be darkened, so the edges will blend in. Do this with lateral movement, or by raising and lowering the burning-in board. Be careful during prolonged burning-in exposures that the negative does not pop out of focus because of enlarger lamp heat. You can correct this problem, if it occurs occasionally, by simply opening the enlarging lens up one or two f/stops and make a corresponding cut in burning-in exposure time.

Mention should be made of the *red safety filter* that is usually in a pivoting

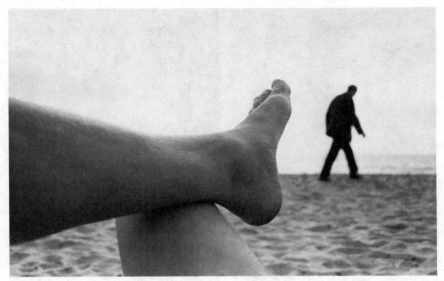

43. *Burning-in darkens selected areas of a print. The photographer wanted a darker sky than he got in this straight print.*

44. *After the initial exposure, a piece of cardboard—cut up to block the leg, foot, man, and sand—was held in the enlarger's light beam while the sky was given additional exposure. The burned-in sky gives better balance to the photograph.*

45. *The photographer decided the background in this picture was distracting.*

46. *To obliterate the background, he overexposed it. After giving the entire print an initial exposure, he held his hand in the enlarger beam to block extra exposure from the girl and baby.*

holder just below the lens of most every enlarger. When swung into the beam of the projected image, it prevents that image from being recorded by black-and-white photo paper. This is helpful when you are going to burn-in and want to hold the burning-in tool at the correct height before making the additional exposure. Be sure you don't jiggle the enlarger head while moving this safety filter in or out of position, or the image may be blurred or misaligned. The red filter can also be used while you realign the enlarging easel that might have been accidentally moved when you inserted the photo paper.

Occasionally it is desirable to make special dodging and burning-in masks to completely eliminate large or irregular image areas. These areas may be made either white or black in the print by *vignetting*.

For vignetting to white, use the burning-in technique and make the *total* print exposure through a hole with the appropriate shape. If the image desired has an irregular shape, turn on the enlarger and trace the shape onto a thin piece of cardboard. Then cut it out, but make the cutout *smaller* than the tracing. This allows you to raise the vignetting board a few inches from the surface of the print paper and keep it moving slightly during the exposure to avoid sharp edges around the image. When you make the exposure through the cutout hole, the rest of the paper covered by the board receives no exposure and remains white.

For vignetting to black, make a dodger by taping the cutout shape to a piece of wire. After the initial exposure, reexpose the print but cover the image area you are preserving by holding the dodger in the enlarger light beam. To avoid sharp edges around the image, hold the dodger a few inches above the paper and keep it moving slightly. To produce an adequate black around the image, it may be necessary to open the lens to its widest f/stop for the reexposure, or to remove the negative.

Burning-in is a common correction made during printing when an enlarger and/or lens does not produce uniform illumination of the projected negative. With some enlarger and negative combinations, you may experience the problem of print corners or edges being lighter than the center of the print. (Carefully inspect your prints for uniformity of exposure.) Burning-in the corners is particularly important because that is where the fall-off of light is most evident. After your initial print exposure, give the corners additional exposure to make them equal in density to the center of the print.

Sometimes unwanted details appear in your print which degrade the impact of the image. Invariably they occur in areas that cannot be cropped

47. *Vignetting during enlarging eliminates distracting elements in a picture.*

48. *In this vignetted result, there's no doubt the celebrating couple are the center of attention.*

out of the print without destroying overall composition. Fortunately, there is a simple technique for subduing such details: *diffused dodging and burning-in.*

The normal opaque dodging mask is replaced with a transparent one of slightly diffused material, and the hole of the burning-in board is covered with similar material. Two handy items that can be taped over the opening in a burning-in board are women's nylon stockings and plastic sandwich bags. Use a single layer, or double the material if greater diffusion is required.

Additional exposure through the diffusion material will burn-in (darken) unwanted details in *dark* image areas. How much diffused burning-in you can do without it becoming obvious in the print depends on the size of the unwanted details, how they contrast with the surrounding areas, and what kind of diffusing material you are using.

Burn-in with the board very low to the photo paper in order to minimize the amount of stray light. Use a burning-in board with a white top surface so you can watch it during the exposure to see exactly where you are burning-in; it is difficult to tell this by looking at the photo paper because the image there is made so fuzzy by the diffusion material.

You can reverse the technique and dodge out unwanted details in a *light* image area. The diffusion material, such as wrinkled cellophane, should be taped with transparent tape to the end of a thin, stiff wire. Or you can smear Vaseline in selected spots on a piece of glass, and hold it in the path of the projected image. How much of the image you want to remove or diffuse depends on how long you use the diffusion dodger during the print exposure, and how dense the diffusion material is.

Sometimes it is necessary to use both devices: dodging out most of the unwanted image, and then burning-in a subtle tone to match the surrounding areas. With either the dodging or burning-in technique, you may not want to completely remove the unwanted details but just diffuse them somewhat in order to subtly change their density and clarity.

Another method of improving the image is *print flashing,* which can subdue harsh highlights or contrast. This is achieved by reexposing the problem area to white light after the basic exposure is made. Commonly a pen-size flashlight is used, with a cone of black paper placed over the bulb so you can control the diameter of light it produces. (If the penlight's intensity is too bright, cut down the amount of light with one or more layers of translucent Scotch tape.)

When done correctly, flashing fogs (darkens) bright areas without seeming to change the density of middle tones or shadow areas. Let's say you've taken a portrait of a lady who has a white rose pinned to her dark dress. When making a "straight" print, the rose turns out too bright and is a distracting element in the photograph. By flashing the rose, you can tone it down and thus improve the picture.

The amount of flashing depends on the subject to be subdued, intensity of the penlight, and the distance you hold it from the photo paper. Make a test strip or print to determine exposure time and best technique for flashing. After the print's initial exposure, use the enlarger's red safety filter (see page 116) so the image can still be projected on the photo paper and used as a guide for flashing.

Large bright areas, such as sunlight glistening off the windows of a big office building, can be flashed with light from the enlarger. Start by cutting a mask from cardboard, with the opening slightly smaller than the image area to be darkened. After the initial exposure, properly position this mask above the easel by aligning the mask with the projected image; use the enlarger's red safety filter so the photo paper will not be reexposed. Now turn off the enlarger light, remove the red filter, and take the negative out of the enlarger. Close down the enlarger lens two or three f/stops, then turn on the enlarger to flash the print. Keep the mask moving slightly during exposure to avoid edges of the mask showing up in the print. Make a test strip to determine the correct exposure time for flashing.

The greatest danger with any of these alterations—dodging, burning-in, or flashing—is overdoing them, resulting in a print that looks unnatural. The best advice is to do nothing to the original image, unless you have a specific reason for altering it and can do that without creating a distraction in the print.

49. *The sharpness of a straight print, like this one, can be reduced with diffusion.*

50. *When half the original exposure time was up, a plastic bag was held in the enlarger beam for the remaining exposure. That partial diffusion softened the image and reduced print contrast, too.*

Something else to consider is *diffusion,* which will soften an image and reduce its sharp lines or vivid details. This is commonly done in portraiture to minimize the subject's facial blemishes or wrinkles. Diffusion also diminishes minor negative defects such as scratches, coarse grain, or retouching marks. Often it is used solely to create more aesthetic or pictorial effects.

Diffusion can be done either when enlargements are being made or at the time the picture is taken. When done during shooting, the highlights are most affected since they reflect most of the light reaching the film. When done during enlarging, the shadows are most affected since they allow the most exposure to reach the paper. Fortunately, the shadows are normally too dark to reveal much of this exaggerated effect in the print.

The greatest disadvantage of diffusing during shooting is that your negative is permanently diffused. However, if diffusion is done during enlarging, a sharp negative can also be printed without diffusion whenever you choose.

Diffusers vary from commercially made optical glass filters to the homemade varieties previously mentioned: Vaseline on glass, nylon stocking hosiery, crumpled cellophane, plastic window screening, or other materials that diffuse the light reaching your print paper or film.

A technique practiced by many photographers is to diffuse the image for only a portion of the total printing time, permitting some of the exposure to go completely undiffused. This provides you some image diffusion, but keeps the highlights clear and sparkling. Whether a little or a lot of diffusion is necessary depends upon the effect you desire.

One thing to remember: diffusion lowers print contrast, so if you plan on diffusion you may need to switch to a grade of paper with higher contrast.

Besides changes you can make during the exposure stage of enlarging, you can manipulate a print's image by *selective development.* A common trick used by photographers is to accelerate the development of certain areas of the print by breathing on them. Because the developer is generally about 70°F (21°C), by blowing your hot breath on the print surface, you can heat an area and increase its development rate.

If this is insufficient to speed development in a selected area, try swabbing it with hot water or stock developer. Rub the water or developer on with cotton, after lifting the print from the developer tray. Several applications may be necessary. (Do not lift the print too close to the safelight or you will fog the image.) Such applications often save you the time and expense of making a new print, so experiment.

8

Refining
Black-and-White Techniques

With practice, you'll find that processing films and printing negatives is rather easy. However, you may not be getting the best results, nor using certain techniques that turn a good (or even a poor) image into a better one. A few common ways to improve prints were just discussed in the preceding chapter—dodging, burning-in, vignetting, flashing, diffusing, and selective development.

A number of other refinements and varied approaches to black-and-white photography are covered here: correcting distortion, toning, using variable developers, intensifying negatives, reducing negatives and prints, and using stabilization processes.

Some creative techniques popular with photographers doing black-and-white work—such as multiple printing and sandwiching, texturing, making photograms, solarization (Sabattier effect), and reticulation—are also applicable to color photography, and these are discussed later in chapter 16.

Correcting and Creating Distortion

Tilting the enlarging easel, the enlarger lens, or negative carrier while printing can correct distortion that occurred when the subject was photographed. Often these techniques are used to straighten vertical lines that seem to be converging. Such distortion occurs when you point your camera down or up, as when photographing a tall building. Architectural photographers frequently shoot with view cameras or perspective-correction (PC) lenses to avoid the problem, but most of us correct converging lines in the darkroom.

There are several ways to make the correction. The easiest to do is to tilt the enlarging easel until the coverging lines of the projected image appear parallel (severe distortion cannot be corrected). Since depth of focus is better at smaller apertures, use a small enlarger lens opening like f/16 to help keep the image in focus. If the easel has been tilted to a considerable angle, the

51. Lines that are parallel but become distorted because of the camera's angle can be corrected in the darkroom.

52. The enlarging easel was tilted until the buildings appeared more normal.

53. *Try changing a straight print with some creative distortion.*

54. *To create this effect of motion, six exposures were made; the easel holding the enlarging paper was moved slightly to the left before each exposure.*

negative carrier should also be tilted in order for the image to remain in focus; alternatively, the enlarger lens should be tilted.

If both your negative carrier and enlarger lens can be tilted, the easel can stay flat; this allows the image to remain in sharp focus even at wide enlarger lens openings.

Of course, by moving or tilting the easel (or negative carrier or enlarger lens) you can also create distortion. Another technique is to bend or twist the photo paper so it is not flat during exposure. (Set a small f/stop on the enlarger lens for sharpest focus.) Practice with a blank piece of paper to see the effects you'll get; the image will be shortened if the paper is held in a concave shape, and it will be lengthened if the paper has a convex bend. Experiment with different subjects until you find the images that work well with purposeful distortion.

Toning Black-and-White Prints

The image color of black-and-white prints can be changed by toning them chemically. Toning is generally used to improve the print by adding color that will enhance the subject. Thus, portraits and sunlit scenes are often bathed in a sepia or brown toner, and snow, water, and night scenes frequently are treated in a blue toner. There are toners that produce other colors, including red, orange, yellow, and green.

The richness of the color change depends on the toner selected, the toning method, and the type of photo paper that is toned. Many toners are single solutions (some can be diluted), and others are two-step types, first requiring a bleach step and then the toner that will bring back the image in the chosen color. Toning can be done in normal room light.

Toning is sometimes done to preserve the image rather than to appreciably change the image color. Many art museums and collectors prefer to purchase photographs that have received protective toning for *archival permanence*. For this purpose, selenium toners and gold toners are preferred. (See page 129).

Very popular for general toning are various brands of toners that produce brown tones, especially sepia tones. Kodak makes a sepia toner as well as several other toners that yield different varieties of brown when used with different cold-tone or warm-tone photo papers. These are brown toner, rapid selenium toner, and Poly-Toner. Kodak also makes a blue toner, and when used on a sepia- or brown-toned print, it produces red tones (with cold-tone papers) or orange tones (with warm-tone papers). A summary of these Kodak toners follows.

Kodak toners. Kodak's Poly-Toner is a single solution that can be diluted to produce a variety of hues ranging from reddish brown to very warm brown. You can actually get three distinct tones by just adding water to the concentrated stock solution of Poly-Toner.

Suggested dilutions and treatment times at 70°F (21°C) are one part toner to four parts water for 1 minute to achieve a cold brown (selenium) tone; one part toner to twenty-four parts water for 3 minutes to produce a brown tone; and one part toner to fifty parts water for 7 minutes to get a warm brown tone.

With 1:4 dilution, image density is slightly increased, so it is best if the print has been underdeveloped by 20 to 30 seconds. With the 1:50 dilution, image density is slightly decreased, so overdevelop the print by about 1 minute. After toning, prints should be washed for 30 minutes and then allowed to air dry; a colder tone is produced if toned prints are heat-dried, and they will require a 2- to 5-minute bath in hardener to protect the emulsion.

Like some other toners, Kodak's Poly-Toner smells like rotten eggs because it gives off hydrogen sulfide fumes. Use adequate ventilation because these fumes are also poisonous. And be aware that hydrogen sulfide will fog unexposed paper and film, so keep them away from the vicinity where you are toning.

Kodak's Selenium toner gives several hues of reddish (cold) brown tones, depending on dilution of the stock solution. It works well with warm-tone papers, but has little effect on cold-tone papers. The solution has no offensive odor. At 68°F (20°C), toning in the recommended dilution of one part toner to three parts water takes from 2 to 8 minutes, depending on the contrast grade of paper. This toner increases slightly the density of the image, so the print's developer time should be reduced by about 10 percent. Different hues are possible by removing the print after only partial toning, or diluting the stock solution with more water.

Kodak's Sepia toner requires two steps, bleaching and then redevelopment in the toner. It works especially well with cold-tone papers to produce a warm-brown image, but varying the hues is not practical. Prints should be fully bleached for about 1 minute, then rinsed in running water at least 2 minutes, before being placed in the second solution. The original image density will reappear in sepia tones in about 30 seconds. Sepia toning requires a print be overexposed 10 to 20 percent because of the bleaching step.

If blue spots appear, it's because the bleach has reacted with iron; chipped enamel trays or even water from rusty pipes may be at fault. Fumes from the toner are smelly and poisonous, so work in a well-ventilated area. Also, use rubber gloves or print tongs because the toner solution is very alkaline.

Kodak's Brown toner requires the same precautions: adequate ventilation and use of rubber gloves or print tongs. It is a single solution that produces warm tones on cold-tone papers. Toning takes 15 to 20 minutes at 68°F (20°C) but can be reduced to 3 or 4 minutes if the toner is used at 100°F (37.5°C). Developer time should be increased to compensate for some loss of contrast that occurs when the brown toner is used.

Kodak's Blue toner comes in two parts (liquid and powder) to make a single odorless solution that produces cold blue tones. Toning takes 8 to 45 minutes at 68°F (20°C) but only 2 to 15 minutes at 100°F (37.5°C). Warm tone papers yield a deep blue, while cold-tone papers give a less rich, slate blue appearance. When prints have been previously toned sepia or brown, bathing them in blue toner will change the image color to red, if a cold-tone paper, or orange, if a warm-tone paper.

Edwal toners. Another company, Edwal Scientific Products Corp., makes single-solution toners that come in brown, blue, red, yellow, and green. In addition, a wide range of colors is possible by first toning the print in one Edwal toner and then in another.

Although these toners have no offensive odor, they will stain trays and hands, so it's a good idea to use rubber gloves or print tongs. You may find it best to save up a batch of prints and tone them all at once. One reason for doing this is that the toners, once mixed, last only six to eight weeks (except the blue toner, which lasts at least one year).

Instructions are printed on the backs of Edwal toner bottles, and should be followed carefully. Inside the cap of each 4-ounce bottle are some reddish crystals that must be poured into the bottle and mixed thoroughly. The mixed 4-ounce bottle of toner is then diluted with water to make 64 ounces of working solution, which is enough to tone about thirty 8 x 10-inch prints.

Temperature of the toner can range from 65°F (18.5°C) to 110°F (43.5°C); the warmer the solution, the faster the toning. Toning normally takes 4 to 10 minutes. Toning speed and brightness of the image can be increased by adding one-half to 1 ounce of 28% acetic acid to the 64 ounces of toner working solution, except this has little effect with the blue toner.

Edwal toners work with most photo papers, cold-tone or warm-tone. Conventional papers that produce glossy prints should be ferrotyped *after* toning, not before.

To tone a print, immerse it in the desired toner and agitate occasionally until it reaches the color you like. Then wash the print in running water for 10 to 20 minutes. Because toners will stain blotters and aprons on print dryers, it is best to air dry the prints (see page 87). Remember, if you are getting blue or green spots on the prints after toning, this is probably due to iron in your wash water (from rusty pipes) or chipped porcelain trays used for processing or toning.

If you decide you want a wider range of colors, do not mix Edwal toners together, but use separate trays and first tone a print in one color and then tone it in another to get the effect of both colors: red and brown produce a nice orange, for example.

For unusual effects, use an Edwal toner full strength and tone a print for a long time—at least 15 to 20 minutes. It is best to use a print that is extremely dark—one that you normally would throw away. Prolonged toning causes the image to become brighter, and eventually most all the silver salts will be converted to a colored image that has chalky tones.

If the toner has converted most of the print but some dark areas remain, you can transfer the print to a second undiluted Edwal toner color for another long period of time. The silver that still remains in those dark areas will eventually be affected by the second toner and produce a colored outline effect that will surprise you.

One of the most inexpensive, common, and colorful "toners" that you can use is *food coloring,* which actually tints the paper's base. This food dye affects the photo paper's color, not the silver image. The longer the print is in the dye, the deeper the color—until it reaches a saturation point.

While it is in the food coloring, be sure to agitate the print so it will be toned evenly. After you have the desired effect, take the print out of the dye and rinse it. Carefully squeegee off all the surface liquid, and put the print on a screen to air dry; if any liquid stands on the surface, it will continue to tone and cause dark spots to appear.

Since food coloring dyes the paper and not the silver image, be careful not to get any water or other moisture on the print after it dries, or the color may run or spot. To a certain extent, you can wash the food coloring out of the paper any time you wish.

Protective Toning

Over a period of years, a photo image may fade or change because its metallic silver has been harmfully affected, particularly by sulfur gases and other air pollution. Fortunately, the images can be protected by toning, and many photographers routinely bathe their prints in a selenium toner solution to give them greater permanence. A gold toner solution also offers protection, but it is more costly and less commonly used.

The following selenium toner solution gives a print protection *without* changing its tone; this is a different formula than the one described for normal toning with Kodak Rapid Selenium Toner. With conventional photo papers, you can combine the protective toning and clearing agent baths to save time (RC papers should not be bathed in clearing agents).

Mix a 1-gallon solution of Kodak Hypo Clearing Agent (other brands, like Perma-Wash, can be substituted), add 1½ ounces of Kodak Rapid Selenium Toner concentrate, and 2½ ounces of Kodak Balanced Alkali. Following the fixer step, prints are put in this solution (at 75°F) and continuously agitated for 3 to 5 minutes, then washed. Mix a fresh clearing agent/toner solution after bathing fifty 8 x 10-inch prints per gallon.

Some photographers increase the amount of Rapid Selenium toner in this solution to a total of 7 ounces, in order to produce an evident change in the print's tone, in addition to giving the image protective toning. The blacks are especially intensified, adding a special richness to the print. Treat as above (fixer to clearing agent/toner solution to wash), leaving the print in the clearing agent/toner until it is visually toned to your personal taste. The results will be different with different brands and contrast grades of paper, as will the rate of toning.

Varying Paper Developers for Contrast Control

If you are consistent in the way you expose and process your film, then you should be producing negatives that are consistent in density and contrast. This, of course, makes routine printing much easier. But you may find, even though your negatives are good, that the mood or feeling you want in a print just isn't there. Sometimes a little more contrast may be required, but switching to a paper grade of higher contrast still won't give the desired result.

One way to get more subtle control of contrast in your prints is to change the developers you are using. With packaged developers, you can either vary their dilution or combine them with other packaged developers. Another approach is to prepare your own paper developers, mixing ingredients according to published formulas. Naturally, the custom developers which you mix yourself permit the greatest control of print contrast results. But for the majority of photographers, varying the packaged developers provides enough contrast control, and is much less trouble.

Let's say you're using Kodak's Dektol, a popular developer for black-and-white prints. This developer gives a good contrast range with neutral- and cold-tone papers when diluted 1:2 as directed (one part stock Dektol to two parts water). But for greater contrast control, in order to obtain intermediate tones that you can't achieve simply by changing paper grades, you should consider using a variety of packaged developers and dilutions.

For instance, you might use Kodak's Selectol-Soft for decreasing print contrast, Dektol diluted 1:2 for normal print contrast, and undiluted Dektol for increasing print contrast.

Selectol-Soft is a warm tone developer designed for use with warm tone portrait papers; it is "softer" in contrast than the regular warm-tone developer called Selectol. Selectol-Soft, if used with a cold-tone paper, such as Agfa's Brovira or Kodak's Kodabromide, reduces print contrast almost a full contrast grade. But it gives a different feeling than if you used a cold-tone developer and simply switched to a paper of lower contrast.

To increase contrast by almost a full contrast grade, use undiluted Dektol. Again, the print will have a different appearance than if you used Dektol at normal 1:2 dilution and simply switched to a paper of higher contrast.

Often it is desirable to get a range of contrast that falls in between the contrast you would get by using either one developer or the other. Do this by processing in both developers. For instance, say you have a negative that prints okay on grade No. 3 paper, but too much detail is lost in the shadow areas. Your answer would be to process it for part of the developer time in Selectol-Soft, which reduces contrast enough to keep more shadow detail, and then finish the developer time in Dektol diluted 1:2, which gives the print back much of the contrast you liked in the original print developed only in Dektol.

You should standardize your variable contrast options. Using your normal developer time for conventional papers (not RC), say 3 minutes, you would set up a list of changes for developers and times that would give you the contrast you desire from any image. For example, to *reduce* contrast, you could develop the print for: 3 minutes in Selectol-Soft; *or* 1 minute in Selectol-Soft and 2 minutes in Dektol (1:2). Each combination would give you a variation on contrast; to retain shadow detail and still get a rich, snappy print, try the latter (1 minute in Selectol-Soft and 2 minutes in Dektol [1:2]).

To *increase* contrast, you could develop the print for: 2 minutes in Dektol (1:2) and then 1 minute in undiluted Dektol (stock solution); *or* 1 minute in Dektol (1:2) and 2 minutes in undiluted Dektol; *or* 3 minutes in undiluted Dektol. The latter offers the most contrast you can get without changing to a paper of greater contrast grade.

The degree of contrast change obtainable by processing in the manners described varies with the type of paper. With some, the effect is minimal. So do some tests to find out what your papers will produce. Kodabromide and Brovira both work well with this method of processing, as do many warm-tone papers like Kodak's Ektalure.

Early photographers had no choice but to mix their own chemistry, and even today, some photographers prefer to concoct their own "soup." Making your own developers takes time, but if you do a lot of printing, this will offer you the greatest control over contrast. And you can save money because buying the chemical components in bulk is less expensive than purchasing packaged developers. You'll need a scale to weigh the powdered ingredients, and you must understand how a developer is composed. Here's a summary.

Commonly, a developer's chemical ingredients include a developing agent, accelerator, preservative, and restrainer. These are dissolved in water to make the developer solution.

The *developing agent,* which is sometimes called a reducing agent, reduces the exposed silver salts (halides) in the emulsion to silver metal, and this forms the image. Common developing agents in modern developers are Elon (or Metol) and hydroquinone.

The *accelerator* is required to activate the developing agent, which is inherently weak. The accelerator is an alkali, most commonly sodium carbonate.

The *preservative* maintains the properties of the developing agent by removing oxygen that accumulates in the developer. Sodium sulfite is the most common preservative.

The *restrainer* helps prevent development of the *unexposed* silver halides, which otherwise would cause overall grayness of the image. A common restrainer is potassium bromide.

The type and amount of these various chemical ingredients determine the characteristics of a developer. For example, for a low contrast developer you'd mix equal parts of Elon and hydroquinone; while for a higher contrast developer you'd mix one part of Elon to seven parts of hydroquinone.

A number of technical photographic books discuss and list various developer formulas, which you should read for more details about using variable developers for contrast control. For starters, a few of the most popular formulas are reproduced here, including the well-known Beers formulas.

Regarding Beers, you mix two developing solutions, A and B, and then combine them in different amounts in order to produce a wide range of contrasts on only one grade of paper. For instance, mix 16 ounces of "A" developer (Beers Formula) with 16 ounces of water, and you'll develop a print with low contrast. Mix 10 ounces of "A" with 6 ounces of "B" and 16 ounces of water, and you'll get a print with medium contrast. Or mix 4 ounces of "A" with 28 ounces of "B" (and no water) and you'll get a print with high contrast.

FORMULAS FOR COMMON PAPER DEVELOPERS

Chemical amounts are in grams; water in liters (note: 1 liter = 1.05 quarts). Mix chemicals in 2 liters of water at 125°F (51.5°C), then add water to make total amount listed. Mix in order listed.

	DEVELOPER			
	D-72			
Chemical (grams)	(for cold-tone papers; same as Kodak's Dektol)	54-D (for cold-tone Agfa papers)	Beers Formulas "A"	"B"
Elon (Metol)	12.4	10.8	16	0
Sodium sulfite	180	160	46	46
Hydroquinone	48	42.4	0	16
Sodium carbonate	320	352	47	63
Potassium bromide	2	0.84	0.57	1.15
Water (total)	4 liters	4 liters	2 liters	2 liters

Intensifying Negatives

Black-and-white negatives that lack density and contrast because of underexposure or underdevelopment can be intensified chemically. The existing density of the image will be built up, as will contrast, so it will be possible to make an acceptable print from a negative that was originally too thin (little density) or too flat (little contrast). One drawback is that graininess also increases.

The procedure for intensifying can be done in normal room light, and the process can be repeated for even greater intensification of a negative. Convenient to use is Kodak's Chromium Intensifier, which consists of two packets of powder that are dissolved to make 16 ounces of bleach and 16 ounces of a clearing bath. You'll also need Kodak's Dektol developer (diluted one part developer to three parts water) to redevelop the image. This treatment stains negatives light yellow, but this does not affect the print result.

If the negatives to be intensified are already dried, soak them in water for at least 10 minutes. Place the wet negatives in the bleach bath for 3 to 5 minutes at 68°F (20°C) until the black image turns yellow. After a rinse in water, treat the negatives in the clearing bath for about 2 minutes until the yellow stain disappears and the negatives seem clear. Rinse again in water, then redevelop the negatives in Dektol (diluted 1:3) until the image reappears and darkens. The final step is to wash the negatives for 10 to 20 minutes. Intensification can be repeated if desired. Do not use this process with color negatives.

Reducing Negatives and Prints

Black-and-white negatives that are too dense because of overexposure or overdevelopment can be treated chemically with a reducer so they will make more acceptable prints. Likewise, overexposed or overdeveloped black-and-white prints can be treated to reduce overall density and to clear up highlights. Do not use a black-and-white reducer on color films or prints; special reducers are made for color work.

Reduction of black-and-white negatives or prints can be carried out in normal room light. The process of reducing negatives is easy to do with Kodak's Farmer's Reducer. Two packets of powder are dissolved to make 1 quart each of solutions A and B. These are mixed to make a working solution, which is active only 10 minutes. One caution before you begin: negatives can be easily ruined by overreducing, so practice with an unimportant negative first.

If the negative is dry, soak it in water for at least 10 minutes. Immerse the negative in the reducer, and carefully watch the image because reduction takes place quickly. When you are satisfied with the image density, take the negative out of the reducer and wash it in running water for 20 minutes. On larger negatives you can also reduce portions of the image by applying diluted reducer (one part to four parts water) with a small brush or swab of cotton.

To reduce black-and-white prints, dilute the working solution of Farmer's Reducer one part to four parts water, and immerse a wet print for 5 to 10 seconds. Rinse with running water and check if reduction is sufficient; return to the reducer as many times as required, then wash for 1 hour (or use a clearing agent to reduce the wash time).

To lighten highlights, portions of the print image can be reduced by applying the reducer directly with a small brush. Afterward, be sure to fix and wash. For best results, follow the reducer's instructions carefully and practice with an unimportant print.

More varied results are possible if you mix your own reducer. For instance, instead of reducing the overall density of a negative, you can formulate a reducer that will reduce highlight density without destroying shadow detail. Instructions of mixing and using a variety of reducers can be found in Kodak's professional data book, *Processing Chemicals and Formulas for Black-and-White Photography,* available through camera stores.

Processing by Stabilization

Many photographers dream of print processing that is simple, fast, and without mess. Surprising to some, it has been available since World War II when the need for quickly processed prints in confined working conditions led to stabilization processing. This involves a tabletop machine and two solutions: activator and stabilizer. The exposed photo paper is inserted in the machine and emerges as a print in just 15 seconds. The paper, a special type, is still damp but it dries at room temperature in a few minutes.

The main drawback, besides the stabilization processor's cost, is that the images are not permanent unless they are eventually fixed and washed in the conventional manner. Normally, stabilized prints keep up to several months. Stabilization processing machines are practical for newspaper work so photographers can more easily meet their deadlines. They are popular with the military, police, and medical professions, too, and some professional

55. *Portions of a picture can be lightened or eliminated by chemical reducing.*

56. *A small brush was used to apply reducer in the background areas of this print.*

photographers have a stabilization processor in order to make proof prints rapidly.

Kodak manufactures the most expensive model, the Ektamatic, which uses

Kodak's Ektamatic chemicals and Ektamatic SC papers; such papers also can be processed in trays using Dektol developer and normal print processing procedures. There are at least a dozen models of stabilization processors, including some made by Ilford, Agfa, and Spiratone, and prices range from $150 to $800.

9

Understanding
Color Photographic Processes

From the time daguerreotypes first appeared and made black-and-white photography popular, it took nearly one hundred years before another invention did the same thing for color photography. This was a three-color positive film, called Kodachrome, first announced in 1935 by Eastman Kodak Company. A number of other important events led to that moment.

The Beginning of Color Photography

The initial problem of scientists searching for a color process was understanding the make-up of light and how it works. A major step was taken in 1861 by Scottish physicist James Clerk-Maxwell when he proved that white light is a mixture of three colors—red, blue, and green—called the additive primaries. Various combinations of these three primaries produce all of the various colors in the visual light spectrum. (Do not confuse them with the primary colors of pigments—red, yellow, and blue—that you may have learned about in art class.)

To demonstrate this *additive* system of light, Clerk-Maxwell began with three black-and-white photos taken of a multicolored tartan ribbon. Each photo was shot from the same position but with a filter of a different primary color in front of the lens. Because a color filter allows light of its own color to pass through, Clerk-Maxwell produced three black-and-white negatives that recorded the ribbon in different shades of gray. Black-and-white positives were made from these negatives, and then Clerk-Maxwell used three projectors to project each positive through the same color filter its negative had been shot with. When these three primary color images were superimposed on a white screen, a full color image of the tartan ribbon resulted. Clerk-Maxwell's demonstration, the first real proof of the additive color theory, set the stage for future developments in color photography.

Later, scientists would say that Clerk-Maxwell's experiment should not have worked, because he used collodion wet plates and they were not sensitive to red and green light. However, it was more recently discovered what was then unknown, namely, that the dyes in the tartan ribbon reflected some ultraviolet light which caused images to be recorded through the red filter, and the green filter passed some blue light which produced images on the film that was to register green light.

Actually, black-and-white films were "color blind" until 1873. That's when German researcher Dr. Hermann Vogel discovered that adding dyes to photographic emulsions would make them sensitive to the green and yellow portions of the light spectrum, instead of only the blue band. The resulting film was referred to as *orthochromatic,* because it is sensitive to every color but red. Later came *panchromatic* film, which is sensitive to all colors including red, the longest wave in the visual spectrum.

Panchromatic film was very important to the development of color photography, because it allowed photographers to record the complete range of gray tones, from black to white, that accurately could represent the full range of colors.

However, color photography with the additive system was complicated, requiring three separate exposures through filters of each of the primary colors (red, blue, green) onto three separate black-and-white films. Then those images were projected through filters of the primary colors and superimposed to re-create the subject in color.

Later there was limited success in making color transparencies with the additive process. Single-exposure methods were devised that utilized color filtering screens to break up the colors of light into fine lines on just one piece of film. After processing, the black-and-white film was placed in register with the same filtering screen so the image could be viewed in color.

Other innovations with the additive system included Autochromes, color transparencies using dyed transparent grains of potato starch to filter the colors of light. Invented and manufactured in the early 1900s by two French brothers, Auguste and Louis Lumières, Autochrome film was popular with professional photographers, including those of the *National Geographic,* who used the Lumières' film to make some of the early color photographs that appeared in that magazine.

But experiments were also being made with an alternative method of reproducing color, the *subtractive* system, which became the basis of the color photography we enjoy today. With the subtractive system, color images are formed by dyes in different layers of the film's emulsion and they superimpose to create a full-color photograph. The dye colors—yellow, magenta, and cyan—are called the subtractive primaries, and they are the complements of the additive primaries.

Kodak's Kodachrome, which produced a positive color transparency, was the first commercially successful color film using the subtractive system. In 1936, the year Kodachrome was made available in 35mm rolls for still cameras, a German firm introduced Agfacolor, the first color negative film to use the subtractive process. With those two films on the market, amateurs as well as professionals became fascinated by color photography.

Subsequent color films and print materials all have been based on the subtractive system. Today there is a great variety of color films available for making positive slide transparencies or color negatives. Materials for making color prints are also quite varied, including Kodak's Ektachrome and Ilford's Cibachrome papers that produce color prints directly from color slides. Printing with color negatives has been simplified, too; one process requires only two chemical steps and no more than seven minutes' processing time.

Previously, color processing and printing was too complex, time consuming, and expensive to encourage many photographers to try it in their home darkrooms. Now there are easier, faster, and less costly home processes for producing color negatives, color slides, and color enlargements. Even photographers who have never had black-and-white darkroom experience are jumping into color. However, even if you only intend to develop color films and make color prints, be sure to read the chapters in this book that deal with black-and-white processing and printing, because the principles and procedures for black-and-white also apply to color.

Summarizing Color Processing and Printing

When considering color photography, remember that color is a quality that is inherent in light, not in matter. You do not photograph an object that has a certain color, but rather you photograph an object that reflects a certain color of light.

Light reacts as both waves and as photon particles. Some of these photons are absorbed by molecules in an object and others are reflected. For instance, a red apple looks red because it absorbs all of the colors in the light spectrum except red. Because the apple reflects red, that's what we see and photograph.

Color photography is based on the principle that white light is composed of equal parts of three basic colors, the primary colors—blue, green, red—and that by varying the mixture of these colors, all other colors can be reproduced. Consequently, the emulsion of color films and color photo papers contains three color-sensitive layers, each affected by one of the primary colors.

When exposed to light, each emulsion layer absorbs light of its own color. Generally, the top layer is sensitive to blue light, the middle layer to green light, and the bottom layer to red light. Wherever there is a color other than blue, green, or red, it will react on two more layers of the emulsion to eventually produce that specific color.

Where part of the image is black, no emulsion is exposed because black does not reflect any of the colors of light. Where white is part of the image, all three layers of emulsion are equally exposed because white light is made up of all three of the primary colors (blue, green, red).

Surprisingly, perhaps, these colors are first developed as superimposed black-and-white negative images in the three separate layers of the emulsion. This is true for all color materials, whether color negative or color positive (slide) films, or color papers that produce prints from color negatives or color positives.

In the next stage, however, the processes differ according to whether the color materials are negative or positive.

With *positive* color films and papers, sometimes called reversal films (slides) or reversal (Type R) papers, the emulsion is exposed a second time, either chemically or with light. The silver halides that were not acted upon during the first developer that produced the black-and-white negative images are now acted upon by a *second* developer to create a positive image.

Also, during this second development stage, colored dyes are produced which transform the three layers of black-and-white images into color.

In each layer, the dye produced is the *complement* of the color of light originally recorded there: yellow dye is formed in the blue sensitive layer, magenta dye is formed in the green sensitive layer, and cyan dye is formed in the red sensitive layer. As complementary colors and superimposed images, the layers of yellow, magenta, and cyan produce an image that has all the natural color relationships of the original subject you photographed.

With *negative* color materials (both films and papers), there is only one developer required. This single developer, in addition to producing black-and-white negative images, also produces color dyes in each of the color sensitive layers. These dyes are the complementary colors—yellow, magenta, and cyan—and appear in the negative. However, some color negative films also have an overall orangish cast, which is a built-in "mask" that helps produce the proper colors during printing.

Color processing and printing require more care and time and cost than black-and-white film processing and printing. The procedures are similar, although some color processes have more steps than black-and-white processes, such as bleach and stabilizer. And, as noted, positive color films require two developers instead of one.

For printing, color negatives and slides must be exposed through filters of various densities and colors (usually yellow, magenta, or cyan) to produce the proper balance of colors in the print. Deciding on the correct filtration for each specific negative or slide is a major consideration in producing the best color prints.

10

Considering Color
Films and Processes

Color Film Characteristics

To repeat, there are two types of color film: *color negative film* and *color positive (transparency) film.* Color negative film is designed for making color prints. As the name implies, the developed film contains negative images; some color negatives also have an orangish color cast, which is a *mask* required to produce "correct" colors in a print. Color negative films usually include the suffix "color" in their brand names, i.e. Kodacolor, Agfacolor.

Color transparency film is designed for producing slides, which are positive images, and these are usually projected. Transparency film is technically referred to as *reversal* film. Such films usually have the suffix "chrome" in their names, i.e. Kodachrome, Agfachrome.

You should be aware that color negative films can also be used to make color transparencies (slides), as well as black-and-white prints. And color transparency films can be used to make color prints.

Until recently, if color prints were desired from color transparency film, an *internegative* had to be made first. Within the last few years, however, positive-to-positive systems of color printing at home have been perfected so that you can make color prints directly from color slides. This is known as *direct positive* or *Type R* printing. One product name for this type of printing is Cibachrome.

Most color films can be processed in a home darkroom with the same equipment that is used for processing black-and-white films. One difference is that color film processing requires more precise time and temperature control than black-and-white processing.

Also, there are some color films which can only be processed by their manufacturer, or photographic labs that are especially equipped to handle them. For example, Kodak's Kodachrome films must be processed in expensive machines by Kodak or other large labs because the process is too complex for home processing.

Kodak's color negative film Type 5247, originally designed for the movie industry, is frequently sold and processed by custom labs that advertise in the photography magazines. Long rolls of this film are cut and spooled into cassettes for use in 35mm still cameras. After processing, the roll of color negatives is contact printed onto another roll of film to make positive color transparencies; then the custom lab sends you both the color negatives (for making color prints) and the color slides (for projection).

In addition to custom processing labs, the major film manufacturers maintain labs that process their own brands of film. In the U.S., such labs are operated by Kodak, Fuji, Agfa, and Sakura.

Many novice photographers shy away from color processing because they feel it is too complicated and/or expensive. But those who try processing color film most often find it is easy. And it's inexpensive, when compared to the cost of having a professional lab do your processing. As was mentioned, color film can be processed with the same equipment that you use for processing black-and-white film. Color processing takes longer, but with some practice, it will become just as routine as developing black-and-white film.

Color film processing kits are available, or you can buy the various chemicals separately in larger quantities, in case you do a considerable amount of color processing.

Most color negative films can be developed in Kodak's Process C-41 (Flexicolor) or C-22 chemicals. Other color negative processes include Beseler's CN2, Unicolor's K-2 and Total Color, and Dignan's NCF-41.

Most color transparency films (except Kodachrome) can be processed in Kodak's Process E-6, E-4, or E-3 chemicals. Unicolor also has a process, called Unichrome, for developing color slide films. Another is Unicolor E-6 Chemistry.

Remember that one of the main reasons for processing your own color film is that you have total control of the results. When film is sent out for developing, it is processed according to laboratory standards that are geared for properly exposed film. Self-processing can help save accidentally overexposed or underexposed film. And by developing your own color film, you also have the option of reducing or increasing development in order to add or reduce contrast. Generally, the big processing laboratories, which are fully automated, can't give your color film the personal attention it deserves.

Color Film Brands and Sizes

Following are lists of color negative films and color transparency (slide) films that are popular with today's photographers. Included are manufacturer and brand names. Also listed are the ASA film speeds and some of the popular film sizes available.

In the charts, cartridge film refers to 126-size, unless asterisked (*) to indicate 110-size is available as well. Cassette refers to 135-size film for 35mm cameras. Roll film refers to 120-size only. And sheet film indicates availability of 4 x 5-inch sheets. Camera stores can tell you if these films are available in other sizes.

COLOR NEGATIVE FILMS

MANUFACTURER AND FILM NAME	ASA FILM SPEED Daylight†	FILM SIZES			
		Cartridge / (126 or 110*)	Cassette / (135)	Roll / (120)	Sheet (4 x 5)
KODAK					
Kodacolor II	100	X*	X	X	
Kodacolor 400	400	*	X	X	
Vericolor II, Type S	100		X	X	X
Vericolor II, Type L	††			X	X
FUJI					
Fujicolor F-II	100	X	X		
Fujicolor N100	100	X	X		
Fujicolor F-II 400	400		X		
SAKURA					
Sakuracolor II	100	X	X		
Sakuracolor N-100	100	X	X		
Sakuracolor 400	400		X		
AGFA					
Agfacolor CNS	80	X	X		
3M					
3M Color Print Film	80	X	X		

†Daylight color films are color balanced for sunlight, electronic flash, and blue flash bulbs or cubes. When other types of illumination are used, filters may be required and film speed is reduced.
††Vericolor II, Type L, is balanced for tungsten light; for use with long exposures (1/50 to 60 seconds); film speed varies according to exposure time.

COLOR TRANSPARENCY FILMS

MANUFACTURER AND FILM NAME	ASA FILM SPEED Daylight† / Tungsten	FILM SIZES			
		Cartridge / (126 or 110*)	Cassette / (135)	Roll / (120)	Sheet (4 x 5)
KODAK					
Kodachrome 25	25		X		
Kodachrome 64	64	X*	X		
Kodachrome 40 (Type A)	/ 40		X		
Ektachrome 64	64	X*	X		
Ektachrome 64 Professional	64		X	X	X
Ektachrome 200	200	X	X		
Ektachrome 200 Professional	200		X	X	
Ektachrome 50 Professional (Tungsten)	/ 50		X	X	X
Ektachrome 160 (Tungsten)	/ 160		X		
Ektachrome 160 Professional (Tungsten)	/ 160		X	X	
Ektachrome 400	400		X		
Ektachrome Slide Duplicating 5071	/ ‡		X		
AGFA					
Agfachrome 64	64	X	X		
Agfachrome 100	100		X		
FUJI					
Fujichrome R-100	100	X	X		
Fujichrome RK-126	64	X			
SAKURA					
Sakuracolor R	100		X		
3M					
3M Color Slide Film	64	X*	X		
3M High Speed Color Slide Film	400		X		

†Daylight color films are color balanced for sunlight, electronic flash, and blue flash bulbs and cubes. When other types of illumination are used, filters may be required and film speed is reduced.

‡Film speed depends on tungsten light source.

Color Film Storage and Care

(A discussion regarding the care and storage of black-and-white and color films begins on page 17.) Many photographers who use color film are concerned whether it should be stored in a refrigerator or freezer. All color films age, which means there is a change in color balance, and this aging takes place faster at warmer temperatures than it does at cooler temperatures. An *expiration date* stamped on the film box indicates the month and year after which the aging effects may be significant.

So-called *amateur* or *consumer films* are designed to allow for the effects of aging (i.e. shift in color balance) when they are stored at room temperature—about 70°F (21°C) or less. So-called *professional films,* however, are more critical in regard to color balance, and they require refrigeration at a temperature of 55°F (13°C) or less. For Kodak's Ektachrome Infrared film and Ektacolor Internegative films, recommended storage is in a freezer with the temperatures between 0° and −10°F (−18° to −23°C).

These storage suggestions apply to both unexposed and exposed films. Regarding Kodak's E-6 Professional films, factory tests have shown there is little or no change when they are stored up to a week at room temperature, although refrigeration at 55°F or lower is recommended.

Two cautions regarding refrigeration or freezing of film should be noted. Some refrigerators or freezers are very humid and can cause water or ice to form on the outside of film packages. Even though unopened packages are moisture-proof, it's a good idea to wrap the film in plastic as extra protection against such moisture.

Also, refrigerated or frozen film must be allowed to warm up before breaking the package seal. Otherwise, water vapor may condense from the air onto the film's surface and cause water spots or make the emulsion stick.

Processed color films also are affected by temperature and humidity, and the color dyes will remain true longer if color negatives and slides are stored at temperatures no higher than 70°F (21°C) and with the relative humidity ranging between 15 and 40 percent.

Color Film Processes

As you recall, the emulsions of color films, both negative and positive types, are composed of three layers that are sensitive to the three primary colors of light: blue, green, and red. Color dyes are formed during processing—yellow, magenta, and cyan—which are complementary to those primary colors.

With color negative films, these complementary colors appear as negative images. When printed, the images become positive and revert in the photograph to their original primary colors. With color positive (slide) films, processing includes a second color developer that turns negative images to positive, and their overlapping complementary colors reproduce the photographer's subject in its original primary colors.

More precisely, here's what happens to color negative and color positive films during processing.

Regarding color negatives, the processing steps (in order) are developer, bleach, wash, fixer, wash, stabilizer, and drying. These steps are for *Kodak's C-41 process.*

A color negative film's multi-layered emulsion is composed of light-sensitive silver halide grains, just as black-and-white films are. The developer reacts on the exposed silver halides to form a negative image (tones in the negative are dark where the subject was bright and light where the subject was dark). At the same time, chemical substances in the film known as *couplers* react to form dyes proportionate to the amount of silver being developed.

| Protective Overcoat |
| Blue-Sensitive AgX with Yellow Coupler |
| Yellow Filter |
| Interlayer |
| Green-Sensitive Fast AgX with Magenta Coupler |
| Green-Sensitive Slow AgX with Magenta Coupler |
| Interlayer |
| Red-Sensitive Fast AgX with Cyan Coupler |
| Red-Sensitive Slow AgX with Cyan Coupler |
| Antihalation Layer |
| Acetate Support |

57. *A cross section of Kodacolor II color negative film indicating its various layers; AgX is an abbreviation for silver halides. The yellow filter layer prevents blue light from affecting silver halides in the green and red sensitive layers.*

In the next step, silver grains are bleached out, leaving the color dyes in the three layers that overlap to produce the color negative image. After a wash to prevent chemical contamination, the image is made permanent by the fixer. Following a second wash, the stabilizer step stabilizes the dye colors and helps prevent spots on the negatives during drying.

As for color positive films available for home processing (which exclude Kodachrome film), the processing steps (in order) are first developer, first wash, reversal bath, color developer, conditioner, bleach, fixer, final wash, stabilizer, and drying. These steps are for *Kodak's E-6 process,* which has three fewer steps than its predecessor, E-4, and cuts processing time by 19 minutes. (E-4 steps are prehardener, neutralizer, first developer, first stop, wash, color developer, second stop, wash, bleach, fixer, wash, stabilizer, and drying.)

With positive color E-6 Ektachrome film, its three-layered emulsion is composed of light-sensitive silver halide grains—just as color negative films and black-and-white films are. The first developer reacts on the exposed silver halides to form a negative silver image. After the first wash to stop developer action and prevent chemical contamination, the film is given a reversal bath. This "fogs" the remaining (unexposed) silver halides.

In the fourth step, the color developer turns the fogged silver halides to positive silver images. It also activates dye couplers in the emulsion layers to form color dye images.

The conditioner prepares the silver images for the next step, the bleach. In the bleach, both negative and positive silver images are converted to silver salts, while the color dye images remain unaffected. The fixer makes the silver salts water soluble, and the final wash removes these salts and other chemicals. This leaves the dyes that produce the final positive color image. In the stabilizer step, the stability of the color dyes is enhanced, and the solution also serves as a wetting agent to promote spot-free drying.

Ektachrome films are favorites of home processers. Improvements in film quality and ease of processing has occurred rather rapidly since the first Ektachrome films were introduced in 1946 for professional photographers. The initial daylight film speed was ASA 12, and do-it-yourself processing took 90 minutes. By the time Ektachrome roll films came on the market in 1955 for amateur use, their daylight film speed was increased to ASA 32 and processing time had been reduced to 67 minutes.

Within four years, the films' color rendition was improved and the ASA boosted to 50; high speed Ektachrome films also appeared, with the daylight type rated at ASA 160. In 1966, a new process for some Ektachrome films, E-4, became available and reduced processing time to 47 minutes. Processing was easier, too, because the earlier E-3 process required reexposure of the film with a bright light to produce the positive images, but E-4 used chemical agents for that reversal step.

In 1976— 77 new professional and amateur Ektachrome films were introduced by Kodak, along with an even newer process, E-6. Speed of the daylight type film was increased to ASA 200, and processing time for roll films in one-pint tanks was cut to 37 minutes. The E-6 Ektachromes have other important improvements. Better color renditions are notable, because blues and greens were overemphasized in the earlier Ektachromes. The E-6 types produce good reds, yellows, and oranges, as well as improved flesh tones, wood colors, and neutrals. Despite faster film speeds, they also have better sharpness and finer grain. Very remarkable is an even faster E-6-type film, Ektachrome 400, which was introduced in 1978 and has a film speed of ASA 400.

As for the difference between Ektachrome professional and amateur films (the latter which Kodak also calls "consumer" films), professional films have more specific film speed information and require more exact handling. Each batch of emulsion made for Ektachrome Professional films (Process E-6) is tested for precise speed, and this information is printed on the data instruction sheet packed with the film. For example, Ektachrome 64 Professional (Daylight) film has an established film speed of ASA 64, but the instruction sheet lists its *effective speed,* as tested at the factory. This effective speed might be faster (ASA 80) or slower (ASA 50), which helps the professional photographer make more accurate exposures.

Color balance of the professional films is more uniform when Kodak's handling instructions are followed. That means the films must be stored at 55°F (13°C) or lower and they should be processed promptly (at least within a week) after exposure.

The emulsions of the amateur/consumer E-6 Ektachrome films have more latitude regarding exposure and handling, so their instruction sheets do not

---

KODAK EKTACHROME 160 Professional Film (Tungsten)

Process E-6

A high-speed color reversal film intended primarily for use under tungsten existing light conditions.

● The following information, determined at the time of manufacture, applies to film packaged herein.

 EFFECTIVE SPEED: ASA 200   24 DIN

The following information, based on average emulsions, is to determine speed under various light sources:

LIGHT SOURCE	SPEED	WITH FILTER SUCH AS:
Tungsten (3200 K)	ASA 160 23 DIN	None
Photolamp (3400 K)	ASA 125 22 DIN	KODAK Filter, No. 81A
Daylight	ASA 100 21 DIN	KODAK Filter, No. 85B

Handling and Storage: *Unexposed film should be kept in a refrigerator at 13°C (55°F) or lower, in the original sealed package.*

---

58. *Instruction sheets packed with Kodak's Ektachrome Professional films indicate the "effective speed" of the particular batch of film, as determined by factory testing. This sheet accompanying a roll of Ektachrome 160 Professional (Tungsten) film, normally a film with a speed of ASA 160, notes that the film has an effective speed of ASA 200.*

have such revised film speed information or exacting storage instructions.

Another type of color positive film, the first to be designed for amateur and professional use, is Kodachrome. Introduced in the mid-1930s, Kodachrome films continue to be improved by their manufacturer, Eastman Kodak Co., except that processing has remained a complex procedure requiring elaborate equipment.

The reason is that Kodachrome film does not contain color dye couplers in its three layers of emulsion, which means three separate color developers are required during processing to produce the color dye images. Therefore, home processing is not possible with Kodachrome films.

For a better understanding of *Kodachrome processing,* here's what happens to the film at a Kodak lab. (This is Process K-14, designed for current Kodachrome films.) Individual rolls are spliced together to a length of about 500 feet, which is equivalent to nearly one hundred rolls of thirty-six-exposure film. The master roll is loaded into an automatic continuous processing machine, where it winds up and down through the various solutions. In the initial chemical, the film's antistatic and antihalation backing is softened. Then the film goes into the first developer, for 2 minutes 10 seconds, and washed for 50 seconds afterward.

For the reversal procedure, the film's three individual emulsion layers are reexposed by tungsten-halogen lights covered with filters that react on a specific layer. First the film passes over a light with a red filter, then enters a cyan developer for two minutes, which deposits cyan dyes in the bottom emulsion layer. After a wash, the film is exposed to a blue light, which acts on the top layer. Then it runs through a yellow developer for three minutes to deposit yellow dyes. Next, after another wash, the film makes a 4-minute run through a magenta developer, which contains a chemical fogging agent that exposes the middle emulsion layer and deposits magenta dyes.

The final steps are a 2-minute wash—1 minute in the bleach, 1 minute in fixer—another 2-minute wash, and then into a dryer for 3 minutes, from which the film emerges ready to be mounted or sleeved. Besides Kodak, some commercial labs process Kodachrome films, but each one has invested at least $250,000 in Kodachrome processing machinery and related equipment!

Color Film Processing Equipment

Excluding Kodachrome processing, equipment needed for color film processing in your own darkroom depends in part on the size of the film you are using. Cassette, roll, and cartridge films—like 135, 120, and 126—can be processed in the same type of *daylight developing tank* used for black-and-white processing.

Nikkor, Brooks, and Patterson are brand names of three popular tanks that have reels on which the film is loaded in total darkness. Once the loaded reels are placed inside the tank, and the tank cover is closed, processing can be done in normal room light (see page 30).

Sheet film, like 4 x 5-inch or larger, can be processed in trays, or in large open tanks using special film hangers which suspend each sheet individually in the chemical solutions (see page 38).

Other equipment which you will need include:

Thermometer
Measuring graduates
Stirring rod
Funnel
Storage bottles
Timer
Rubber gloves
Film cassette opener
Scissors
Sponge or squeegee
Washing device
Film clips
Drying cabinet
Negative sleeves.

(For details regarding this equipment, see chapter 2.) Besides these items, you'll need a dark room or changing bag, and the processing chemicals.

Precautions for Color Film Processing Chemicals

When mixing chemicals, follow the manufacturer's directions carefully. Be sure that powdered chemicals are completely dissolved. Cleanliness is imperative in order to avoid contamination. After each solution is mixed, all of the equipment used in the mixing process (i.e. graduate, stirring rod, thermometer) should be thoroughly washed in hot water.

When mixing chemicals for color processing, use distilled water, or filter your water supply. Without these precautions, mineral ingredients in ordinary water may affect the activity of your chemicals. If you want to filter water rather than buy distilled water, investigate some of the filtering systems offered by Pako, Fisher, and others. These systems cost from $50, up.

If you plan to process your film immediately after mixing the solutions, you'll save time by mixing with water adjusted to the proper processing

59. *A water bath can be used to establish and maintain chemical solution temperatures required for processing.*

temperatures. However, it's also a good idea to let the chemicals stand in their bottles for several hours to make sure they are thoroughly dissolved. Once the chemicals are mixed, the developing process can begin if the chemicals are at correct temperature. An easy way to do this is to put the chemical storage bottles in a *water bath* that is maintained at the proper developer temperature. For Kodak processes E-6 and C-41, for instance, the developer temperature must be kept at 100°F (37.8°C).

If the chemicals are extremely cold and you want to speed up the warming process, immerse the bottles in very hot water and keep a close watch on the thermometer. Conversely, if your chemicals are too hot, you can reduce the temperature quickly by using an extremely cold water bath.

Keeping chemicals at their recommended temperature is crucial. Because color film has very little *latitude,* especially when compared to black-and-white film, you need to be very careful about the developers' temperature: with the C-41 process, it must be within ¼°F± (.15°C±) of the recommended temperature.

Subsequent steps usually have more latitude, as with Kodak Process E-6, where the temperature of all solutions except the developers can range from 92° to 102°F (33.5 to 39°C). Be sure the wash water is within this temperature range, too.

Color film chemicals have a storage life of two to six weeks, depending on how you store them. The best storage is in dark glass bottles that are completely filled and have their caps on tight. Air oxidizes chemicals and reduces their useful life. That is why it is important to fill bottles to the top and to use glass bottles rather than plastic, especially with developers, since plastic tends to "breathe".

Another problem with chemicals can be using the wrong one accidentally. Help avoid this by painting the storage bottles a different color for each chemical. That way you won't confuse developer with bleach, or C-41 Stabilizer with E-6 Stabilizer. Another important thing is to label each bottle plainly with both the name of the chemical and the name of process. Also number the bottle according to the chemical's sequence in the process. Include the solution's mixing date and its exhaustion date, so you'll know when it should be replaced.

Each time you process film, the chemicals lose some of their strength. In order to get consistent results, compensate for this depletion by increasing development time, or by replenishing the chemicals with special replenisher solutions. The amount of increased development, or replenisher, depends on how much film has been processed in the solutions. Keep a record and follow manufacturers' recommendations on the processing data sheets.

Unless you are processing large amounts of film on a regular basis, it is not practical to use replenishers because they deteriorate within several weeks after mixing. What most photographers do is adjust the developer time to compensate for the amount of film previously developed in the solution. For example, if you processed two rolls of thirty-six-exposure 35mm film in freshly mixed C-41 chemicals, before processing any more film, you should increase the developer time by 14 seconds—to a total of 3 minutes and 29 seconds (see page 155).

A special note of caution should be made regarding the handling of color processing chemicals. They can irritate your skin, so it is wise to wear a pair of clean rubber gloves when mixing or pouring the solutions. Be sure to read the warnings that appear on the chemical packages and in the chemical instructions. Also be certain your darkroom has adequate ventilation.

11

Processing Color Films
Step by Step

This chapter describes the procedures for processing both color negative and color transparency (positive) films. The mechanical aspects of loading roll film on processing reels and sheet film in hangers, using processing tanks, and giving proper agitation were discussed in chapter 3, "Processing Black-and-White Films Step by Step." Be sure to read that chapter if you are unfamiliar with those techniques.

Processes for Color Negative Films

Film manufacturers constantly strive to improve their films, as well as the processing procedures required. One reason, in our energy and ecology conscious times, is to use processes that are less wasteful in regard to water and energy, as well as less polluting.

When Eastman Kodak Co. brought out their newest color negative films, Kodacolor II and Vericolor II Professional, they also introduced new processing chemistry, Process C-41, with Flexicolor chemicals. C-41 replaces Kodak's Process C-22, which is for developing Kodacolor-X and Ektacolor Professional films. Although such films are no longer manufactured (Kodak replaced them with Kodacolor II and Vericolor II Professional films), some supplies may still be around. So Kodak continues to make Process C-22 chemicals in order that the older films can be developed, and also to develop Ektacolor Internegative films. (A new color internegative film has been introduced by Kodak that can be developed in the newer Process C-41.)

Other film manufacturers, like Fuji and Sakura, have introduced color negative films that can also be developed in the newer Kodak chemistry, C-41, while some other non-Kodak color negative films can be processed in C-22. Data sheets packed with every film indicate the proper process to use for that particular film. Following is a list of various processes—Kodak's and other brands—and the films for which they are intended. Afterward there is a summary of the processes, in order to give you an idea of the steps, temperatures, and times required. Be warned, however, that the processes occasionally are improved and undergo alteration, so *be certain to read and follow the instructions packed with the processing kit you purchase.*

COLOR NEGATIVE FILM PROCESSES

Processes	Films
Kodak's C-41; Beseler's CN2; Unicolor's K2 and Total Color; and Dignan's NCF-41.	Kodak's Kodacolor II, Kodacolor 400, and Vericolor II; Fujicolor F-II and Fujicolor F-II 400; Sakuracolor II and Sakuracolor 400; and Kodak's Type 5247.
Kodak's C-22 and Unicolor's F	Kodak's Kodacolor-X and Ektacolor S and L; Fujicolor N100; Agfacolor CNS; 3M Color Print Film; Sakuracolor N-100; and Kodak's Type 5254 and Ektacolor Internegative films.

Summary of Steps for Kodak's Process C-41 (Flexicolor Chemicals)

You can develop Kodak's popular color negative film, Kodacolor II (ASA 100) and Kodacolor 400 (ASA 400), at home with a Kodak Flexicolor Processing Kit, Process C-41. Kodak's Vericolor II Professional films can be personally processed in C-41, too. Follow the kit's directions exactly.

A summary of the steps follows. Total time is 24¼ minutes, plus drying. Use a daylight film developing tank and load it in total darkness. After the first two steps (developer and bleach) are completed, you can remove the tank's top and continue the processing steps in room light.

KODAK'S C-41 PROCESSING KIT (100°F)

Step	Temp. (F)	Time* (Min.)	Remarks
1. Developer	100± ¼	3¼	Total darkness
2. Bleach	75—105	6½	Total darkness
(remaining steps can be done in normal room light)			
3. Wash	75—105	3¼	Running water†
4. Fixer	75—105	6½	
5. Wash	75—105	3¼	Running water†
6. Stabilizer	75—105	1½	
7. Dry	75—110	10 to 20	

*Includes 10-second drain time in each step.
†Use fresh water changes throughout the wash cycles. Fill the processing tank as rapidly as possible from a running water supply for about 4 seconds. When full, agitate vigorously for about 2 seconds and drain for about 10 seconds. Repeat this full wash cycle. If desired, use a running water inflow-overflow wash with the cover removed from the tank.

The C-41 processing kit contains two units of developer and one unit each of bleach, stabilizer, and fixer. You'll use two pints of developer before the other chemicals are exhausted, but mix only one pint of developer to start. Instead of chemically replenishing the developer, developing time is increased according to the amount of film that has been processed. When a certain number of rolls has been developed, discard the developer and mix another pint.

The chart that follows indicates the film capacity of one pint of C-41 developer, and the increased developer time that is required after a certain number of rolls are processed.

C-41 DEVELOPER TIME IN MINUTES AND SECONDS

Film Size	Rolls*	Processes						Developer's Film Capacity Rolls†
		1st	2nd	3rd	4th	5th	6th	
110—12	3	3'15"	3'20"	3'26"	3'31"	3'37"	3'43"	18
110—20	3	3'15"	3'22"	3'30"	3'37"	3'45"		15
126—12	2	3'15"	3'21"	3'28"	3'36"	3'45"		10
126—20	2	3'15"	3'25"	3'37"				6
135—20	2	3'15"	3'23"	3'33"	3'45"			8
135—36	2	3'15"	3'29"	3'47"				6

*Rolls of film processed per pint before each time increase.
†Discard solution after developing this number of rolls per pint.

Replenishment is recommended when developer tank volumes are greater than one pint. For chemical storage life, refer to the C-41 data sheet packed with the Flexicolor Processing kit.

The C-41 process is more critical in regard to temperature and agitation than is the other color negative process, C-22. C-41 developer must be maintained at $100\pm\frac{1}{4}°F$ ($37.8 \pm .15°C$). The bleach, washes, fixer and stabilizer are not as critical temperature-wise, but they should be maintained between the recommended temperatures of 75° to 105°F (24° to 40.5°C).

The best way to control temperature is to use a water bath at the correct temperature (see page 151). Bring the bottle of chemicals to proper temperature just before you begin processing, and then keep them in the water bath during the process. The processing tank should be placed in the water bath, too, removing it only during agitation and when pouring out solutions after each step.

Because of C-41's extremely short developer time (3¼ minutes), agitation is very critical. If a daylight developing tank is used, spacers should be added to hold the film reel (or reels) in place. That's because movement of reels during inversion agitation can cause *surge marks* (see page 45).

To prevent this, cut off pieces of plastic (not wood) clothespins and force them between the reel(s) and side of the tank to hold the reel(s) firmly in place.

Vigorous inversion of the tank should be done with the developer for the first 30 seconds, with rapping of the tank on a tabletop to dislodge air bells. After this initial agitation, agitate the film every 13 seconds for 2 seconds. For the bleach and fixer, agitate every 30 seconds for 5-second durations. With the stabilizer, no agitation is required after an initial 30-second agitation.

Once processed, remove the film from the reel(s) and hang it up to dry. Squeegeeing should not be necessary, provided you mixed the stabilizer with distilled water. The film dries fast; it should only take 10 to 20 minutes with good air circulation.

In addition to Kodak's C-41 chemistry for processing many brands of the most current color negative films (usually indicated with a II, as in Kodacolor II, Vericolor II, Fujicolor II, and Sakuracolor II), there are other processes on the market. These are offered by Color By Beseler, Dignan Photographic, and Unicolor. The main advantage of the first two is that Beseler's CN2 and Dignan's NCF-41 can be used at 75°F (24°C); Unicolor's K-2 and Total Color require a temperature of 100°F (38.7°C), as does Kodak's C-41.

Summary of Steps for Beseler's CN2 Processing Kit

Color By Beseler's CN2 processing kit can be used at 75°F (24°C) or 85°F (29.5°C). There are just three chemical steps, plus a water wash. At 75°F (24°C), total processing time is 29½ minutes. The one-pint kit will process up to six rolls of thirty-six-exposure 35mm film or equivalent.

The kit contains complete instructions for use, but a summary is given here.

BESELER'S CN2 PROCESSING KIT (75°F)

Step	Time*	Remarks
1. CN2 developer	16 min.	Increase developer time 5 percent for each roll processed.
2. CN2 bleach-fix	9 min.	
3. Water wash	4 min.	Open tank; use running water.
4. CN2 wetting agent	½ min.	

*Includes 15 seconds for draining from tank.

Summary of Steps for Unicolor's K-2 Processing Kit

Unicolor's K-2 kit for processing color negatives has four steps, including a water wash. The temperature required is 100°F (37.8°C), but total processing time is only 13¼ minutes. Chemicals are supplied in 1-quart and 1-gallon sizes. Each quart will develop up to twelve rolls of thirty-six-exposure 35mm film or equivalent.

Complete instructions are packed with the kits; a summary of steps follows.

Unicolor also has a process called Total Color which has two chemicals, Developer and Blix (plus an optional Stabilizer), that can be used to develop both color negatives and color prints. Color negative processing is identical to the K-2 process outlined below, including procedure, temperature, and processing times, except the stabilizer step can be eliminated in the Total Color process.

UNICOLOR'S K-2 PROCESSING KIT (100°F)

Step	Time	Remarks
1. Color developer	3¼ min.	Includes time for draining from tank; increase developer time 15 seconds for each subsequent roll.
2. Blix (bleach-fix)	6 min.	Agitation required.
3. Water wash	3 min.	Open tank; use running water.
4. Stabilizer	1 min.	Mix with distilled water to prevent water spots on film.

Summary of Steps for Dignan NCF-41 Processing Kit

An independent manufacturer of a color negative process is Dignan Photographic, 12304 Erwin St., North Hollywood, Calif. 91606. The company produces a NCF-41 processing kit that can be used at 75°F (24°C). There are five chemical steps, plus a water wash, and total processing time is 21 minutes. The one-quart kit will process up to thirty-two rolls of thirty-six-exposure film or equivalent.

A summary of the required steps is given below; complete instructions come with the kit, which is available in some camera stores, or by writing the Dignan address above.

DIGNAN NCF-41 PROCESSING KIT (75°F)

Step	Time*	Remarks
1. Color prebath	3 min.	Save for reuse.
2. Color activator	6 min.	Discard after one use.
3. Stop Bath	1 min.	Discard after one use.
4. Bleach-fix	5 min.	Save for reuse.
5. Water wash	5 min.	Open tank; use running water.
6. Stabilizer	1 min.	Save for reuse.

*Includes 15 seconds for draining from the tank.

Summary of Steps for Kodak's Process C-22

As mentioned previously, Process C-41 supersedes Process C-22. The color negative films Kodak made for C-22—Kodacolor-X and Ektacolor Professional films—have been replaced by Kodacolor II and Vericolor II Professional films, and these newer color negative films are developed in C-41. (Ektacolor Internegative films continue to be manufactured, until Kodak replaces it with a color internegative film that can be developed in C-41.) You may encounter some film that requires C-22 processing (it will be marked on the film box, cassette, or roll), and processing kits will be available from Kodak until there is no longer a demand.

The steps for processing Kodacolor-X or Ektacolor Professional films in C-22 are summarized here. Carefully follow the instructions packed with the chemicals, especially regarding temperature and agitation. Note that the C-22 process takes more than twice the time of the newer C-41 process (52 minutes vs. 24¼ minutes).

KODAK'S C-22 PROCESSING KIT (75°F)

Step	Temp. (°F)	Time* (min.)	Remarks
1. Developer	75±½	13	Total darkness
2. Stop Bath	73—77	4	Total darkness
3. Hardener	73—77	4	Total darkness
(Remaining steps can be done in normal room light)			
4. Wash	73—77	4	Running water
5. Bleach	73—77	6	
6. Wash	73—77	4	Running water
7. Fixer	73—77	8	
8. Wash	73—77	8	Running water
9. Final Rinse	73—77	1	Kodak Photo-Flo Solution
10. Dry	110 (not above)		

*Includes 10-second drain time for each step.

Kodak's C-22 processing kit contains five solutions: two units each of developer and stop bath, and one unit each of hardener, bleach, and fixer. Do not mix the extra units of developer and stop bath until the first units are exhausted. The hardener, bleach, and fixer will process twice as much as a comparable amount of developer and stop bath. For further technical information and advice, refer to the C-22 data sheet included with the chemicals.

Processing Errors with Color Negative Films

Processing problems sometimes are apparent only after negatives are printed. For instance, you may see a greenish cast in the shadow areas of a print. This often is the result of an overall reddish stain on the negative which is not easily detected if the negative has a built-in color mask (i.e. orangish tint). Such staining on the negative may have been caused by one of the following processing errors:

a)   overdevelopment, because of a higher than normal developer temperature or prolonged developer time
b)   handling the film under a green safelight (color negative film must be processed in complete darkness)
c)   fixer contaminating the developer
d)   omitting the hardener and fixer, or shortening the time of any of the steps between the developer and the bleach.

To check the minimum density of any negative to see if it might be stained, compare it with an unexposed but properly processed piece of the same type of color negative film. (Also look for mechanical errors that may occur during processing; see a description beginning on page 43.)

Viewing Color Negatives

Some color negatives, such as Kodacolor, Vericolor, and Ektacolor, have an overall orangish tint. This is a so-called *color mask* that is required in order to produce correct colors in a print. Although this orangish color should be disregarded when studying a color negative, it prevents you from easily determining the individual colors or color balance of that negative.

Saturated colors are fairly obvious, even though complementary to the actual colors photographed (for example, yellow appears as violet, and red as green). But pastel tints, "cool" shades, and near neutral colors are difficult to judge in a color negative.

As for appraising exposure when viewing a color negative, the highlight areas should not be excessively dense, and there should be adequate detail in the shadow areas, too.

Push Processing Color Negative Films

For the best photographic results, color film should be exposed and processed according to its recommended film speed (ASA) and processing instructions. However, when color negative film is accidentally underexposed, you can overdevelop it to try saving the results. (There will be an increase in contrast, graininess and fog, however.) Also, you can decrease development to try salvaging overexposed color negative film.

Before deciding to alter development, remember that color negative films have some *exposure latitude*. If developed normally, even films that have been over- or underexposed up to one f/stop will produce satisfactory prints.

Also, if you want to check results at normal development before developing an entire roll, you can make a *snip test*. Just cut off about 6 inches of film beyond the leader, and process that strip. (Photographers who are uncertain of what film speed [ASA] they used when exposing a film can make a snip test before developing the entire roll.) If your snip test results are overexposed, decrease developer time. If underexposed, increase the time.

| | ASA EQUIVALENT | | APPROXIMATE |
| CAMERA | Kodacolor 400 | Kodacolor II | CHANGE IN |
EXPOSURE	Fujicolor F-II 400	Vericolor II	DEVELOPER TIME
4 times (2 f/stops) underexposure	1600	400	Increase by 75 percent
2 times (1 f/stop) underexposure	800	200	Increase by 35 percent
NORMAL ASA	400	100	Use normal time*
2 times (1 f/stop) overexposure	200	50	Decrease by 30 percent
4 times (2 f/stops) overexposure	100	25	Decrease by 50 percent

*Refer to the data sheets accompanying Process C-41 chemicals.

To overdevelop or underdevelop color negative film, a change is made in the processing time of the developer only; times for all other steps remain normal. The previous chart is a guideline for the percentage of change in developer time for Kodacolor 400 and Fujicolor F-II 400 (both ASA 400), and for Kodacolor II and Vericolor II Professional, Type S (both ASA 100). All these films are processed in Kodak's C-41 or other brands of equivalent chemistry. For best results, exposure and processing tests are recommended.

Processes for Color Transparency (Positive) Films

Color transparency films produce positive images for projection, or for viewing with a light source behind them. These are popularly called color slide films, and technically called color reversal films.

Color prints can be made directly from color transparencies on positive-to-positive print papers. Or you can first make a color internegative from a color transparency and then use that internegative to produce a color print on negative-to-positive print papers.

Like color negative films, most color transparency films can be processed at home, *except* for Kodak's Kodachrome films. These color slide films, including Kodachrome 25 and Kodachrome 64, involve complicated processing procedures. That's because Kodachrome requires three color developers to form its color dyes.

Other color slide films, including Kodak's Ektachrome films, have emulsions of different chemical make-up that include the color dye couplers, and these films can be processed at home. As you recall, the couplers are incorporated in the emulsion but do nothing until acted upon by the developer, which turns them into dyes and controls the color of the image.

Over the years, Kodak has improved Ektachrome films and their processes. In 1976—77, the company introduced new E-6 Ektachrome films and their developing chemistry, Process E-6. The E-6 films were Ektachrome 64, Ektachrome 200, Ektachrome 50 (Tungsten), and Ektachrome 160 (Tungsten), as well as professional Ektachrome films. Ektachrome 400 was introduced a year later.

They replaced the familiar Ektachrome-X (ASA 64), High Speed Ektachrome (Daylight) (ASA 160), and High Speed Ektachrome (Tungsten) (ASA 125), and their developing chemistry, E-4. Since supplies of the older films will be around for a while, so will Process E-4, including kits for home processing.

Another, and even older process, E-3, once required for most Ektachrome professional sheet films, will be phased out by Kodak in favor of E-6.

There have been significant improvements in the developing processes for Ektachrome films. Because these color transparency films are reversal films, the black-and-white negative images first produced during processing must be reversed to positive images. In the oldest process, E-3, this is done physically, by exposing the film to a No. 2 Photoflood light. In the E-4 and E-6 processes, the film images are reversed chemically.

The later processes also allow a hotter developer temperature, and thus a shorter processing time. Developers for E-6 are used at 100°F (37.8°C), E-4 developers at 85°F (29.5°C), and E-3 developers at 75°F (24°C). Processing times in one-pint tanks, excluding drying, are 37 minutes for E-6, 56 minutes for E-4, and 67 minutes (plus reversal exposure) for E-3.

Remember that all Ektachrome films are marked on their package and cassette or roll regarding the particular process to use for that film: E-6, E-4, or E-3. *Never* develop the film in any process except the one specified.

Unicolor also offers processes for developing color transparencies. The newest is *Unicolor E-6 Chemistry* for E-6 films. The other is called *Unichrome,* and it will process color films of the type designed for Kodak's Process E-4. That means you can use the 1- or 2-quart kits of Unichrome chemistry to process the older Ektachromes (Ektachrome-X and High Speed Ektachrome), Agfachromes, Fujichrome, and 3M slide films. The process takes about 45 minutes (at 80°F); it involves twelve steps, including a reexposure step that is done physically (with a No. 2 Photoflood light), instead of chemically as in the E-4 process. (More details are given following a discussion of Kodak's E-6, E-4, and E-3 processes.)

Here is a list of processes for specific color transparency films.

COLOR TRANSPARENCY FILM PROCESSES

Processes	*Films*
Kodak's Process E-6; and Unicolor E-6 Chemistry	Kodak's Ektachrome 64, Ektachrome 200, Ektachrome 400, Ektachrome 50 (Tungsten), and Ektachrome 160 (Tungsten)
Kodak's E-4 Process; and Unicolor's Unichrome	Kodak's Ektachrome-X, High Speed Ektachrome, and High Speed Ektachrome Tungsten; Agfachrome 64; Fujichrome R-100 and RK-126; Sakuracolor R; and 3M Color Slide Film
Kodak's E-3 Process	Kodak's Ektachrome Professional Daylight and Type B, Ektachrome 6115, and Ektachrome Duplicating Film 6120

Summary of Steps for Kodak's Process E-6

Process E-6 is Kodak's most recent color transparency process, introduced in the summer of 1976, and it is for the new Ektachrome films introduced at that same time and in 1977. There are numerous advantages over the previous Ektachrome processes (E-4 and E-3).

Important to photographers doing home processing is that the total processing time with manual agitation (but excluding drying) is 37 minutes. There are just nine wet steps, including two water washes, and the seven chemicals required are supplied in easy-to-mix liquid concentrates.

Kodak offers E-6 processing kits in 1-pint and 1-gallon size. The kits contain first developer, reversal bath, color developer, conditioner, bleach, fixer, and stabilizer. (Descriptions of the purpose and action of each E-6 chemical were outlined in the previous chapter.)

The quality and life of E-6 processing solutions depend on the cleanliness of the equipment in which the chemicals are mixed, stored, and used. Even the smallest amount of fixer is harmful to the other solutions. For that reason, always mix the fixer in separate equipment. A second set of mixing equipment should be used for the first and color developers, and a third set for the other chemicals.

Storage life of the solutions, once they are mixed for use, vary according to the chemical and the manner in which it is stored. *Fresh* first developer, reversal bath, and conditioner will last eight weeks in a full, tightly capped glass bottle; if these solutions have been used, their storage life in a full, tightly capped bottle is four weeks. Whether fresh or used, in *partially full* bottles they will last only one week. Fresh color developer lasts twelve weeks in a full, tightly capped bottle; eight weeks if used. Fresh or used, its life in a partially full bottle is six weeks. Bleach and fixer have a storage life of twenty-four weeks, whether fresh or used, or in a full or partially full bottle.

The amount of film the solutions will process, without replenishment, depends on the film size. The list below indicates the number of rolls that can be processed in the 1-pint size E-6 processing kit.

Film Size / No. of exposures	Rolls Per 1-Pint Kit*
110 / 20	36
126 / 20	16
127	16
35mm / 20	12
35mm / 36	8
120	8

*There are *two* 1-pint units for both the first developer and the color developer. Mix one pint of each at a time, and discard them after *half* the number of rolls listed above are processed; then mix the second set of one-pint developer units.

Refinements in the E-6 process are expected, so always reread the instruction sheet packed with each E-6 processing kit or any separate E-6 chemicals you purchase.

KODAK'S E-6 PROCESSING KIT (100°F)

The following steps apply to all E-6 roll films in one-pint tanks, and the times given are for film processed exclusively with manual agitation. Total processing time is 37 minutes, plus drying.

Step	Temp (°F)	Time* (min.)	Remarks
1. First developer	100±½	7	First three
2. First wash	92—102	2	steps in
3. Reversal bath	92—102	2	total darkness.
(Remaining steps can be done in normal room light.)			
4. Color developer	100±2	6	
5. Conditioner	92—102	2	
6. Bleach	92—102	7	
7. Fixer	92—102	4	
8. Final wash	92—102	6	Two tanks; Counterflow
9. Stabilizer	92—102	1	
10. Dry	not to exceed 120		Remove films from reels before drying.

*Includes drain time of 10 seconds in each step.

Agitation is especially important in the E-6 process, and it varies for each solution; read the processing kit's instructions carefully. Only the reversal bath, conditioner, and stabilizer do not receive any agitation, but you should initially rap the developing tank to dislodge any air bubbles that may be clinging to the film in those solutions.

The tank also should be rapped to dislodge air bubbles in the other steps: First developer, first wash, color developer, bleach, fixer, and final wash. In addition, initial agitation is required in each of those six steps. Do this by turning your invertible tank over and back once per second for the first 15 seconds the film is in each solution. Afterward, 5 seconds of inverting agitation is required every 30 seconds in those solutions. Other methods of manual agitation are described in the E-6 processing instruction sheets.

PROCESSING ERRORS WITH E-6 COLOR TRANSPARENCY FILMS

After inadequate film storage or improper exposure are eliminated as causes of poor quality Ektachrome transparencies, incorrect processing in Kodak's Process E-6 may be the problem. Errors can occur in mixing chemicals, order of processing, solution temperatures, agitation rates, washing, and contamination of solutions. The following list will help you identify such errors with Process E-6.

Appearance of Film	Probable Fault
Very high maximum density (no image apparent)	First developer and color developer reversed. First developer omitted.
Dark overall	Inadequate time or low temperature in first developer. First developer diluted, exhausted, or underreplenished. Color developer starter added to first developer.
Very dark (overall or in random areas)	Bleach or fixer (or both) omitted, reversed, diluted, exhausted, or underreplenished.
Light overall	Excessive time or high temperature in first developer. Film fogged by light prior to processing. First developer too concentrated. First developer overreplenished. First developer contaminated with color developer.
Light overall, blue color balance	First developer contaminated with fixer.
Overall density variation from batch to batch	Inconsistencies in time, temperature, agitation or replenishment of first developer.
Blue	Reversal bath too concentrated. Color developer alkalinity too low. Color developer replenisher mixed with Part B only. Process E-4 used in error.
Cyan	First and color developers underreplenished.
Yellow	Color developer alkalinity too high. Color developer starter added to first developer. Color developer replenisher mixed with only Part A.

Appearance of Film	Probable Fault
Low densities blue green, high densities yellow	Color developer contaminated with first developer. Color developer contaminated with fixer.
Blue red with high maximum density	Color developer replenisher too dilute.
Green	Reversal bath exhausted, diluted, or underreplenished. Film fogged by green safelight. Wash used between reversal bath and color developer.
Very yellow	Film exposed through base. Film fogged by room lights during first developer step.
Scum and dirt	Stabilizer requires replacement.

Summary of Steps for Unicolor E-6 Chemistry

Besides Kodak, Unicolor makes chemistry for processing Ektachrome films of the E-6 type, including Ektachrome 64, Ektachrome 200, Ektachrome 400, Ektachrome 50 (Tungsten), and Ektachrome 160 (Tungsten).

With Unicolor's E-6 Chemistry, there are ten steps, which take about 29 minutes. Two rolls of 120-size or thirty-six-exposure 35mm film can be developed in 8 ounces of working solutions, but the first developer time must be increased 20 seconds for the second roll.

If push processing, increase the first developer time by 30 percent for one f/stop underexposure (film rated at double its normal ASA film speed), or by 60 percent for two f/stops underexposure (film rated at four times its normal ASA film speed). Following is an outline of the processing steps.

UNICOLOR'S E-6 CHEMISTRY PROCESSING KIT (100°F)

Step	Temp (°F)	Time (min)	Remarks
1. First developer	100	6½	Pour developer in tank, agitate continuously for first 15 seconds. Agitate 2 seconds each 15 seconds thereafter. Include drain time in total time for this step.

UNICOLOR'S E-6 CHEMISTRY PROCESSING KIT (100°F) (Cont.)

Step	Temp (°F)	Time (min.)	Remarks
2. Water rinse	92—102	2—3	Fill tank with water and drain. Repeat five times. Note: total of six rinses is more important than absolute rinse time.
3. Reversal bath	92—102	2	Agitate initial 10 seconds only and rap tank to dislodge air bubbles.

(Remaining steps can be done in normal room light.)

Step	Temp (°F)	Time (min.)	Remarks
4. Color developer	99—101	6	See Step 1.
5. Stop bath	92—102	1	See Step 1.
6. Water rinse	92—102	2	See Step 1.
7. Bleach	92—102	3	See Step 1.
8. Fixer	92—102	2	See Step 1.
9. Water rinse	92—102	2—3	Use water flow sufficient to change water in film tank at least 6 times. Time not critical.
10. Stabilizer	Room temp.	30 sec.	Agitate gently initial 10—15 seconds only.
11. Dry	Not over 104		

Summary of Steps for Kodak's Process E-4

Process E-4 should not be used to develop the newer Ektachrome films; it is designed for Ektachrome-X, and High Speed Ektachrome (Daylight) and (Tungsten). As supplies of these films are depleted, and demand for Process E-4 diminishes, Kodak will stop producing E-4 chemicals.

A summary of steps follows for E-4 processing in 1-pint tanks only. Read instructions packed with the E-4 processing kit carefully. In one pint tanks, processing takes 56 minutes, requiring a total of twelve steps, plus drying.

KODAK'S E-4 PROCESSING KIT (85°F)

Step	Temp (°F)	Time* (min)	Remarks
1. Prehardener	85±1	3	First four steps
2. Neutralizer	85±2	1	in total darkness.

KODAK'S E-4 PROCESSING KIT (85°F) (Cont.)

Step	Temp (°F)	Time* (min)	Remarks
3. First developer	85±½	7	
4. First stop bath	85±2	2	
(Remaining steps can be done in normal room light.)			
5. Wash	85±5	4	Running water
6. Color developer	85±2	15	Be careful; see warning on label.
7. Second stop bath	85±2	3	Don't use First stop bath.
8. Wash	85±5	3	Running water
9. Bleach	85±2	5	
10. Fixer	85±2	6	
11. Wash	85±5	6	Running water
12. Stabilizer	85±2	1	Be careful; see warning on label.
13. Dry	Not over 110		Remove film from reels before drying.

*Includes 10-seconds for draining.

Agitation is important. Begin after pouring in the prehardener, by rapping the daylight developing tank on the tabletop to dislodge any air bubbles clinging to the film. For *each* solution, you give the film initial agitation by turning invertible tanks over and back once per second for the first 15 seconds. In the first developer, continue this type of agitation without stopping for the first 2 minutes. Additional agitation should be avoided when the film is in these solutions: prehardener, neutralizer, and stabilizer. But all other solutions require subsequent agitation every 30 seconds by turning the tank over and back four or five times.

Summary of Steps for Kodak's Process E-3

This early process for Ektachrome films will be dropped from production by Kodak, because of its replacement by improved films and processes. Process E-3 is primarily used to develop these films: Ektachrome Professional, Daylight Type, and Type B, roll size 120 only; Ektachrome 6115, Daylight Type, and Type B, sheet film only; and Ektachrome Duplicating Film 6120, sheet film only.

Do not use Process E-3 to develop Ektachrome films designated for processing in E-6 or E-4.

The major difference between Process E-3 and other color transparency processes is the physical reversal step that is necessary. Rather than chemically reversing the image from negative to positive, reversal is accomplished by exposing the film to a bright white light. Following the third step (the hardener), there is a 3-minute wash, and then the exposure which reverses the negative image which is done with No. 2 Photoflood bulbs. For film on developing reels, Kodak recommends a 15-second exposure between *two* No. 2 Photofloods located 2 feet apart. With sheet film, a 5-second exposure is suggested.

If Kodak's E-3 processing kits (1- or ½-gallon sizes) are still available, they each contain seven chemicals. Processing takes approximately 67 minutes, requiring a total of fourteen steps.

KODAK'S E-3 PROCESSING KIT (75°F)

Step	Temp (°F)	Time* (min)	Remarks
1. First developer	75±½	10	Steps 1 through 3 in total darkness.
2. Rinse	73—77	1	Running water
3. Hardener	73—77	3	
(Remaining steps can be done in normal room light.)			
4. Wash	73—77	3	Running water
5. Reversal exposure	Reexpose as prescribed for specific equipment.		
	Drain films at least 1 minute before color development.		
6. Color developer	73—77	15	
7. Wash	73—77	5	Running water
8. Clearing bath	73—77	5	
9. Rinse	73—77	1	Running water
10. Bleach	73—77	8	See warning on label.
11. Rinse	73—77	1	Running water
12. Fixer	73—77	6	
13. Wash	73—77	8	Running water
14. Stabilizer	73—77	1	See warning on label.
15. Dry	Not over 110		Remove sheet films from hangers and roll films from reels.

*Includes 10 seconds drain time in each step.

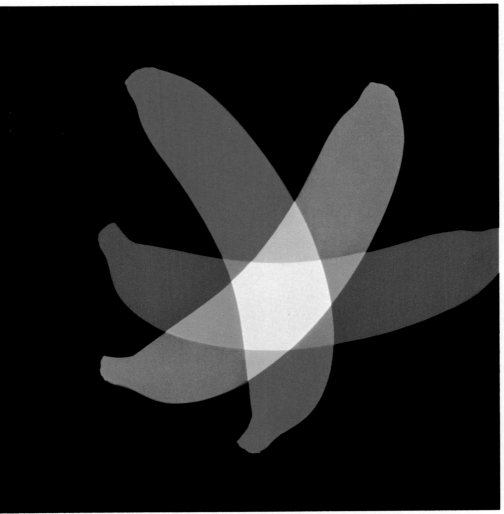

1. The six colors shown here are the keys to color photographic processes: red, green, and blue, called the additive primaries; and cyan, magenta, and yellow, called the subtractive primaries. To show their relationships, light was projected through banana-shaped filters of the three additive primaries. A mixture of red and green light produces yellow; red and blue light produce magenta, and blue and green light produce cyan. When all three additive primaries overlap, white light is produced.

In addition, the subtractive primaries are complements to the additive primaries; specifically each color is complementary to the additive primary it lacks. Thus, yellow (a mixture of red and green light) is complementary to blue; magenta (a mixture of red and blue) is complementary to green; and cyan (a mixture of blue and green) is complementary to red. For simplicity in this book, red, green, and blue are referred to as primary colors, and cyan, magenta, and yellow are referred to as complementary colors. See Chapters 9, 12, and 14.

2. Too
Green

Too
Magenta

3. Too
Red

Too
Cyan

4. Too
Blue

Too
Yellow

5. When making color prints, it is important to recognize various color casts so they can be corrected with different filtration in order to achieve good color balance, as is evident in the final print above. The test prints opposite show the primary colors and their complementary colors.

The manner of filter correction depends on whether the print is to be made from a color negative or color positive (slide). For example, if a print from a color negative is too green, filtration of its complementary color, magenta, is subtracted. If a print made from a color slide is too green, magenta filtration is added. Guidelines for adjusting filtration to produce correct color balance in a print are given in Chapter 14.

6. Because only one sheet of color printing paper can be processed at a time in a processing tube or drum, it saves time to make several test prints on one sheet of paper. Four test images were printed on this 8" x 10" sheet by using a cardboard mask to block the light from three-quarters of the paper while separate exposures were made of the individual negatives. Three of the negatives were being tested for proper filtration, while the image in the upper left-hand corner was being tested for correct exposure by masking off portions of the image for different exposure times. See Chapter 14.

7. Color printing papers are made specifically for color negatives or color positives (slides). This flower was photographed with flash in Hawaii on Kodachrome slide film and printed directly on color reversal paper to show its natural red color.

8. When the same slide is printed directly on color negative paper, it produces a negative image in complementary colors (i.e., red becomes cyan and the black background becomes white). An internegative must first be made of the slide before the image can be printed in its natural colors on color negative paper.

9. *Selective filtration can be used to alter and enhance an image. The nude in this California scene was too similar in color to her surroundings and was "lost." To make her more evident, the photographer used a dodging tool with a cyan filter during printing to "warm up" the model with a light reddish cast around her body. See Chapter 14.*

10. *Color was added directly to this Caribbean beach scene by the photographer who used a blue felt-tipped pen to fill in much of the bright areas in the slide. The print was made directly from the slide on color reversal paper.*

11. The subjects in this informal portrait were unhappy with the colors in a straight print made from the color negative.

To please them, the photographer applied dyes called Kodak Retouching Colors directly to the print with cotton. He added color to everything but the girl's dress, including a light blue to the sky.

13. When a color slide film is developed in color negative chemistry, such as Kodak's C-41, a negative image with increased contrast is the result (see Chapter 11). Negative prints, like this one, can be made directly on color reversal paper.

14. To make a print that turns the negative transparency image to a positive in its more natural colors, use color negative paper. Because of its increased contrast, note that both the shadows and highlights lack detail.

Processing Errors with E-4 and E-3 Color Transparency Films

Faulty processing of Ektachrome films in processes E-4 or E-3 can change their color balance and give other unpleasing results. The following chart summarizes Kodak's suggestions for identifying such processing errors.

Appearance of Film or Other Problem	Possible Causes or Remedies
Very dark, almost opaque	Bleach or fixer omitted.
Dark overall	Inadequate time, temperature, or agitation in first developer. First developer underreplenished, exhausted, or diluted.
Light overall	Excessive time, temperature, or agitation in first developer. First developer overreplenished.
Overall density variation from batch to batch	Inconsistencies in time, temperature, or agitation in first developer; or variations in first developer replenishment rate.
Red	Color developer improperly mixed.
Bluish magenta	Color developer diluted, exhausted, or underreplenished.
Magenta areas and streaks	Uneven or insufficient agitation in first color developers.
Yellow	Film fogged by room lights during first developer step (may show partial negative image).
Yellowish green	Film fogged by yellow green safelight. Color developer overreplenished or too alkaline.
Blue specks	Chemical contamination. Do not allow metallic particles or chemical dust to come in contact with film.

(Mechanical errors during processing can affect your transparencies in other ways; see descriptions of these problems beginning on page 43.)

Summary of Steps for Unicolor's Unichrome Process

This process is designed for the same types of color films that can be processed in Kodak's E-4 Process, including Ektachrome-X, High Speed Ektachrome, Fujichrome, Agfachrome, and 3M color slide films. The process varies slightly according to the type of film, and full instructions are included in the 1- and 2-quart Unichrome kits.

For Ektachrome-X, High Speed Ektachrome, and Fujichrome films, there are twelve steps that total about 45 minutes. In the fourth step, the films are converted to positive images by reexposure with light from a No. 2 Photoflood.

Two rolls of thirty-six-exposure 35mm film can be processed per 8 ounces of working solutions; for the second roll, processing time must be increased by 30 seconds in the first developer and by 2 minutes in the color developer. Following is an outline of the steps.

UNICOLOR'S UNICHROME PROCESSING KIT (80°F)

Step	Temp. (°F)	Time (min.)	Remarks
1. First developer	80 ± ½	8	Careful agitation required.
2. First stop bath	75—80	2	
(Remaining steps can be carried out in normal room light.)			
3. Water rinse	75—80	3	
4. Reexposure			Approx. 30 seconds each to top and bottom of film reel with No. 2 Photoflood 12—18 inches from film.
5. Color Developer	80 ± ½	8	
6. Second stop bath	75—80	2	Do not use first stop bath.
7. Water rinse	75—80	3	Important to follow precise rinse techniques.
8. Bleach	75—80	5	
9. Water rinse	75—80	1	
10. Fixer	75—80	2	
11. Water rinse	75—80	6	
12. Stabilizer	75—80	1	Do not squeegee film.
13. Dry	Not over 110		Bluish cast of wet film disappears when film is dry.

Viewing Color Transparencies

When wet, Ektachrome transparencies of good density and color balance often appear somewhat opaque and too warm in color balance. If it is necessary to evaluate transparency film without waiting for it to dry, bathe it in Kodak Rapid Fixer Concentrate, undiluted Solution A only (*do not* add Solution B), for 1 minute after the fixer step. This temporarily eliminates the misleading color and density of wet transparencies. When finished viewing the film, continue with the wash that normally follows the fixer step.

Push Processing Color Transparency Films

While color transparency films have less exposure latitude than color negative films, some Ektachrome films have more latitude in developer times to compensate for over- or underexposure.

With the newer Ektachrome films designated for developing in E-6, Kodak does not recommend purposely under- or overexposing them for push processing. Underexposed film that is overdeveloped shows a decrease in exposure latitude, a shift in color balance, and an increase in contrast. Overexposed film that is underdeveloped gives a shift in color balance and lower contrast. However, if you have no other choice to correct an exposure mistake, you can compensate on a limited basis by changing the first developer time of the E-6 process. If your camera exposure is the equivalent of four times (two f/stops) underexposed, *add* 5½ minutes to the first developer time. For two times (one f/stop) underexposure, increase first developer time by 2 minutes. For a two times (one f/stop) overexposure, decrease the time by 2 minutes.

Despite Kodak's concern for exposing E-6 Ektachrome films at their normal ASA film speeds, photographers are accustomed to "pushing" the other Ektachrome films to higher (faster) film speeds. There is some loss in color quality with the E-6 films, but you have the advantage of being able to shoot at film speeds from two to four times (one to two f/stops) faster than normal. To do this, you must compensate by extending the first developer time of Process E-6. For example, Ektachrome 400 (ASA 400) can be rated at ASA 800 if processed 9 minutes in the first developer instead of the normal 7 minutes for roll films. And it can be rated at ASA 1600 if processed 12½ minutes in the first developer.

So, if you purposely or accidentally under- or overexpose Ektachrome films, you can compensate by increasing or decreasing the first developer time in the E-6 process to get acceptable results.

Use the following compensation chart as a guideline. For best results, exposure and processing tests are recommended.

CAMERA EXPOSURE	ASA EQUIVALENT Ektachrome 160, Tungsten	Ektachrome 200	Ektachrome 400	APPROXIMATE CHANGE IN FIRST DEVELOPER TIME
4 times (2 f/stops) underexposure	640	800	1600	Increase by 80 percent
2 times (1 f/stop) underexposure	320	400	800	Increase by 30 percent
NORMAL ASA	160	200	400	Use Normal Time*
2 times (1 f/stop) overexposure	80	100	200	Decrease by 30 percent
4 times (2 f/stops) overexposure	40	50	100	Decrease by 50 percent

*Refer to data sheet accompanying Process E-6.

Altering the Density and Color Balance of Color Films

When exposure or processing mistakes are made with color transparency film, you are luckier if the slides are slightly underexposed or underdeveloped rather than overexposed or overdeveloped. If the film image is too dense, you still have something to work with, while film that is too light does not offer much hope.

Underexposed or underdeveloped film can be saved by bleaching, called *reducing,* if the problem is not too extreme. Normally, if film has been underexposed or underdeveloped one f/stop, it can be saved. If it is off more than one f/stop, bleaching will improve it but never to a "properly exposed" condition.

One brand of color reducer is Colorbrite Overall Transparency Reducer, and it can be used to cut the density of Kodak's Ektachrome slide films.

Colorbrite also makes *selective reducers* that will alter the color balance of Ektachrome slides. They act individually on magenta, cyan, or yellow to change the film's color cast.

Another brand called Starer Emulsion Infiltration Dye will also alter the color balance of processed transparencies, including Ektachrome E-6 and Kodachrome films, as well as color negatives (and color prints on RC paper). Films (or prints) are bathed in Starer's magenta, cyan, or yellow dyes which are absorbed into the emulsion to make the color corrections.

Processing Color Transparency Film as Color Negatives

If you like to experiment, try processing Ektachrome transparency film in color negative chemistry. This produces color negatives with higher contrast than is obtainable with regular color negative films. Because color transparency film does not have the orangish tint (color mask) of color negative film, the Ektachrome's colors are vibrant and rich. Expose according to the film's normal ASA.

The resulting Ektachrome negatives can be used to make positive prints of higher-than-normal contrast by using the normal negative-to-positive color printing paper. Or you can make *negative prints* using reversal (Type R) color printing paper, or with the internegative method. Also, the Ektachromes can be mounted and projected as negative slides.

Because of the high contrast yielded by this process, you can try shooting on overcast days in order to minimize contrast. In sunlight, if you take an averaging meter reading for a scene or subject with normal contrast, you will retain the middle values and lose detail in the shadows and highlights. If you expose for the details in shadows you lose detail in the highlights, and vice versa.

Try choosing subject matter that will be enhanced by such excessive contrast. For instance, if you shoot seascapes, expose for the shadows. This causes the highlights on the water to block up, leaving rock forms suspended in white space.

To process the Ektachrome films as color negatives, use the appropriate color negative processing kit: Kodak's Process C-41 for E-6 Ektachrome films or Kodak's C-22 for E-4 or E-3 Ektachrome films. No changes in the processing procedures are required. Just follow the instructions in the kit, substituting the Ektachrome film for the usual color negative film. If you do not want to do your own processing, ask a custom lab to do it for you in either C-41 or C-22, according to the type of Ektachrome film you used.

Once processed, the unmasked (no orangish tint) negative images are quite beautiful in themselves. If making negative prints, the internegative process allows more contrast control than the Type R processes. For positive image prints, expose the Ektachrome negatives like any other color negative and do not worry about the lack of the usual orange colored mask. It may take a little testing with the filtration to get the colors you want, but it is fun to experiment, and the dramatic results are worth your time.

12

Preparing to Make Color Prints

There are two basic ways to make color prints: the negative-to-positive method, and the positive-to-positive method. The first, once commonly called Type C process, uses a color negative to make a positive color print. This process is the oldest of the two, and traditionally offers the greatest control over a print's color and contrast.

The other is known as a reversal (or Type R) process, and uses a positive color transparency, a slide, to make a positive color print. Only recently have reversal-type color prints begun to approach the color and quality of prints made with the negative-to-positive process. In the past, getting the best print from a transparency first required making a color negative of the slide image, called a color internegative, and then printing that internegative with the negative-to-positive process.

Besides selecting the chemical process and photo paper appropriate for a color negative or a color slide transparency, you have a choice of two ways to expose the print paper: the *white light subtractive exposure method* or the *tricolor additive exposure method*. Both require filters to be used during the enlarging procedure.

There are many factors that can affect the colors in your prints: the light falling on your subject when photographed, the type of color film you used, the film's processing, the type of light source in your enlarger and its intensity, the type of color print paper, and the paper's processing. By filtering the enlarging light while it projects the color negative or slide image on the photo paper, you determine the colors that appear in a print.

With trial-and-error test printing, or with the aid of other devices like color analyzers or color calculators, you select the color filters that finally produce colors in the photograph that are like those of the original subject or scene. In short, photographers say that filters are used during enlarging to give the print good *color balance*. Of course, sometimes filters are chosen to alter colors in order to improve a photograph, change its mood, or create a bizzare effect.

What color filters do you use for color printing? A detailed explanation is given in chapter 14. Meanwhile, it is beneficial to know about the colors of white light, and the nature of color photo papers, in order to understand why you need to use filters in your enlarger to make a color print.

To begin with, it is important to remember that white light—including sunlight and that from an enlarger lamp—is composed of three colors called the *additive primaries:* red, blue, and green.

Color photo papers have three light-sensitive layers, and each of these emulsion layers is sensitive to only one of those three primary colors. However, photographic color images are produced when three other colors called the *subtractive primaries*—yellow, magenta, and cyan—are combined, or overlayed, within the color paper.

Each of these colors is really a mixture of two additive primary colors:

yellow = red + green
magenta = blue + red
cyan = blue + green

Because each lacks one additive primary, it is called the *complementary* color to that missing primary color. Thus, yellow is complementary to blue; magenta is complementary to green; and cyan is complementary to red. A

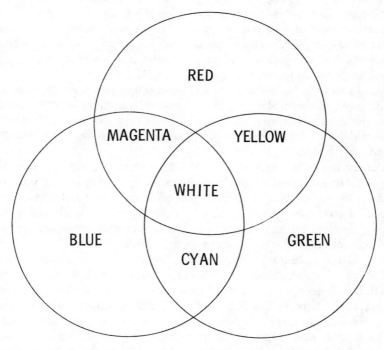

60. *Overlapping color wheels showing the relationship of the important colors in photography. White light is a mixture of red, blue, and green, called the additive primaries. Their complementary colors are the subtractive primaries, cyan, yellow, and magenta.*

good way to memorize these important relationships is to think of three simple abbreviations: BY (blue/yellow), GM (green/magenta), and RC (red/cyan).

For simplicity, in this book the additive primaries will be referred to as primary colors and the subtractive primaries as complementary colors.

When color photo paper is exposed and processed, its blue sensitive emulsion layer forms an image in yellow, its green sensitive emulsion layer forms an image in magenta, and its red sensitive emulsion layer forms an image in cyan. These images overlap within the print and produce the full color photographic image.

Regarding exposure methods, with the tricolor additive method, the color photo paper is exposed three times, each time through a different primary color filter. You should remember that a color filter allows light of the same color to pass through it. This causes red filtered light from the enlarger to expose the photo paper's red sensitive emulsion layer, green filtered light to expose the green sensitive emulsion layer, and blue filtered light to expose the blue sensitive emulsion layer.

The order of the exposures through these primary color filters does not matter. Exposure times will vary for each filter, however, while the enlarger's f/stop is kept the same for all three exposures.

Why can't you expose through the three primary colors all at once, instead of making three individual exposures? The reason is that when any two primary color filters are put together, they prevent the transmission of light. Consequently, separate exposures are necessary.

However, a color print can be made by a single exposure when you use filters of the complementary colors (yellow, magenta, cyan) because when complementary color filters are placed together, they do not block the light as the primary color filters do.

With white light exposure, the subtractive method, the complementary color filters actually subtract light of their opposing primary color. That means a yellow filter subtracts blue light from the image projected by the enlarger, a magenta filter subtracts green light, and a cyan filter subtracts red light.

The *density* of the filter determines how much light is subtracted. In order to produce a print with a good color balance, you must select filters of the colors and densities that are appropriate for the specific color negative or slide transparency you are exposing.

The white light subtractive exposure method is much easier and faster than the tricolor additive exposure method. For one thing, with the additive method, you must be careful not to move the enlarger or the enlarging easel holding the photo paper. If either one is jarred between exposures, the result will be misregistered colors; the three images will not align with each other and your subjects will have multicolored outlines. (Of course, you can deliberately misregister exposures in order to create a special effect.)

The subsequent exposure information in this book concentrates on the most popular color printing exposure method, white light subtractive exposure, which involves filters of the three complementary colors—yellow, magenta, and cyan.

Equipment for Making Color Prints

The equipment needed to make color prints is the same whether you use color negatives or color transparencies (slides). With a few additions, you can produce color prints in any well-equipped black-and-white darkroom. Of course, color printing is more expensive, complex, and time-consuming than black-and-white printing.

Following are a list and discussions of color printing equipment—some items are necessary, some not, depending on how much printing you plan to do. To make occasional prints for fun or for friends, you can start with basic equipment. As your print production increases, so will your investment in other equipment, in order that you can make superb color prints in the easiest, most efficient manner. Such optional equipment is marked by a †.

Starred (*) items were discussed in the equipment listing in chapter 4, "Establishing a Darkroom." So be sure to read about those items in more detail in that chapter.

Enlarger*
Color-corrected enlarger lens
Color printing filters
Heat-absorbing glass
Enlarging easel*
Enlarging timer*
Enlarging magnifier*
Paper cutter*
Antistatic brush, cloth, or can of compressed air*
Processing device (tubes and trays)
Thermometer
Measuring graduates
Stirring rod
Funnel
Storage bottles
Processing timer*
Color print paper
Processing chemistry
Rubber gloves
Towels
Safelights*†
Voltage regulator/stablizer*†

Color analyzer*†
Color calculator†
Color print viewing filters†
Enlarger color head*†
Refrigerator†
Hot water regulator†
Print dryer*†

Enlarger

So delicate is the balance among color hues in color printing that it must be controlled by filtration during exposure. The enlargers commonly used for printing color negatives or slides have a drawer or slot where filters can be placed. The filter drawer is located in the enlarger head below the enlarger's light source and just above the optical condensors.

If an enlarger does not have such a drawer to accommodate filters, they can be placed in a filter holder that is attached beneath the enlarger lens.

There are also enlargers specifically for color printing that have a built-in filtration system referred to as a *color head.* (Some black-and-white enlargers can de adapted with a color head.) These color heads feature *dichroic filters,* which do not fade with age or exposure to light. Fading is a problem with ordinary acetate color printing filters that are placed in an enlarger's filter drawer. Because color head filters are built in, they also are protected from dust and damage.

To select the filtration for exposing your color negative or slide, you turn the color head's appropriate dials (magenta, yellow, cyan) to the specific densities desired. The range of a color head's dial-in filters densities is much greater than you can achieve with individual color printing filters used in a drawer.

Color heads use quartz halogen lamps, from 75- to 250-watts, and a cooling fan or other type of heat dissipater is a necessary part of high-wattage models. A significant drawback is the extra cost of color head enlargers. For this reason, you may decide to start with an enlarger that has only a filter drawer. But a good idea is to make sure that that enlarger can also be equipped with a color head, in case you decide to buy one later.

One bonus of owning a color head is that you can use it for making black-and-white prints on variable contrast papers without using additional filters. You dial in dichroic filter combinations on the color head that are equivalent to the variable contrast filters ordinarily used with such black-and-white papers, like Kodak's Polycontrast or Ilford's Ilfospeed Multigrade.

However, since most color heads are of the diffusion type, black-and-white

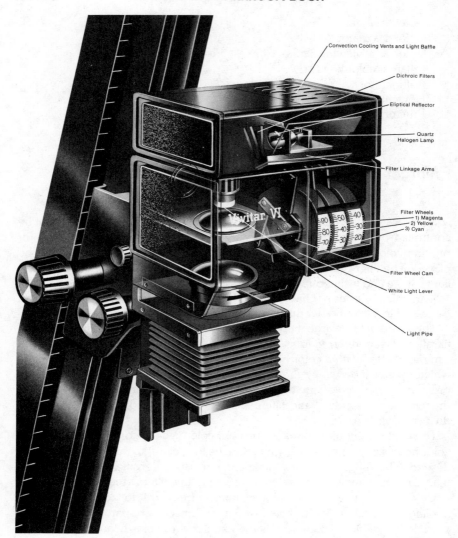

61. Enlargers with color heads feature built-in dichroic filters that "interfere" with the light coming from the enlarger lamp in order to alter its colors. With this model, the photographer controls the degree of filtration (i.e. interference) by rotating the filter wheels.

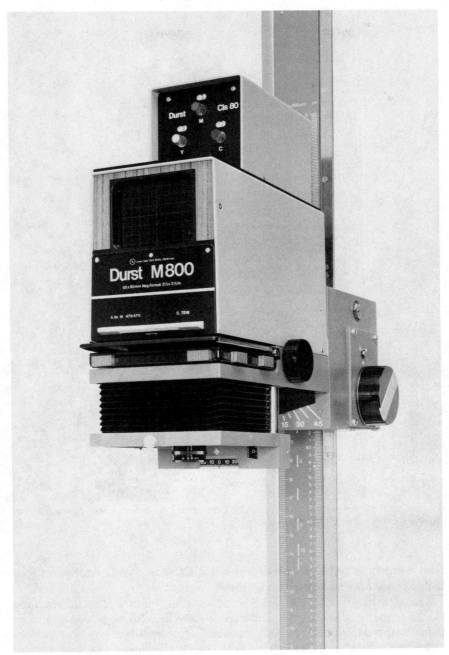

62. *Small knobs on this color head are turned back and forth to regulate various amounts of magenta, yellow, and cyan filtration.*

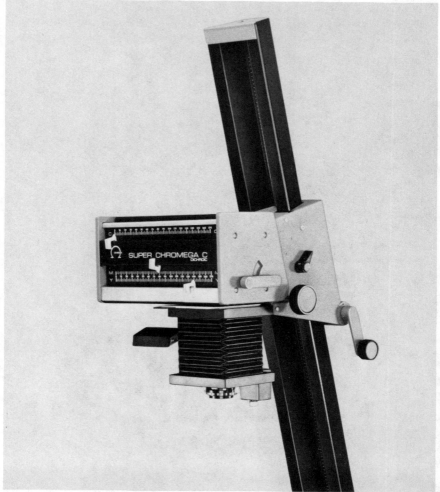

63. On this model, levers are moved along scales to select specific amounts of filtration.

print contrast is reduced unless you select filtration that is equivalent to a higher grade of contrast than you normally would use.

There are some color head models that feature condensor-type illumination, but these tend to show more flaws in color negatives and slides than do the diffusion type. Also, contrast of color slides may be excessive when printed with condensor-type color heads. However, this type of color head also produces the sharpest prints and best contrast when used for black-and-white printing.

Photographers who do equal amounts of quality color and black-and-white printing often have a modular type of enlarger—one that is easily converted from one optical system to another by changing the lamphouse or head.

(Other considerations regarding enlargers were discussed in detail in chapter 4. These include enlarger sizes, illumination systems, lenses, negative carriers, focusing, types of support, and baseboards.)

Color-corrected Enlarger Lens

An enlarger lens for color printing must be carefully designed and ground to insure that the light passing through it will not distort colors. So be sure you buy a lens that is color-corrected; inexpensive enlarging lenses often are not. Besides being color-corrected, the more costly lenses will give a sharper image, too. Remember to test out any new lens you buy, and exchange it if the lens does not appear to perform satisfactorily. (See also page 58.)

Color Printing Filters

There's a choice of two types of color filters used for color printing, *color printing (CP)* or *color compensating (CC)*. The CP type fits in the filter drawer in the head of an enlarger. This type, relatively inexpensive, is made of fairly stable acetate. Because CP filters are placed above the negative, fingerprints or dust or small flaws will be diffused and not seriously affect the final image.

You must use the more expensive CC filters if your enlarger does not have a filter drawer or a color head. These are made of a high quality gelatin or glass, and must be kept free of dust and scratches. That's because CC filters are placed beneath the enlarger lens, and any flaws in them will distort the image. CP and CC filters commonly come in densities varying from .025 to .50.

Another filter that is necessary is an *ultraviolet (UV) filter*. This filter must be used at all times to prevent color imbalance caused by ultraviolet light from the enlarging bulb. It is placed between the bulb and negative or slide. For color negative papers, use filter No. 2B; for color reversal papers use filter No. 2A. It is impossible to attain true colors in a print without using a UV filter. This filter appears clear and it does not affect exposure times. In enlargers with a color head, such UV filtration is built in.

For the tricolor additive exposure method, only three filters are required:

red (Kodak No. 25 with color negatives; No. 29 with slides), green (Kodak No. 99 with color negatives; No. 61 with slides), and blue (Kodak No. 98 with color negatives; No. 47B with slides). But for the white light subtractive exposure method, you need different colors and many more filters. Following is a list of the filters in three colors (magenta, yellow, and cyan) that you should purchase in various densities; the suggested number to buy is indicated in parenthesis ().

Designated are the most common CP filters that are for use in the enlarger's filter drawer. (If your enlarger does not have a filter drawer, use CC filters and place them in a holder beneath the lens.)

Magenta	Yellow	Cyan*
CP025M (1)	CP025Y (1)	CP025C (1)
CP05M (1)	CP05Y (1)	CP05C (1)
CP10M (2)	CP10Y (2)	CP10C (2)
CP20M (1)	CP20Y (1)	CP20C (1)
CP40M (3)	CP40Y (3)	CP40C (3)
	CP80Y (1)	

*Kodak produces cyan CP filters that are more specifically balanced for Kodak's Ektacolor RC papers, and these are designated with the suffix -2, i.e. CP10C-2. Do not use them with Kodak's Ektachrome 2203 color reversal paper.

Remember, a UV filter must also be used in the filter pack: No. 2B for color negative papers, and No. 2A for color reversal papers.

Heat-absorbing Glass

Like color filters, heat-absorbing glass is a special requirement for color printing. Since both negatives and CP filters are sensitive to heat, this glass must be used to prevent their damage by heat from the enlarger lamp.

The greenish hue of heat-absorbing glass also helps correct the color of the light reaching the print paper. The glass should be installed in the enlarger head between its light bulb and the filter drawer. In some enlargers, this is done by lifting up the lamp housing and laying the glass on top of the condensor lenses.

Heat-absorbing glass also is necessary when CC filters are used; heat from the lamp will not reach filters placed beneath the enlarger lens, but heat can affect the negative or slide that's being enlarged. Enlargers with a color head already have heat-absorbing glass or a similar feature built in.

64. *On most enlargers without color heads and dichroic filters, acetate color printing (CP) filters are placed in a special filter drawer (arrow) located between the light source and the negative carrier.*

Enlarging Timer

Unless you purchase an expensive *electronic* timer, it is unlikely your timer will be very accurate for short exposures. To assure consistency, some photographers select a standard time for all exposures. Ten seconds, for example, is long enough to allow for dodging, but not too long to make exposing a laborious process. With a standardized exposure time, adjustments in exposure are made by changing the enlarger lens aperture. As long as you have a good lens, there should be no problem with distortion, even when the lens is wide open, or when it is closed down to its smallest f/stop.

Exposure time will be consistent because you never change the timer. Working in this manner also allows you to become accustomed to judging exposure by the intensity of light falling on the enlarging easel. After considerable practice you can figure exposures quite accurately, without always having to test exposures.

Processing Devices

Tube-type processors were behind the mid-1970s revolution in home darkroom color print processing. These small, plastic cylinders make it possible to process with the room lights on. Commonly called *tubes* or *drums*, the devices come in popular print sizes—8 x 10 through 20 x 24—and are loaded in the dark, usually with a single sheet of exposed color print paper. Once the end cap is in place, lights can be turned on. Chemicals are poured in and out through light-tight openings.

Some tubes are designed so a used chemical can be drained from one end while the next chemical enters from the opposite end. This avoids the delay that occurs in other tubes that use the same end for draining and filling the tube. Draining techniques and times will vary according to the tube manufacturer, which includes Devtech, Cibachrome, Paterson, Beseler, Chromega, and Unicolor.

The amount of chemical required will differ by tube brand, too, but usually ranges from 1½ to 3 ounces of solution for each 8 x 10-inch print processed.

65. *There are several types of tubes, also called drums, which are used for processing color prints. Some have openings in each end for filling and draining chemicals, and others include a water bath tray for maintaining the temperature of the solutions.*

66. For manual agitation with a processing   67. Motorized devices can also be used
tube, roll it back and forth on a tabletop.   to provide agitation.

Usually the chemicals are dumped out after each use, but some can be reused or replenished, depending on the process you choose. Agitation techniques are given in instructions packed with the brand of tube you buy. Usually you agitate the tube manually by rolling the cylinder back and forth on a tabletop. The chemical solution stays along the bottom of the tube, and the print's emulsion surface is covered by this solution with every revolution of the tube.

Motorized devices to rotate the tubes for agitation can also be purchased; the best ones have off-center rollers that slightly tilt the tube back and forth while it rotates.

Processing color prints in *trays* is the other method commonly used in home darkrooms. There are advantages and drawbacks. Trays are less expensive than a small tube processor, but trays usually require greater amounts of chemicals for use. Tubes will process only one print (or two smaller prints) at a time, but skillful photographers can process up to six prints at once in a tray (a maximum of three is initially recommended).

Because some color papers must be handled in total darkness in the initial processing steps, or under very dim safelight, you must get used to working by "feel" if you use trays. In addition, the emulsions of color print papers are more delicate than black-and-white papers (especially Cibachrome color paper), so using your fingers instead of print tongs is recommended. Rubber gloves are required, especially if you have sensitive skin or a cut on your hands.

Agitation is critical for color papers, so certain techniques must be followed for tray processing. For single sheets, trays can be rocked gently, and the print occasionally lifted from the solutions. When tray processing more than one RC or Cibachrome print at a time, interleaf them carefully or—move the group of prints slowly about as they float in the tray. Read the specific instruc-

supplied with the color paper and/or print processing chemistry you are using.

Most color processes require several water rinse steps, and if you have running water, this is not a problem. Without it, you should set up two trays of water for each rinse step. The first will rinse away most of the previous chemical solution, while the second tray of fresh water will finish the wash job and prevent contamination that may otherwise stain your print. The final wash should be done in running water.

Some print processes require high and constant temperatures, so you will need another set of larger trays (or a sink) with a hot water bath in order to keep your chemicals at the proper temperature. For tray processing, you may want to choose those print processes that can be used at room temperatures, although you must compensate by increasing processing times.

Processing in an electrically-operated *drum processor* is another method, and this works well for small-volume color printing. Until tube-type processors were manufactured, a drum was the most popular device for advanced amateurs and professional photographers making their own color prints. The most commonly used drum is Kodak's Rapid Drum Processor, which gives excellent results but costs several hundred dollars.

Compared to tubes and trays, drum processing cuts down on processing times, and the machine automatically takes care of agitation. All you do is add chemicals, and then dump them out after each step, which minimizes contamination problems and increases consistency in color print quality.

Another processing system, *basket-and-tank,* is normally used by professional photographers and photofinishers who do a larger volume of color printing. Individual tanks are used for each chemical, and usually hold 3½ gallons of liquid. Prints are inserted in a stainless steel "basket" which is then moved from one chemical to the next. Prints of a wide variety of sizes can be processed easily this way.

Agitation is done manually, and by bursts of nitrogen gas that bubble through the chemicals. Such bursts occur for 1 out of every 10 seconds. If the agitation is too great or too little, you get uneven processing and so-called basket marks. The basket-and-tank system is very economical regarding chemistry, because the solutions are replenished after each run, not just dumped out.

Continuous-roll processing machines are used by large volume photofinishing firms. These expensive and sophisticated processors are designed for continuous rolls of color print paper. Then the prints are cut apart and sorted for delivery to customers.

Thermometer

Color processing solutions, especially the developers, demand exact temperature control. Buy a good thermometer and use it exclusively. Your thermometer may not give the same reading as another thermometer, but if you gear your processing to the temperature readings of only one instrument, you shouldn't have a problem. Be sure your thermometer gives readings in both Fahrenheit and Celsius, and in divisions at least as small as ½°F (0.3°C).

Processing Timer

An accurate and easy-to-read darkroom timer, such as those made by Omega, is essential for the precise timing required when processing color prints. A big wall clock with a second hand is a less expensive option. For tray processing in total darkness, your timer should make an audible signal when time is up and should be convenient to reset. It is helpful if the hands are luminescent and can be seen in the dark.

Color Print Paper

While black-and-white photo papers vary in many respects, you have fewer things to consider in selecting a paper for your color printing. Color papers are of two basic types: one type for printing from color negatives, the other for printing directly from positive color transparencies (slides). The latter is sometimes called reversal print paper.

In addition, color papers are designed for use in two types of chemistry: one is oil-base and known as Type A, the other is water-base and known as Type B. Color papers are sometimes called Type A or Type B for this reason.

Some color papers are manufactured for a specific chemical process and cannot be processed in any other chemistry. An example is Cibachrome color paper, which must be processed in Cibachrome chemistry.

Three Kodak papers are more compatible with other appropriate brands of processing chemistry. Kodak's Ektacolor 74 RC and Ektacolor 78 (and their predecessor Ektacolor 37 RC) color print papers are designed for printing color negatives. They can be processed in Kodak's Ektaprint 2 (and its predecessor Ektaprint 3) chemistry, as well as some other Type A color negative print processes, including Beseler's 2-Step Color Print Chemistry. The other Kodak paper is Ektachrome 2203 color reversal print paper, designed for direct printing of color transparencies (slides). It works in Kodak's Ektaprint R-1000 process, and in reversal print chemistry of other manufacturers, like Beseler and Unicolor.

Always check the instructions or data sheet packed with the color paper to make sure you process it in the proper chemistry.

Here are some other facts about color print papers. The same paper is used for both contact printing and enlarging. Unlike black-and-white papers, there are no contrast grades or variable contrast color papers.

Color papers are medium weight. Their surfaces are usually limited to glossy, lustre, and/or silk. Most current color papers are the resin-coated (RC) type, which dry rather rapidly without needing a heated print dryer. One type of Cibachrome paper is on a plastic base, which does not dry as rapidly. Glossy surfaces are self-glossing; ferrotyping is neither required nor recommended.

Color print papers are available in larger standard sizes, usually including 8 x 10, 11 x 14, 16 x 20, and 20 x 24. They are packaged in envelopes or boxes, most commonly in quantities of ten, twenty-five, fifty, or one hundred sheets per package.

Color papers require more careful storage and handling than black-and-white. Most must be refrigerated at 50°F (10°C) or lower, or changes in the paper's speed and color balance will result. (Cibachrome is a notable exception, because it can be stored at room temperature.) To avoid moisture condensation after removal from refrigeration, the paper should be given 2 to 4 hours to warm up to room temperature before being exposed and processed.

The emulsions of color print papers are more susceptible to damage than black-and-white emulsion, and care is required especially for tray processing. In addition, some are fogged by safelights, and those papers must be handled in total darkness, even before and after exposure. Read the paper's data sheet for specific instructions regarding storage and handling.

Processing Chemistry

There are two basic types of processes for color print papers. One is for papers exposed with color negatives, the other is a reversal process for papers exposed directly with positive color transparencies (slides). In the latter process, the reversal step is usually done chemically, but it may require reexposure of the print paper to a bright light.

The processes, which are discussed individually in the following chapter, vary according to their manufacturers. The trend is toward fewer chemical steps, higher processing temperatures, and shorter processing times. Some processes permit flexible processing times, based on solution temperatures. Especially convenient for home darkrooms are processes that can be used at room temperature. Otherwise a constant temperature water bath is required to bring the chemicals to proper processing temperature, and keep them there.

Stains are frequently problems in color print processing, and some processes require numerous water rinses or baths to prevent chemical contamination.

The storage life of color processing chemicals, and their useful life after mixing, are limited. Powdered chemistry can be kept longer before mixing, but it is less convenient to mix than liquid concentrates. Most solutions are discarded after one-time use, especially in tube or tray processing, but some can be reused if replenished and/or properly stored, or if processing times in those used solutions are increased.

Be sure to label all storage bottles so you'll use the correct chemicals, and mark down the mixing date so you are sure the solution is still fresh before using it. Always read the data packed with the print processing chemistry for special instructions about storage, mixing, and use.

Chemical sizes vary according to manufacturer, but most are available in small quantities (1 quart or 1 gallon); home processing kits contain all the required chemicals and are especially convenient, although not the least expensive way to purchase color processing chemicals.

Rubber Gloves

If your skin is sensitive, or your hands have cuts, be sure to wear rubber gloves while working with color print chemistry. This is especially important when mixing the chemicals or if processing in trays.

Towels

As in all darkroom work, chemical contamination is a problem. Keep your hands and work areas clean and dry. Use lint-free paper or cloth towels; be sure cloth towels are frequently laundered because dried chemicals can circulate in the air as chemical dust and still cause contamination.

Note: The following equipment marked with a † can be considered optional items for color print processing unless you regularly make considerable numbers of color prints.

Safelights†

Color printing materials are sensitive to all colors of light. Consequently, some color papers must be handled in total darkness, like Kodak's Ektachrome 2203, used for making direct positive prints from color slides. The manufacturer indicates on each paper's data sheet whether safelights can be used, and what color, bulb wattage, duration, and distance are permitted.

For example, with Kodak's color negative print paper, Ektacolor 74 RC, you can use an amber (No. 13) safelight at least 4 feet from the paper, with a 7½-watt bulb. Exposure of the paper to safelight should be no longer than 3 minutes before the enlarger exposure, and no longer than 3 minutes afterward.

To make items in your darkroom stand out a little better, mark them with bits of fluorescent tape. But the best advice is to have everything so conveniently organized that you can literally find it in the dark.

Voltage Regulator/Stabilizer†

A voltage regulator/stabilizer compensates for fluctuations in electrical current. It is plugged into the wall socket and your enlarger or enlarger timer is plugged into the stabilzer. Even small current changes, such as 5 volts, have a significant effect on the brightness and color of light from the enlarger lamp, and this can change the density and color balance of a print.

A voltage regulator/stabilizer isn't necessary until you decide to do a considerable amount of color printing. If you ordinarily print during times when your family or neighbors are not using many electrical appliances that are turning on and off, household voltage should remain fairly constant and not cause adverse effects during exposure.

Color Analyzer†

This can be an expensive addition to your darkroom, but it will make life much easier for photographers who make a great number of color prints. A color analyzer is like a small computer with a memory that enables you to determine the filtration and exposure of any negative or slide without always making the usual trial-and-error test prints. Once you are a practiced user, a color analyzer should save you considerable time and paper.

Generally, a light-sensitive probe is used at the enlarger easel (or baseboard) to pick up the projected image of the color negative or slide. You turn the analyzer's dials until it indicates the correct filtration and exposure to

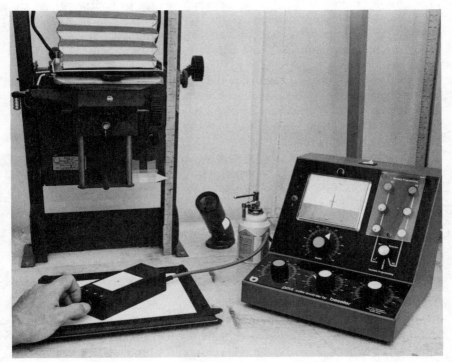

68. *After a color analyzer has been programmed, its sensor reads the light projecting a color negative or slide, and the photographer adjusts the analyzer's dials until they indicate correct filtration and exposure.*

use with that negative or slide. Some analyzers can make both overall (integrated) readings of the projected image and spot readings of selected areas.

In order for the color analyzer to be used correctly, it must first be programmed with the filtration and exposure data of your "standard" color negative or slide (see page 230). Let's say this standard negative or slide is a daylight exposure of a girl's face taken with your favorite daylight color film. With this negative or slide, using a method of trial and error, you make what you consider a perfect print.

The print's exposure data—filtration and time—is then programmed into the analyzer. (This procedure varies with different models, so follow the analyzer's instructions carefully.) Now it will "read" any similar color negative or slide of the same film type, indicating the proper filtration and exposure time.

In other words, as long as you expose the same type of film with a similar subject under similar lighting, you should get a good print by exposing the paper according to your analyzer's reading. (Some photographers make test strips anyway, before exposing a full sheet of paper for the final print.)

Of course, if the film is different, or the lighting, or the type of subject, the analyzer can't compensate without being reprogrammed. (Some analyzers have extra memory banks that hold exposure data for a variety of "standard" negatives or slides.)

Regardless, the analyzer's exposure data should put you on the right track for making exposure and filtration corrections for subsequent negatives or slides. Consider a color analyzer a helpful tool, but at least until you learn its limitations, always make several test prints or test strips to be sure you are getting the best result possible.

If you plan to purchase a color analyzer, check to see if it can also be used for black-and-white printing. Some models will read black-and-white negatives and indicate the correct exposure and paper contrast grade (or variable contrast filter) to use.

Color Calculator†

There are some less expensive, non-electronic calculators that can help you determine the proper filtration and exposure for color negatives and slides. These are commonly called color calculators for subtractive printing, and similar types are made by Beseler, Unicolor, and Chromega. They involve a diffuser that is placed below the enlarger lens, a matrix of magenta, yellow, and usually cyan filter material that is placed on the color print test paper, a comparison card to determine neutral gray, and detailed instructions. Even with such calculators, a test print or two is necessary in order to establish correct filtration and exposure for the final print. When making prints from color negatives only, try Kodak's Ektacolor FilterFinder Kit.

Color Print Viewing Filters†

These filters are useful for viewing color test prints to determine what changes, if any, need to be made in filtration in order to improve the color balance of the print. Kodak has a filter viewing kit, with filters of varying densities in six colors: magenta, red, yellow, green, cyan, and blue. Kodak's "Color Dataguide" also has a set of viewing filters, with instructions for their use, and how to figure corrections in filtration.

Enlarger Color Head†

This is a superior but somewhat expensive alternative for color filtration, instead of using color printing (CP) filters in the enlarger's filter drawer. (Color heads are described under "Enlarger" in this section.)

Refrigerator†

Because of its sensitivity to heat and humidity, most color print paper must be stored in a refrigerator, at least 50°F (10°C) or lower. Unless this precaution is taken, changes in the paper's emulsion speed and color balance can result. (Cibachrome is one exception; it can be stored at room temperature.) Packages of refrigerated paper should be allowed from 2 to 4 hours to warm up to room temperature in order to avoid moisture condensation on the paper's emulsion. The temperature of your darkroom should be about 70°F (21°C).

Color chemistry has a much more offensive odor than the chemicals used in black-and-white printing, so be sure *ventilation* in your darkroom is adequate. An exhaust fan, or small air-conditioner, is a refreshing suggestion. If ventilation is poor, at least mix the chemicals outside the darkroom or away from the processing area.

Hot Water Regulator†

This is a nonessential and somewhat expensive item for your darkroom, but it is especially helpful if you have trouble controlling the temperature of the wash water. Such a regulator also conserves water, because you don't have to run the water while trying to reach the desired temperature.

Print Dryer†

Since most color print papers are of the resin-coated (RC) type, they air dry rather quickly at room temperature. For better air circulation, some photographers squeegee and lay the wet prints on plastic window screen mesh stretched over frames. Others use hand-held hair dryers to speed up drying. There are also some special forced air print dryers designed for RC papers. Heated print dryers are fine, if the temperature is not set too high. Remember that glossy color papers should not be ferrotyped. Instructions packed with color papers usually advise the safest methods for drying that particular paper.

13

Processing Color Prints
Step by Step

With the necessary equipment at hand, as described in the previous chapter, you are ready to make color prints.

There are two aspects of color printing you must understand: how to properly expose color print papers and how to process them. Before discussing how to figure correct exposure and filtration when printing color negatives and slides (see chapter 14), here is an explanation of color print papers, processes, and procedures.

While the procedures for processing black-and-white prints were discussed in earlier chapters and may be familiar to you, color print processing has some unique variations. First, there are two basic processes: one for color prints made from negatives and another for color prints made from transparencies (slides). The latter process also requires a reversal step, and this is accomplished chemically in most processes and by reexposure of the print paper to a bright light in other processes.

In addition to the solutions necessary for black-and-white print processing (developer, stop bath [rinse], and fixer), your color process may require other chemicals like bleach, stabilizer, and a second developer.

Color print processing is most often done in home darkrooms in a small tube-type processor, which is light-tight. If trays are used, some initial processing steps must be carried out in total darkness.

Because of continuing chemical and technical advances, color print processes are always being refined and improved. The most recent color print chemistry, used at high temperatures, has dramatically cut the number of steps and amount of time required for processing. Because processes occasionally are improved, *always remember to carefully read and follow the manufacturer's instructions enclosed with any color print materials you purchase.*

Processes for Making Color Prints from Color Negatives

There are several color processes currently on the market for printing color negatives, and these are summarized below. A few of the most popular are Kodak's Ektaprint 2 chemicals; Beseler's 2-Step Chemistry; and Unicolor's Universal A^r Chemistry and Total Color Chemistry.

COLOR NEGATIVE PRINTING PROCESSES

Process Brand	No. of Steps Tube*	/	Tray	Total Time Required† Tube	/	Tray	8 x 10-inch Prints Per Gallon**
Beseler 2-Step	4	/	3	9	/	9	100
Kodak Ektaprint 2	6	/	3	8	/	8½	48
Unicolor Universal A^r	6	/	6	10	/	10	50
Total Color	6	/	5	10½	/	11½	50

*Includes prewet step.
†Processing times can vary according to the temperatures used, except Ektaprint 2 which is developed at 91°F; times for other processes based on developer temperature of 80°F.
**Approximate number only, based on 2.5 ounces per print; actual amount of solution required depends on specific tube or tray.

Most of the home systems for color print processing are designed for use with a small tube-type processor, which is sometimes called a processing drum. Once the processor is loaded with the exposed paper, processing can be done with the room lights on. Some popular brands of tube processors are made by Beseler, Unicolor, Chromega, and Paterson (see also page 188).

Trays can also be used for processing color prints, but careful agitation is required to avoid streaks and uneven development. In addition, some of the initial steps in tray processing must be done in total darkness.

There are a few brands of color negative printing papers, and the one you choose may depend on the specific process you are using. Commonly, the manufacturer of a color printing process also makes color print paper to use with that process. Some papers, like Kodak's Ektacolor RC, can be used with some of the other processes; instructions packed with each process will specify the brand name(s) of paper to be used.

Color print papers in popular use are medium weight and resin coated. They usually come in glossy, lustre, and/or silk surfaces. And most are available in common sizes, including 8 x 10, 11 x 14, and 16 x 20 inches. Some photographers buy professional rolls of color paper and cut off pieces as needed.

Two of the most popular color print papers are Kodak's Ektacolor 74 RC and Ektacolor 78 because they can be processed in several different chemistries, including Kodak's Ektaprint, Beseler 2-Step, and Unicolor's Universal A^r and Total Color.

Kodak's Ektacolor RC Color Negative Print Papers

Kodak was a pioneer company in creating papers and processes that allowed photographers to make their own color prints, beginning in the mid-1950s. And great strides were made in the early 1970s that made home color processing easier, faster, and of better quality.

One big step was the introduction by Kodak of a resin-coated color paper, Ektacolor 37 RC, used for printing color negatives. The resin coating required less chemicals, saved wash water, and sped up processing times. In 1977, Ektacolor RC was improved and made twice as sensitive in order to cut exposure times. This faster paper is called Ektacolor 74 RC; Ektacolor 37 RC is still available in rolls for commercial processing machines. Later, in 1979, Kodak introduced Ektacolor 78, a resin-coated paper that is identical to Ektacolor 74 RC except that it produces images with higher contrast.

Ektacolor 74 RC and Ektacolor 78 papers are processed in Kodak's latest color negative print chemistry, Ektaprint 2, a two-chemical process that was introduced in 1976. The paper can also be processed in the forerunning chemistry, Ektaprint 3, which requires three solutions. Ektacolor 74 RC and Ektacolor 78 can also be processed in many of the color negative print processes offered by other manufacturers.

Ektacolor 74 RC and Ektacolor 78 papers are for use with Kodak's color negative films, including Kodacolor II, Kodacolor 400, and the professional Vericolor and Ektacolor films. They also work with other brands of color negative film, such as Agfacolor and Fujicolor.

Here are some details about these popular papers. They come in four surface types: silk lustre (Y), smooth lustre (N), smooth glossy (F), and a new surface Kodak calls Lustre-Luxe (E). Because of its resin coating, the F surface paper should not be ferrotyped to obtain a gloss; the gloss will appear after drying.

Ektacolor RC paper is affected by high temperature and/or high humidity, so unexposed sheets should be refrigerated in their original foil-lined package at a temperature of 50°F (10°C) or lower. Before use, the paper must be warmed to room temperature to avoid moisture condensation. To reach an average room temperature of 70°F (21°C), allow 2 hours' warmup time if the paper is 50°F or above, 3 hours if down to 35°F (2°C), and 4 hours if the paper has been stored as low as 0°F (−18°C).

You can handle Ektacolor 74 RC or Ektacolor 78 color paper under an amber (No. 13) filter with a 7½-watt safelight, if the safelight is at least 4 feet from the paper. After exposure with the enlarger, the maximum time the paper can be exposed to safelights before fogging occurs is 3 minutes.

One problem with Ektacolor papers is that prints have a bluish cast which only disappears when the paper is completely dry. This makes it difficult to tell a wet print's true colors or judge color balance.

Following is a survey of several processes available for making prints from color negatives, and the step-by-step procedures for processing Ektacolor 74 RC, Ektacolor 78, and similar papers.

Kodak's Ektaprint 2 Color Print Process

The Ektaprint 2 process uses only two chemicals, developer and bleach-fix, which come in 1- and 3½-gallon sizes. Since 1976, it has been Kodak's replacement process for Ektaprint 3, which required an additional chemical, stabilizer.

Below are instructions for using the Ektaprint 2 process in small tube-type processors and in trays. The procedures vary in steps, times, and techniques. In addition, you'll need different amounts of chemicals, depending on whether you process in a tube or trays. One sheet of 8 x 10-inch paper in a tube-type processor requires 2 to 3 ounces of Ektaprint 2 Developer, which is discarded after one use. For tray processing, if developer time is increased for each sheet processed, up to twelve 8 x 10-inch prints can be processed per quart of Ektaprint 2 Developer.

Do not mix the chemicals too far in advance; it's always best to use fresh solutions. The storage life of mixed but unused Ektaprint chemicals, kept at room temperature in full, tightly capped glass bottles, is six weeks for developer and eight weeks for bleach-fix.

Summary of Steps for Ektaprint 2 Processing in Tubes

Although Ektaprint 2 is basically a two-chemical process, developer and bleach-fix, it requires additional steps when used in a tube in order to prevent streaks on the print. One is a pre-wet water bath and the other is an acid stop bath.

The recommended temperature for developer is 91°F (32.8°C), and the

other chemicals can be the same, or range between 86° to 93°F. Total processing time is 8 minutes, plus drying.

Step	Temp. (°F)	Time* (min.)	Remarks
1. Prewet	91±0.5	½	Use water.
2. Developer	91±0.5	3½	Special mixing required.
3. Stop bath	91±0.5	½	Diluted 28 percent acetic acid.
4. Rinse	91±0.5	½	Use fresh water.
5. Bleach-fix	91±0.5	1	
(Remove print from tube and place faceup in tray for final wash; this can be done in normal room light.)			
6. Final wash	91±0.5	2	Change water every ½ minute; rock tray side to side to agitate print every 2 seconds.
7. Dry	not over 200°F (93°C)		Air dry or use hand-held hair dryer.

*Includes 10-second drain time.

Streaking may result when developer is poured in the tube and first
contacts the dry print paper, so a prewet step is required. However, this water
bath will dilute the developer. To avoid underdevelopment that would result,
the developer must be mixed according to special instructions so it is 20
percent more concentrated than normal for nontube use. Follow these
instructions instead of the regular Ektaprint 2 Developer mixing directions.
The amounts given below are for the 1-gallon size package, which has four
bottles of chemicals marked Part A, B, C, D. After emptying, rinse each bottle
with small quantities of water and add the rinse to the mixing vessel so that the
entire contents are transferred to the solution.

1. Start with 78 fluid ounces (2.3 liters) of water at 90° to 100°F (32° to
38°C).

2. With stirring, add contents of the bottle, Part A. Stir until the solution is
uniform. (It is not possible to overmix Part A.)

3. With stirring, add the contents of the bottle, Part B. Stir until the solution
clears.

4. With adequate ventilation and stirring, add the contents of the bottle,
Part C, which will cause the solution to turn a purplish color. (Do not
excessively mix the solution once Part C has been added.)

5. With stirring, add the contents of the bottle, Part D. After the contents of
Part D are added, the purplish color from Step 4 will disappear and the
solution will become the usual slightly amber developer color.

6. Add sufficient water to bring the total volume to 102 fluid ounces (3.0

liters). When mixed, the developer will appear somewhat hazy, but this effect is normal.

To make the stop bath solution, start with 1 quart (32 ounces) of water and stir in 1½ ounces of 28 percent acetic acid. (You can make 28 percent acetic acid by diluting three parts of glacial acetic acid to eight parts of water. Remember to add the acid to water and never water to acid.)

As for the bleach-fix, mix normally according to the instructions furnished with the 1-gallon size of that chemical.

Processing temperatures must be those recommended by the manufacturer, especially the developer, so the chemicals should be maintained in a water bath at a constant temperature. If your processing tube is water-tight, it should be placed in the water bath along with the bottles of chemicals; an 11 x 14 processing tray will do unless you prefer a deeper tray, such as an oblong plastic pan made for kitty litter. During processing procedures, agitation of the water-tight tube should also be done in the water bath. To maintain the 91°F temperature required for Ektaprint 2 Developer, if your average room temperature is 75°F, the water bath temperature should be 92°F.

If your processing tube is not water-tight, the tube must be kept out of the water bath. Because the temperature of the chemicals will be reduced when used in a tube processor that is outside the water bath, you must run a test to determine correct water bath temperature so the temperature of developer at the time of its use *averages* 91±½°F. As an example, when the room temperature is 75°F, and the water bath temperature is 95°F, the developer's temperature after the processing step will read about 88°F. The average of the developer's temperature before use (94°F) and after use (88°F) will be 91±½°F.

You can conduct the test by using scrap Ektacolor RC print paper and water instead of actual developer. Do both the prewet and developer steps, using volumes recommended for your particular tube, and conduct the test for the proper times of both steps: ½ and 3½ minutes.

Once you've determined the water bath temperature that will give a developer temperature that *averages* 91°F after use, you can establish the water bath temperature for all future processing, as long as your room temperature remains fairly constant.

Correct agitation is important so the prints will be processed evenly. To do this, rotate the tube on a *level* surface from thirty to sixty revolutions per minute, *and* simultaneously tilt or rock the tube end to end about four to six times per minute. For the final wash steps in the tray, rock the tray so the print will move side to side every 2 seconds.

Follow loading instructions provided with your particular tube processor. *The tube must be clean and dry before each print is processed.* Otherwise water spots and steaks will ruin your print.

Load the exposed print paper in the tube in a completely dark room. The emulsion (exposed) side should be facing in, not touching the walls of the tube. Be sure the tube is correctly capped and light-tight before turning on room lights.

Make certain the water bath with your bottles of chemicals is at the correct constant temperature. Your timer can run continuously once processing is started because drain time is included in each step. Action starts when the chemical contacts the print paper.

If you have never processed prints in a tube, practice one or more times—using water instead of the actual chemicals—in order to become familiar with the order of processing steps, filling and draining and agitation techniques. Be sure to test how long it takes to drain your tube (10 seconds is average), because this time must be included in the total time for each step.

You also can use trays for processing color prints in Ektaprint 2 chemicals, and the special procedures are outlined below.

Summary of Steps for Ektaprint 2 Processing in Trays

These steps, times, and temperatures are for processing in trays, or baskets in tanks, with Kodak's Ektaprint 2 chemicals. The recommended developer temperature is 91°F (32.8°C). Total processing time is 8½ minutes. With optional stop bath and wash steps, to prevent streaks on prints, total time is 10½ minutes.

Tray processing may carry over excess developer into the bleach-fix. This, plus low agitation, can result in patterns or streaks on your prints, so increase

Step	Temp. (°F)	Time* (min.)	Remarks
1. Developer	91 ± 0.5	3½	No. 13 Safelight Filter.
(Optional)†			
(a. Stop bath)	86—93	1	
(b. Wash)	86—93	1	Running water.
2. Bleach-fix	86—93	1½	
(Remaining steps can be done in normal room light.)			
3. Wash	86—93	3½	Running water.
4. Dry	Not over 200		Air dry (do not ferrotype).

*Includes a 20-second drain time in each process step. Baskets of complex design can be drained for 30 seconds to prevent excessive carry over.
†Optional steps are suggested if marks or streaks are observed on the surface of prints. Excessive developer carry over and inadequate agitation are usually responsible for such marks.

agitation to prevent such patterns from forming. If increased agitation does not stop the streaking, you will need to include two extra processing steps. After the developer step, treat the prints in stop bath and replenisher from Kodak's Process C-22 or equivalent for 1 minute. Follow this with a 1-minute wash in running water, then proceed to the bleach-fix step.

Regarding agitation, if only one sheet is processed at a time, agitate by rocking the tray from side to side and then end to end. When multiple sheets are processed, agitate by *interleafing*. For best results, especially with larger sizes of paper, not more than three sheets should be tray-processed at one time. With practice, up to six sheets can be processed at the same time by using the following technique.

Initially, fan out the prints in one hand so that they can be handled individually. Immerse the prints in the developer, one at a time, emulsion side down and then turn them emulsion side up. Continuously interleaf the sheets by pulling the bottom sheet from the stack, placing it on top without draining, and reimmersing it completely in the solution. Twenty seconds before the end of the solution time, remove all the sheets from the solution, being sure that the print which was immersed first is on the bottom. During the 20-second drain time, fan the sheets out again so that they will be individually accessible for the next processing solution. At the end of the 20-second drain time, immerse the prints in the next solution one at a time, starting with the same first print as in the developer step.

The position of the first sheet in the stack can be determined by counting the number of times the prints are interleafed or by clipping off a corner.

When processing more than one 8 x 10-inch sheet per batch, increase the developer time by 5 seconds for each successive sheet, up to the exhaustion point of twelve sheets per quart. Do not increase the time in the bleach-fix. The useful life of unreplenished solutions in open trays is 4 hours.

Regarding Kodak's Ektacolor RC papers being tray-processed in Ektaprint 2 chemicals, a safelight can be used during the developer step and for the first 30 seconds of the bleach-fix step. From then on, the remainder of the processing can be done under normal room light. You can use an amber (No. 13) safelight filter with a 7½-watt bulb.

For drying Ektacolor RC papers, squeegee off excess water and lay out the prints in a clean, dust-free place to dry. To speed drying, use forced warm air, as from a hand-held hair dryer, but make sure the temperature doesn't exceed 200°F (93°C). Never ferrotype RC prints; glossy surface RC papers are self-glossing.

Processing Errors with Ektaprint 2

If your color prints do not turn out as you expected, it's time for troubleshooting. Some problems and possible causes during processing are listed below. These regard Ektacolor RC papers processed in Ektaprint 2.

Problem	Possible Cause
1. Cyan stain and/or high cyan contrast (pink highlights and cyan shadows)	a) Bleach-fix contamination of developer or in prewet. b) Developer temperature too high.
2. Magenta-blue streaks	Insufficient stop bath action (stop bath is bad, or no stop bath was used).
3. Light and dark streaks (uneven development)	a) Prewet not used. b) Insufficient developer agitation. c) Processing tube not level.
4. Blue-blacks	a) Diluted developer. b) Insufficient developer time. c) Insufficient drain time after prewet. d) Developer temperature too low.
5. Low contrast (especially magenta-pink highlights and green shadows)	a) Diluted developer. b) Insufficient volume of developer. c) Not enough agitation.

Besides Kodak's Ektaprint 2 process, there are three other popular processes for making color prints from color negatives, and they are manufactured by Unicolor and Beseler.

Summary of Steps for Beseler's 2-Step Color Print Process

In recent years, the Beseler Photo Marketing Co. has been determined to make color printing easier for the nonprofessional. That seems only natural, because Beseler has a large line of color enlarging equipment, darkroom hardware, and printmaking materials geared for home darkroom use.

But Beseler has really been a color pioneer, especially by making available two-step, variable temperature chemistry for all brands of color papers made for printing color negatives. For instance, Beseler's 2-Step Color Chemistry, Type A, will process Kodak's Ektacolor RC paper and Beseler's own resin-coated color paper, while their Type B chemicals can be used with Unicolor B and Agfacolor nonresin-coated papers. All of these papers can be processed at temperatures from 64°F (18°C) to 125°F (51.5°C). And developing times are short. For example, with Kodak's Ektacolor or Beseler's color paper in the Type A chemistry at a temperature of 107°F, total processing time is 2 minutes. After 1 minute in Step 1 (developer) and 1 minute in Step 2 (bleach-fix), and a 2½- to 5-minute wash, you're done. At a room temperature of 75°F, Step 1 takes 6 minutes and Step 2 takes 2½ minutes. This is the quickest and easiest color print processing yet available, and the results are good, too.

Beseler's own color paper can be processed in trays, tubes, or any of the other processing devices available. It comes in two surfaces, glossy and luster. Sizes are 8 x 10, 11 x 14, and 16 x 20. This print paper is resin-coated, and should be processed in Type A chemicals.

Be sure when you buy Beseler's 2-Step Color Print Chemistry to ask for either Type A or Type B, depending on what type of print papers you'll be using. It comes in 1-quart, 1-gallon, and special 4-quart packages for mixing four individual quarts of chemistry. A 1-gallon size will process approximately one hundred 8 x 10-inch color prints. Once mixed for use, the solutions can be kept eight to ten weeks when stored in well-filled, tightly capped, brown glass bottles.

Beseler's 2-Step Color Chemistry is easily adaptable to your processing situation. By consulting a time/temperature chart, you can figure the correct processing times when the two chemicals are at room temperature. Or you can heat the two chemicals to speed up processing times. Instructions packed with the Beseler process tell you how to do this, whether for tray processing or tube processing.

TIME/TEMPERATURE CHART

CHEMICAL TEMP. (°F)	STEP #1 (Developer)	STEP #2 (Bleach-Fix)
107	1	1
101	1½	1
96	2	1
92	2½	1
89	3	1½
86	3½	1½
83	4	1½
81	4½	2
79	5	2
77	5½	2
75	6	2½
72	7	2½
70	8	2½
68	9	3
66	10	3

When using a tube to process a print, you can reuse the chemicals up to four times, as long as it's within a period of a few hours. For each print processed, you increase the time in each chemical by 10 percent, and add fresh Step 1 and Step 2 chemistry (½ ounce per 8 x 10, 1 ounce per 11 x 14, or 2 ounces per 16 x 20). The chemicals also are reuseable when processing in trays; for each 8 x 10-inch print processed, you add 1 ounce of fresh chemistry and increase process times by 2 percent.

Detailed instructions for agitation in tubes or trays are included with packages of Beseler's 2-Step Color Print Chemistry.

Summary of Steps for Unicolor's Total Color Process

Unicolor's unique Total Color can be used to process all the current resin-coated negative print papers, including Ektacolor RC, Unicolor RB, and Agfacolor RC, *and* it can also be used to process color negative films designed for Kodak's C-41 process, including Kodacolor II and Kodacolor 400. The chemicals must be mixed differently for the print and negative processes.

Solutions used for developing negatives can be remixed for use as print developing solutions, but print solutions can not be reused to develop negatives. Follow Total Color's mixing instructions carefully.

To process prints, there are six steps plus drying. Total processing time depends on solution temperatures, which can vary considerably. For tube processing, when you use a water pre-soak at 100°F, the developer at 80°F, and the other solutions between 70° and 100°F, total processing time is 10½ minutes.

Steps	Time (min.)
1. Water pre-soak	1
2. Developer	4*
3. Stop bath	½
4. Blix	2
5. Water rinse	2
6. Stabilizer	1
7. Dry	

*Varies according to water pre-soak and developer temperatures, as indicated on chart accompanying chemicals; 4 minutes' developer time is used when developer is 80°F and pre-soak is 100°F.

If blix and/or water rinse temperatures exceed 100°F, time in each of those solutions can be reduced to 1 minute. The stop bath is an optional step, but recommended. The stabilizer also is an optional step (which should be done in a tray, not a tube); if this step is omitted, time in the water rinse should be doubled.

When prints are processed in trays, the water pre-soak is omitted, and developer time is increased according to the chart included with Total Color's instructions (at 80°F, developer time would be 6 minutes).

Total Color comes in two separate units: Total Color (1) Developer and Total Color (2) Blix. The Blix package also contains chemicals for the optional stop bath and stabilizer steps. Each unit makes 48 ounces of working solutions, enough to process twenty-four 8 x 10-inch prints, or equivalent, in tubes using 2 ounces of chemical per print.

Summary of Steps for Unicolor's Universal A^r Process

Unicolor also offers chemistry for processing some nonresin-coated color negative print papers, like Unicolor B (not RB) and Agfacolor, and this same chemistry can be used to process Kodak's Ektacolor RC color paper.

Unicolor's Universal A^r process requires six steps plus drying, and total processing time is 10 minutes.

Step	Temp. (°F)	Time (min.)
1. Water pre-soak	105—110	1
2. Developer	75—80	3½
3. Stop bath	70—90	½
4. Blix	70—90	2
5. Water rinse	70—90	2
6. Stabilizer	70—90	1
7. Dry		

For tray processing in Universal A^r chemicals, the water pre-soak step is eliminated, and a water rinse is added after the stop bath step. Developer times will vary according to developer temperature, from 7 minutes at 70°F to 2 minutes at 100°F.

Each quart of the working solutions will process twelve 8 x 10-inch prints when used in trays, or sixteen 8 x 10 prints in a tube processor using 2 ounces of chemical per print.

If you'd like to make color prints directly from color slides, different color papers and processes must be used than the ones which produce prints from color negatives.

Processes for Making Color Prints from Color Transparencies

There are several color reversal print processes currently available for home use that are used for making prints directly from slides. A few of the most popular are Ilford's Cibachrome P-12 chemistry; Kodak's Ektaprint R-1000 chemicals; Beseler's 3-Step Print Chemistry; and Unicolor RP-1000 Chemistry for direct positive printing.

All these processes feature chemical reversal; the reversal step no longer is accomplished by reexposing the color print paper to a bright white light during processing.

Most of the home systems for color print processing are designed for use with a small tube-type processor, which is also called a processing drum. Once the processor is loaded with the exposed paper, processing can be done with the room lights on. Some of the popular brands of tube processors include Cibachrome, Beseler, Unicolor, Chromega, and Paterson.

COLOR REVERSAL PRINTING PROCESSES

| | No. of Steps | | Total Time Required | | 8 x 10 prints |
Process Brand	Tube	/ Tray	Tube	/ Tray	per gallon†
Kodak Ektaprint R-1000	13	/	13¼*	/	50
Beseler 3-Step	9	/	11*	/	50
Unicolor RP-1000	12	/ 6	11½*	/ 9½*	50
Cibachrome P-12	5	/ 5	12**	/ 12**	40
Cibachrome P-18 (Professional)	5	/ 5	13**	/ 13**	40

*Time based on solution temperatures at 100°F; processing times of Beseler and Unicolor can be altered by changing solution temperatures.
**Processing times can vary according to temperature of solutions; these times based on developers' temperature of 75°F.
†Approximate number only; actual amount of solution required depends on specific processing tube.

Trays can also be used for processing color prints, but careful agitation is required to avoid streaks and uneven development. In addition, some of the initial steps in tray processing must be done in total darkness.

There are a number of brands of color reversal printing papers, and the one you choose may depend on the specific process you are using. Commonly, the manufacturer of a reversal printing process also makes color print paper that is to be used with that process. Some papers, like Kodak's Ektachrome 2203, can be used with other reversal processes except Cibachrome; instructions packed with each process will specify the brand name(s) of paper to be used.

Color reversal papers are medium weight and resin-coated. They usually come in glossy, lustre, and/or silk surfaces. And most are available in popular sizes, including 8 x 10, 11 x 14, and 16 x 20.

Some of the most popular processes for making color reversal prints will be discussed in detail, including Ektaprint, Beseler, Unicolor, and Cibachrome. They vary in regard to temperature, number and length of processing steps, reversal procedure, processing method (tube or tray), and print paper. All but Cibachrome can be used to process one of the most popular papers for making color prints directly from color slides, Kodak's Ektachrome 2203.

Kodak's Ektachrome RC Color Reversal Print Paper

Ektachrome 2203 paper is used to make prints from Kodak's transparency films, including Ektachrome and Kodachrome, as well as other brands of slide films like Agfachrome and Fujichrome.

This color paper can be processed in Kodak's R-5 and R-1000 chemistry, Beseler's 3-Step Chemistry, Unicolor's RP-1000 chemicals, and others.

Ektachrome 2203 is resin-coated, which allows faster processing times with less chemicals and less wash water than previous reversal-type color papers. Excessive contrast is less of a problem, too. The paper is medium-weight and available in various sizes, including 8 x 10, 11 x 14, 16 x 20, and 20 x 24 inches. It comes in silk (Y), high lustre smooth (J), and glossy smooth (F) surfaces. As a resin-coated (RC) paper, the gloss occurs upon drying; ferro-typing is neither required nor recommended.

Like most color printing papers, Ektachrome 2203 should be refrigerated to prevent changes in the emulsion that affect its speed and color balance. Store it in the original sealed package at 50°F (10°C) or lower. Avoid moisture condensation on the paper before use by allowing the unopened package to warm up to a room temperature of about 70°F. Figure 2 hours for warmup if stored at 50°F or above. When stored down to 35°F (2°C), allow 3 hours warmup. Wait 4 hours if the paper was kept at 0°F (−18°C).

To avoid a change in color balance and density, the paper should be processed right after exposure; even a few hours' delay can make a difference in print color and quality.

Ektachrome 2203 color paper should be handled in *total darkness only,* or some fogging may be evident.

Kodak's Ektaprint R-1000 Color Reversal Print Process

After a positive transparency image is exposed on Ektachrome 2203 paper, it can be processed with Kodak's Ektaprint R-1000 chemicals in small tube-type processors. Solution temperatures must be maintained at 100°F (38°C). There are thirteen steps, and total processing time is 13¼ minutes.

Regarding chemicals, tube processors require from 2 to 3 ounces of each developer per 8 x 10-inch print, and then they must be discarded.

Descriptions of the Ektaprint chemicals and processing steps required for tube processing are given below, but follow the explicit directions from Kodak packaged with the Ektaprint R-1000 Color Developer.

Summary of Steps for Ektaprint R-1000 Processing in Tubes

Remember, to process with Ektaprint R-1000 chemicals in small tube-type processors you must maintain the chemicals at 100°F (38°C). The method for doing this will be described in the instructions accompanying your tube processor. Some models, with chemical inlets and outlets that can be closed or capped, are used in a constant-temperature bath of 100°F. Other models, with nonclosing openings for the solutions, must be used with chemicals pre-warmed to a temperature greater than 100°F (see page 204).

There are five Ektaprint R-1000 chemicals required for processing Ekta-chrome 2203 paper: first developer, stop bath, color developer, bleach-fix, and stabilizer. They are packaged as separate units and are available in 1 quart and 1 gallon sizes.

Besides the R-1000 chemicals, you will need fresh water for the prewet, wash, and rinse steps.

Steps (All solutions at 100 ± ½°F)	Time* (min.)
1. Prewet (water)	1
2. First developer	2
3. Stop bath	½
4. Wash	1
5. Wash	1
6. Color developer	2
7. Wash	½
8. Bleach-fix	3
9. Wash	½
10. Wash	½
11. Wash	½
12. Stabilizer	½
13. Rinse (water)	¼
14. Dry	

*All include a 10-second drain time. Be sure to add the next solution on time for the next step, which begins when the solution contacts the paper.

After mixing, the solutions can be stored in airtight bottles at normal room temperature. The mixed solutions will last as follows: first developer and color developer, 4 weeks (only 2 weeks in a partially full bottle); bleach-fix, 4 weeks; and stop bath and stabilizer, 8 weeks. Remember to discard each chemical after one-time use in the processing tube.

Be sure the exposed Ektachrome 2203 paper is loaded into the processing tube in total darkness. To prevent contamination and streaks, always *clean* and *dry* the tube after each sheet of paper is processed.

Regarding other color reversal print processes for home darkroom users, most manufacturers have systems designed for tube processors. Two popular processes are by Beseler and Unicolor, and descriptions of them follow. Both are for Kodak's Ektachrome 2203 paper, and the reversal step is done chemically. Their main advantage over Kodak's reversal process is that the solutions can be used at a wide range of temperatures.

Summary of Steps for Unicolor's RP-1000 Color Reversal Print Process

Unicolor's RP-1000 chemistry comes as a kit of three chemicals to process Ektachrome 2203 paper in either a processing tube or trays. A nice feature is that the chemicals can be used at a variety of temperatures when processing in a tube; Unicolor's RP-1000 directions give processing times for chemical solutions maintained at 70, 85, and 100°F. For tray processing, the chemicals should be kept at 100°F.

The three chemicals are first developer, color developer, and blix (bleach-

Steps for Tube Processing (All solutions at 100°F)	Time* (min.)
1. Presoak (water)	1
2. First developer	1½
3. Wash	½
4. Wash	½
5. Wash	½
6. Wash	½
7. Color developer	3
8. Wash	½
9. Blix	2
10. Wash	½
11. Wash	½
12. Wash	½
13. Dry	

*Instructions packed with the chemicals indicate correct processing times at other solution temperatures.

fix). In addition, fresh water is required for presoak and wash steps; it must be used at 100°F.

For tube processing, 12 steps are required, plus drying. Using the chemicals at 100°F (38°C), total processing time is 11½ minutes. At 85°F (29°C), processing time is 2 minutes longer. At an average room temperature of 70°F (21°C), it takes 15 minutes to process a print in the Unicolor chemicals.

The same three chemicals can be used for processing Ektachrome 2203 paper in trays. The procedure requires 6 steps and takes 9½ minutes.

Processing must be done in total darkness until the print is placed in the color developer. For the wash steps, place the print in a tray or sink and rinse with running water for the required times.

Keep the print face down in the trays of chemicals to avoid scratching the paper emulsion. Use print tongs gently to agitate the print in the solutions. Avoid splashing the chemicals into other trays, or contamination and a ruined print may result.

Steps for Tray Processing (All solutions at 100°F)	Time (min.)
1. First developer	1½
2. Wash	1½
3. Color developer	2½
4. Wash	½
5. Blix	2
6. Wash	1½
7. Dry	

Regarding storage of Unicolor's RP-1000 chemistry, mixed solutions will last up to 2 weeks in full glass bottles. After opening bottles of the chemical concentrates, squeeze them to remove the air before storing them, and the chemicals will last up to 12 months.

Summary of Steps for Beseler's 3-Step Color Reversal Print Process

Another process designed for Kodak's Ektachrome 2203 paper is Beseler's 3-Step reversal print chemistry. It comes in a kit of three chemicals: first developer, color developer, and bleach-fix. After mixing, they'll keep about 4 weeks in full airtight bottles.

Processing times in a tube can be varied according to the temperature of the chemicals and wash water. With all solutions maintained at 100°F (38°C), the process requires 9 steps and takes 11 minutes.

When processing is done with chemicals and wash water at a room temperature between 70-75°F (21-24°C), the procedure takes 21½ minutes. If the chemicals are kept at 70-75°F but the wash water is 120°F (49°C), processing time is reduced to 12½ minutes. Instructions in Beseler's 3-Step kit give details of the processing alternatives. The chart printed here outlines the fastest procedure in a processing tube.

Steps (All solutions at 100°F)	Time (min.)
1. First developer	1½
2. Wash	½
3. Wash	½
4. Wash	½
5. Wash	½
6. Color developer	2½
7. Wash	½
8. Bleach-fix	2½
9. Wash (running water)	2
10. Dry	

Ilford's Cibachrome Color Reversal Print Process

One of the most popular processes for making color prints directly from color transparencies is called Cibachrome. It is quite different from the Kodak, Beseler, and Unicolor color reversal processes, and it will not work with the most common color reversal print paper, Kodak's Ektachrome 2203.

In fact, the Cibachrome process has fewer steps, shorter processing times, and lower processing temperatures. It also produces prints that are sharper, brighter, and more stable than those made with other color reversal papers and processes.

Because of its considerable latitude, Cibachrome will yield acceptable prints even when you are careless with exposure or processing times. The major complaint with this fine color product has been excess contrast.

Current Cibachrome print material is identified as Type A and Type D for making prints, and Transparent material for making large transparencies for display purposes. Type A, which is designed for home use, offers great latitude and can be purchased in small sizes and quantities. It is developed in Cibachrome's Process P-12 chemistry.

Until 1979, Cibachrome's sole Type A print material had a glossy surface and a plastic base. Then another Type A variety was introduced, which has a matte surface and a resin-coated (RC) paper base. In recent Cibachrome literature, the original glossy and plastic-based print material is referred to as Cibachrome Hi-Gloss, while the newer matte and resin-coated paper is called Cibachrome Pearl. Remember that both are Type A materials and are to be developed in Cibachrome's Process P-12 chemistry.

Professionals and others who want better color control, and who produce a large quantity of Cibachrome prints, use Type D print material. Available only with a glossy surface on a plastic base, it is developed in Cibachrome's Process P-18 chemistry. (For Cibachrome's Transparent material, Cibachrome's Process P-10 is used.)

High volume printers are expected to switch over to newer professional Cibachrome print materials, PS-Brilliant (glossy and plastic-based) and RC-Pearl (matte and resin-coated), which are designed for development in Cibachrome's newer Process P-3 chemistry.

Although Cibachrome's plastic print materials (Type A and Type D) technically are not paper, they are commonly called paper by most photographers, and they will be referred to as paper in this book. References to Type A papers mean both the glossy, plastic-based (Hi-Gloss) paper and the matte, resin-coated (Pearl) paper.

What makes Cibachrome papers different from Kodak's Ektachrome and other color reversal print papers? Read on.

Cibachrome's Type A and Type D Color Print Papers

There are pure azo dyes incorporated in the emulsion layers of Cibachrome color print papers. During processing, the unwanted portions of those dyes—as determined by exposure—are bleached out and washed away. This is unlike the other color reversal print processes, called *chromogenic,* in which dyes are formed by color couplers during processing.

The high quality dyes in Cibachrome paper have much better color saturation than most conventional chromogenic papers, including Ektachrome RC, and much better stability. Tests have shown that Cibachrome prints are fade-resistant, even when exposed to sunlight all day for months; other color print papers will start to fade within a week or so of continuous exposure to sunlight.

The image sharpness of Cibachrome is exceptionally good because the dyes incorporated in the emulsion layers act as a screen to help prevent light from scattering during exposure. In the emulsions of papers like Ektachrome RC, light scatters as it bounces from one silver halide crystal to another during exposure, so the image is never quite as sharp as a Cibachrome image.

Cibachrome paper keeps well in storage before exposure. While most color papers must be refrigerated in order to retain their speed and color balance, Cibachrome can be stored at room temperature (about 70° to 75°F) for several months. Longer storage is possible if the paper is kept at 50°F or lower. To avoid condensation on the emulsion, refrigerated papers must warm up to room temperature before use. Once opened, packages of Cibachrome paper should not be refrigerated.

Cibachrome's latent image stability is also very good. Unlike other color papers, which should be processed immediately or soon after exposure, Cibachrome can be processed one or two days after exposure, and there will be no apparent change in color.

Total darkness is recommended for all color reversal papers, including Cibachrome.

As mentioned, Cibachrome paper has a plastic (triacetate) base and glossy surface or a resin coated (RC) paper base and matte surface. Common sizes of Cibachrome's Type A paper are 4 x 5, 8 x 10, 11 x 14, and 16 x 20 inches. A specially packaged and priced Cibachrome Discovery Kit, to introduce photographers to the process, features 4 x 5-inch sheets of Type A print paper (Hi-Gloss or Pearl) and Process P-12 chemistry. The regular home processing kit offered by Cibachrome includes 8 x 10-inch paper. For volume Cibachrome printing, and more control of print results, use Cibachrome Type D paper and its companion chemistry, Process P-18.

Following is a summary of processing steps for Type A papers with P-12 chemistry, the most popular Cibachrome process for home use. You can use a tube-type processor or trays, and the processing steps can be completed in about 12 minutes when solutions are at the recommended temperature of 75°F (24°C). Temperature range for processing can be from 65° to 85°F (18.5° to 29.5°C), but processing times must be changed (see chart below).

CIBACHROME TEMPERATURE/TIME CHART

Step	68° ± 3°F (20 ± 1½°C)	75° ± 3°F (24 ± 1½°C)	82° ± 3°F (28 ± 1½°C)
1. Developer	2½ min.	2 min.	1½ min.
2. Rinse	(10 sec.)	(10 sec.)	(10 sec.)
3. Bleach	4½ min.	4 min.	3½ min.
4. Fixer	3½ min.	3 min.	2½ min.
5. Wash	3½ min.	3 min.	2½ min.
Total time	14　min.	12 min.	10　min.

An increase or decrease in contrast can be achieved by varying developer time up to plus or minus (±) ½ minute. Shorter times will lower contrast, while longer times increase contrast.

Chemicals should be carefully measured in the graduated beakers furnished with the Cibachrome kit. With a Cibachrome-brand processing tube, use 3 ounces (90 ml.) for each 8 x 10-inch print, and 6 ounces (180 ml.) for each 11 x 14 print. One quart of Cibachrome chemistry is enough to make ten 8 x 10-inch prints, or five 11 x 14 prints.

Cibachrome chemicals should be stored at room temperature, and they will keep for several months in their original, tightly sealed bottles. Storage life of the working (mixed) solutions, in sealed bottles at room temperature, is up to three weeks for the developer, up to five weeks for the bleach, and up to a year for the fixer.

Summary of Steps for Cibachrome Processing in Tubes

The recommended temperature for processing Cibachrome reversal color prints in small tube processors is 75°F (24°C). At that temperature, total processing time is 12 minutes, including developer, rinse, bleach, fixer, and wash.

Total darkness is recommended while inserting the exposed Cibachrome print into the processing tube.

Curve the exposed sheet into a cylindrical shape with the emulsion side facing in. Make sure the tube is absolutely dry so the print will easily slide all the way in, and will not be damaged when you replace the end cap on the tube. Water spots or streaks may occur if the tube is not completely dry.

Once the cap is securely in place, room lights may be turned on for the remainder of the process.

The following summarizes processing steps for Process P-12 chemicals at 75°F. When using a Cibachrome-brand processing tube, use 3 ounces (90 ml.) of each chemical for each 8 x 10-inch print, and 6 ounces (180 ml.) for an 11 x 14-inch print. Instructions with other tubes indicate the amount of chemical required in order to cover the print paper. Complete processing details are found in Cibachrome's *Color Print Manual.*

1) *Developer—2 minutes.* Pour in the developer and agitate the tube uniformly and gently for 2 minutes. Proper agitation is to roll the tube back and forth during the entire cycle. Start draining the developer 10 seconds prior to Step 2.

2) *Rinse—(10 seconds).* When the developer has drained from the tube,

rinse the tube with water at about 75°F and drain immediately. This will remove remaining developer and prevent a whiff of unpleasant odor that occurs if developer and bleach are mixed.

3) *Bleach—4 minutes*. Pour in the bleach and agitate uniformly for 4 minutes. Agitating for less than 4 minutes can cause staining, but overtreatment is not harmful. After 4 minutes, drain the bleach for 10 seconds prior to Step 4.

Important: Pour the used bleach into a polyethylene pail or bucket, or glass bottle, of at least ½-gallon capacity and neutralize with Cibachrome Neutralizer tablets as directed on package. Do not cover the container. The solution will fizz, and when the fizzing stops, pour the bleach down the drain. If you do not have enough neutralizer tablets, use one tablespoon of bicarbonate of soda for each 3 ounces of used bleach.

4) *Fixer—3 minutes*. Pour in the fixer and agitate uniformly and gently for 3 minutes. Start draining the fixer 10 seconds prior to the wash.

5) *Wash—3 minutes*. Wash the print thoroughly in running water for 3 minutes. Be sure to wash the print as recommended in the manual in order to insure maximum stability of the image.

To dry, carefully remove the print from the tube and wipe away the print's surface water with a soft rubber squeegee or clean chamois cloth. Use caution because the wet print surface is delicate. Hang up the print or lay it flat on a blotter or drying rack with the emulsion side up. You also can use a print dryer designed for resin-coated papers or a hand-held hair dryer. Approximate time for room air drying is 1½ hours. With an electric fan, figure 15 to 18 minutes, or speed up drying by using a heated hair dryer for 6 to 8 minutes.

A wet Cibachrome print will look somewhat more magenta than a dry print, so be sure a print is dry before deciding if you need to reprint it.

Summary of Steps for
Cibachrome Processing in Trays

The main advantage of tray processing over tube processing is the ability to process more than one print at a time. Disadvantages are working in total darkness for 5 minutes and the increased possibility of scratching the prints. Also in tray processing, you should wear clean rubber gloves to avoid contact of the Cibachrome solutions with your skin.

Plastic, hard rubber, or stainless steel trays are recommended, but enameled trays may be used if they are not chipped or rusted. For processing a single 8 x 10-inch print in just 3 ounces of each solution (or an 11 x 14-inch print in 6 ounces), it is important that the bottom of the trays be flat, with no ridges or depressions.

Although first-timers are advised to start tray processing with one print at a time, the more experienced photographers usually prefer to process several prints at a time. This can be done successfully with Cibachrome print material provided that adequate solution volumes are used (at least 3 ounces per 8 x 10-inch print) and care is taken to avoid scratching or gouging the swollen and fairly delicate print emulsion. It is also essential that each print be given the correct amount of time in each solution. You can do this by immersing and removing the sheets in 10-second intervals, always maintaining the same order.

For processing a single print, constantly agitate by raising and lowering each of the four sides of the tray to make sure that the entire surface of the sheet is swept over by solution throughout each processing step. For processing several prints, the Cibachrome manual recommends you agitate by interleafing, continually taking a print from the bottom of the tray and placing it on top of the other prints. Processing prints face down helps reduce the possibility of scratching the emulsion. Some photographers prefer to let the stack of prints "float" in the tray, which they constantly rock from each side to provide agitation.

Because Steps 1, 2, and 3 are recommended to be done in total darkness, you should prepare one tray with developer and one tray with bleach before the lights are turned off. The recommended temperature for processing Cibachrome reversal color prints in trays is 75°F (24°C). At that temperature, total processing time is about 12 minutes.

1) *Developer—2 minutes.* Immerse the print into the developer in total darkness. Agitation must be continuous for the entire time. Start draining the developer 10 seconds prior to Step 2.

2) *Rinse—(10 seconds).* Rinse briefly in running water at 75°F to remove excess developer and avoid an unpleasant odor that results if developer mixes with the bleach.

3) *Bleach—4 minutes.* After 3 minutes in the bleach, you can turn on the room lights. Continue to agitate the solution for the full 4 minutes, then drain the bleach prior to Step 4. It is important to neutralize used bleach before disposal, as described in Step 3, page 221.

4) *Fixer—3 minutes.* Agitate continuously. Start draining the fixer 10 seconds prior to washing the print.

5) *Wash—3 minutes.* Wash the print thoroughly in running water for 3 minutes, using procedures recommended in the manual in order to insure maximum stability of the image.

(See page 221 regarding methods for drying Cibachrome prints.)

Some photographers who tray process Cibachrome prints have figured out personal ways to handle the paper safely while processing several prints at one time. Most start with a 30-second water bath to presoak the prints. This helps keep their emulsions from sticking together and allows the developer to act instantly and more evenly.

Four prints are convenient enough to handle at one time in the solutions. Alternate them face up and face down. Their backs will stick to each other if you press them together while in the presoak, and this makes them easy to handle as two pairs of prints.

To prevent carry-over of the developer into the bleach, you can add 2 to 3 percent acetic acid to the rinse water.

The bleach step is where many problems occur if care is not taken that the prints are immersed quickly and evenly in the tray. Agitate by rocking the tray and by moving the bottom pair of prints to the top every 15 seconds.

A water wash can be added between the bleach and fixer steps to cut down on contamination; bathe the prints for 30 seconds. Some photographers also extend the final wash (following the fixer) to 5 minutes instead of 3 minutes to be sure residual chemicals and dyes are washed away.

You will save chemicals by processing more than one print at a time. Eight ounces of each solution will process four 8 x 10-inch prints together, plus another 8 x 10-inch sheet used to make test exposures of the four slides that are to be printed. To process five sheets individually would require a total of at least 15 ounces of each solution.

Photographers working with Cibachrome have found that they can substitute a regular black-and-white film or paper developer for the Cibachrome Developer, and the results usually produce a better print—one that is less contrasty. The key chemical you must not change, however, is Cibachrome Bleach.

Because of its great latitude in exposure, Cibachrome most always produces an acceptable print, unless there are errors in handling or processing.

Processing Errors with Cibachrome

The following are a number of problems that may affect your Cibachrome prints if handling and processing are not done carefully.

Problem	Cause	Remedy
Picture dark reddish in tone and image reversed	Partial or complete exposure through the back of the print material.	a) Reprint the picture, being careful to have emulsion side up. b) Try using a black enlarging easel.

Problem	Cause	Remedy
Blue spots	Due to static, which occurs in a dry atmosphere.	Handle print material carefully when removing from its envelope.
Black picture or no picture	a) No exposure, or b) omission of Part A or B in either developer or bleach, or, c) omission of developer step, or d) omission of bleach step.	Reprint and follow directions closely.
Fogged and dull print	a) Probably due to incorrectly mixed bleach solution (too diluted), or b) insufficient bleaching due to low temperature or insufficient bleaching time, or c) Developer not drained before bleach was added, or d) traces of fixer in the developer (usually because processing tube not sufficiently rinsed before reuse) or e) reversal of fixer and bleach steps.	Check if bleaching conditions were correct and mixing instructions carefully followed. Reprint and follow correct processing procedures.
Formation of yellow stain after relatively short time	Insufficient final wash	Wash print to stop further degradation.
Dark and flat print	Developer time too short.	Reprint and follow correct processing times.
Spots or streaks	Processing tube not completely dry when paper was inserted.	Make sure tube is absolutely dry before beginning the process.

Besides learning about the various methods for processing color prints, you must thoroughly understand how to properly expose color papers in order to get the best possible results from your color negatives and slides. Read the next chapter carefully.

14

Exposing
Color Print Papers

Exposing a color print is much the same as exposing a black-and-white print: a color negative or slide is placed in the enlarger and its image is projected onto the color print paper.

However, with color printing you must also select filters to use in the enlarger in order to get true colors in the print. The filtration you choose determines a print's *color balance.*

Understanding Filtration

There are several reasons why it is necessary to use different combinations of filters for each color negative or slide you print in order to achieve good color balance in the photograph. For one thing, pictures are taken under a variety of conditions where the color of light is not always the same. Also, the color dyes in each batch of color paper that is manufactured vary slightly in sensitivity to colors and to light. In addition, the color characteristics of the light source in an enlarger change according to its age and the voltage supply. And there are usually variations in the processing chemistry that affect colors, too.

There are three basic types of filters you can use for exposing color papers. Acetate filters that go in an enlarger's *filter drawer,* between the light source and the negative (or slide) carrier, are called *color printing filters* and are abbreviated *CP.* For enlargers without filter drawers, there are gelatin *color compensating (CC) filters* placed in a holder beneath the enlarger lens. And enlargers designed especially for color printing have filters built in the enlarger head. These are *dichroic filters* with color and density chosen by the photographer who turns selection dials located on the enlarger's so-called *color head.*

The combination of filters you select to use when exposing a color negative or slide is called a *filter pack* or *filtration.*

Filtration for a specific color negative or slide is determined in a number of ways: with trial-and-error test printing, color calculators, electronic color analyzers, color viewing filters, and experience.

Filters have different colors and densities. In color printing, the most commonly used filters—with their letter abbreviations—are yellow (Y), magenta (M), and cyan (C). Density is indicated by numbers: the higher the number, the greater the filter's density. Sometimes these numbers are referred to as *degrees of density*.

A 20Y filter, for instance, is a yellow filter with a density of .20.

It is important to remember that a filter absorbs (subtracts) only its complementary color and transmits all other colors, including its own color.

You'll recall that white light is composed of three primary colors: red, green, and blue. When filters are placed in the path of the enlarger light projecting the color negative or slide image, the color and intensity of the light is changed before it strikes the color print paper. The filters act in this manner:

| | Colors of Light | |
Filter Color	Absorbs	Transmits
Yellow	Blue	Red & Green
Magenta	Green	Red & Blue
Cyan	Red	Blue & Green

This is the basis of *white light subtractive exposure method* commonly used for exposing color prints and the method that is featured in this book. (An alternative is the tricolor additive exposure method; see page 179.)

The proportion of a color that a filter subtracts depends on the filter's density. A 20Y (yellow) filter, for example, acts as .20 neutral density to the blue light (more technically, it reduces the blue light by .20 log exposure units).

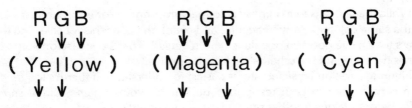

69. *How the filters used in color printing—yellow, magenta, and cyan—absorb and transmit the primary colors of white light.*

From a practical standpoint, you should remember that a 10 degrees' change in filtration will give a *slight* change of color in the print, 20 degrees will make a *moderate* change, and altering filtration 30 degrees will make a *significant* color change. Here are some other facts about filters used in color printing.

When filters of the *same color* are placed together, their densities *add* together. In other words, when you combine a 20Y (yellow) filter and a 40Y filter, the total density will be 60Y.

When filters of *all* three complementary colors (yellow, magenta, cyan) are placed together, they do not change the *color* of the light if their densities are equal; they only reduce the *intensity* of the light. For instance, adding filters of 20Y and 20M and 20C produces .20 *neutral density* to *all* the colors of light (blue, green, red); the color balance will not be changed, although the brightness of the light will be reduced. This means there will not be a change in a print's colors but a longer exposure will be required.

Since photographers like to speed up the printing process, it's best to use as few filters as possible in order to achieve the color balance you desire with the shortest exposure time. For example, say you were using 20Y and 20M and 10C filters. The color change is really only 10Y (subtracting 10 blue) and 10M (subtracting 10 green). But there is also .10 neutral density (10Y + 10M + 10C), which only increases exposure without affecting the print's color. So it would be smarter to use a filter pack with just 10Y and 10M, instead of 20Y and 20M and 10C.

Another thing to keep in mind is that filters of two complementary colors will produce the equivalent of a primary color. The pairs of filters act in this manner:

Complementary Colors		Primary Color
Yellow + Magenta	=	Red
Yellow + Cyan	=	Green
Magenta + Cyan	=	Blue

For this reason, with the white light subtractive exposure method you need to use only filters of the complementary colors in order to change any color in the print.

While the filters used to expose color negatives and color transparencies are of the same colors (yellow, magenta, and cyan), the concepts for selecting the filters to achieve good color balance are reversed. That's because one type of film is negative and the other (slide film) is positive.

Figuring filtration for *slides* seems easiest to understand. If there is too much of a certain color in your test print, you simply *subtract filters of that same color* before making another print. Here's what you'd do:

Excess color in print (from a slide):	Filter(s) to subtract:
Yellow	Yellow
Magenta	Magenta
Cyan	Cyan
Blue	Magenta + Cyan (= Blue)
Green	Yellow + Cyan (= Green)
Red	Yellow + Magenta (= Red)

As an alternative, filters can be *added* in order to change the color balance of a print. But this increases exposure, so you should always try to subtract filters from the filter pack. If there is nothing left in the filter pack to subtract, then you can do the following:

Excess color in print (from a slide)	Filter(s) to add (only when unable to subtract filtration)
Yellow	Magenta + Cyan (= Blue)
Magenta	Yellow + Cyan (= Green)
Cyan	Yellow + Magenta (= Red)
Blue	Yellow
Green	Magenta
Red	Cyan

Of course, the *amount* of color you eliminate from a print depends on the density of the filters you subtracted (or added) in the filter pack.

When printing *color negatives,* you must think opposite of slides in determining the filters to use for correct color balance. If there is too much of a certain color in your test print, you *subtract filters of the complementary color* before making another print. Do the following:

Excess color in a print (from a color negative)	Filters to subtract
Yellow	Magenta + Cyan (= Blue)
Magenta	Yellow + Cyan (= Green)
Cyan	Yellow + Magenta (= Red)
Blue	Yellow
Green	Magenta
Red	Cyan

As an alternative, filters can be *added* in order to alter the print's color balance, but this will increase exposure. Nonetheless, if there is nothing left in the filter pack to subtract, you can add filters as such:

Excess color in print (from a color negative)	Filter(s) to add (only when unable to subtract filtration)
Yellow	Yellow
Magenta	Magenta
Cyan	Cyan
Blue	Magenta + Cyan (= Blue)
Green	Yellow + Cyan (= Green)
Red	Yellow + Magenta (= Red)

In summary, when printing a slide, subtract filters of the same color as the color you wish to reduce in a print. When printing a color negative, subtract filters that are complementary colors to the color you wish to reduce in a print. And to avoid neutral density (which makes no color correction and only increases exposure), never use more than *two colors* of filters in your filter pack.

Furthermore, most color corrections can be made by using only yellow and magenta filters; cyan filters are added only when yellow and/or magenta filters can no longer be subtracted from the filter pack.

Confused? Perhaps, but read on. The reasons for using certain filters, and the methods for selecting their color and density, will be discussed in detail in this chapter. First are the procedures for exposing color negatives.

Exposing Color Negatives Step by Step

With experience you'll find that it's fairly simple to comprehend and carry out the steps required for making a color print. The main challenges are figuring the proper filtration and exposure and doing the actual processing.

Your first consideration when making your first print should be the color negative itself. It should be properly exposed, and contain colors that you can easily judge so there will be little problem to make filter corrections. Try to include a person (for flesh tones) and subject matter with bold colors, like a red car or green grass. A good choice is a negative for which you already have an excellent commercially made color print that you can use for comparison with the print you are going to make.

One problem in judging a color negative is that some color negative films have built-in color masks that give an overall orangish cast to the images and camouflage their actual colors.

Some first-time color printers purchase a *standard negative* and color print, which are available at most camera stores, as well as being included in copies of the *Kodak Color Dataguide.* This properly exposed negative has subject matter with various colors, and the accompanying print can be used for comparison with your test prints. Some photographers call a standard negative a "Shirley," because the picture traditionally features a pretty girl.

A color negative is placed in the enlarger's negative carrier in the normal manner: emulsion side down. Since both sides of color negatives seem shiny, the emulsion side is more difficult to identify than the dull emulsions of black-and-white negatives and color slides.

As an aid to determine the emulsion side of a color negative, Kodak prints arrows along one edge of its roll films, including 35mm. By holding the negative so the arrow is along the *bottom* edge and points to the *right,* the emulsion side is facing *away* from you. Place this emulsion side down in the negative carrier so it will face toward the enlarging easel and photo paper. Use an antistatic brush or can of compressed air to be sure the negative is free of dust.

(The equipment you need to make color prints was listed and discussed in chapter 12, "Preparing to Make Color Prints," but special mention should be made again regarding the enlarger.)

When color printing (CP) or color compensating (CC) filters are going to be used, the enlarger must have a piece of *heat-absorbing glass* placed between its light bulb and the filter drawer. This protects the negatives (and CP filters) from heat from the enlarger lamp and it also helps correct the color of the light reaching the print paper. Enlargers with color heads already have heat-absorbing features built in.

Also required in the enlarger is an *ultraviolet (UV) filter* to prevent color imbalance caused by ultraviolet light coming from the enlarger bulb. Normal tungsten bulbs used in enlargers are No. 212 or No. 302, but some models have tungsten-halogen bulbs. The filter, a No. 2B, is placed above the negative carrier, usually in the filter drawer. This clear-looking filter is used with every color negative, and it does not affect exposure times. Enlargers with color heads have UV filtration already incorporated.

Unless you have an enlarger with a color head and built-in dichroic filters, you'll need a set of color printing (CP) filters to place in the enlarger's filter drawer. These squares of acetate are sold in packages containing various colors and densities. You can start with any set sold in a camera store and then increase the number and variety of filters later as needed.

Most often you'll be working with yellow and magenta, and occasionally cyan. The common densities available are 05, 10, 20, and 40.

These are combined to produce the exact density desired, such as 65Y, which would require three yellow filters: 40Y, 20Y, and 05Y. Having at least *two* filters for each of the four common densities, for both yellow and magenta, makes it easy to put together an accurate filter pack.

Usually with built-in dichroic filters, you can dial in filtration in amounts from 0 to 200.

Now you're ready for the major concerns in exposing color negatives: filtration and exposure. These are usually determined by making a series of test prints. The first step is to establish what is called a *starting filter pack.* This initial filtration depends on the type of color film and color paper you are using, the enlarger light source, and the type of filters in your enlarger.

The examples which follow are for the currently most popular type of color negative print papers, Kodak's Ektacolor 74 RC and Ektacolor 78. (Their predecessor, Ektacolor 37 RC, which is only half as sensitive to light, is still available in rolls but not sheets.) Ektacolor RC, described in the previous chapter, can be used to print any of Kodak's color negative films, including Kodacolor, Vericolor, and Ektacolor, and it works with other brands like Agfacolor and Fujicolor.

Kodak suggests filtration to begin with when printing Kodak color negatives on Ektacolor 74 RC or Ektacolor 78 paper. (See the chart below.)

Type of color negative film	No. 212 or 302 bulb with CP or CC filters	Tungsten-halogen bulb with CP or CC filters	Tungsten-halogen bulb with dichroic filters
Kodacolor II or Kodacolor 400	45M + 25Y	45M + 55Y	50M + 100Y
Vericolor II Professional	55M + 35Y	55M + 65Y	60M + 110Y
Ektacolor Professional	30M + 10Y	30M + 40Y	30M + 70Y

As an example, to make your initial test print with a Kodacolor II negative using normal tungsten enlarger bulbs No. 212 or No. 302, you would insert CP filters in the filter drawer in amounts totaling 45M (magenta) and 25Y (yellow). Don't forget the usual No. 2B ultraviolet (UV) filter, too.

After making a print to test for exposure (see page 233), you will begin analyzing and adjusting this filtration in order to get the best color balance for your final print.

There are two more things to know about Ektacolor 74 RC and Ektacolor 78 color papers. They can be used under an amber (No. 13) safelight equipped with a 7½-watt bulb. Keep the paper at least 4 feet away and do not expose it to the safelight for longer than 3 minutes before or after exposure.

Every package of Ektacolor paper has some important information on the package sealing label. One is the paper's *emulsion number,* indicating the batch in which the paper was manufactured. The color and speed characteristics of Ektacolor paper change slightly from batch to batch, so filtration and exposure corrections are printed on the label for that particular batch.

The filtration information, called *White Light Data,* tells you what to add or subtract from the filter pack you used with the *previous* batch of Ektacolor paper. (Instructions are packed with the paper.) Of course, if you purchased a number of packages of paper with the same emulsion number, you needn't make filter corrections when opening a new package. In fact, some photographers purposely buy several packages of paper with the same emulsion number in order to avoid making such filtration corrections.

An *Exposure Factor* also is listed on the Ektacolor package label to indicate how much to adjust the exposures you used with the preceding batch of paper. Instructions accompanying the paper explain how to recalculate exposure.

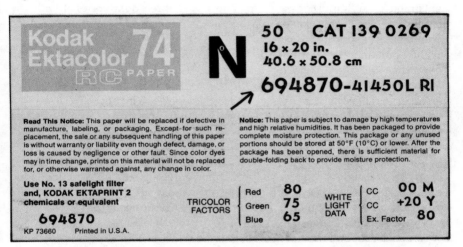

Kodak Ektacolor 74 RC PAPER

N° 50   CAT 139 0269
16 x 20 in.
40.6 x 50.8 cm

694870-41450L RI

Read This Notice: This paper will be replaced if defective in manufacture, labeling, or packaging. Except-for such replacement, the sale or any subsequent handling of this paper is without warranty or liability even though defect, damage, or loss is caused by negligence or other fault. Since color dyes may in time change, prints on this material will not be replaced for, or otherwise warranted against, any change in color.

Notice: This paper is subject to damage by high temperatures and high relative humidities. It has been packaged to provide complete moisture protection. This package or any unused portions should be stored at 50°F (10°C) or lower. After the package has been opened, there is sufficient material for double-folding back to provide moisture protection.

Use No. 13 safelight filter and, KODAK EKTAPRINT 2 chemicals or equivalent

694870
KP 73660   Printed in U.S.A.

TRICOLOR FACTORS		WHITE LIGHT DATA	
Red	80	CC	00 M
Green	75	CC	+20 Y
Blue	65	Ex. Factor	80

70. *The label on each package of Ektacolor color printing paper includes its emulsion number (arrow), and data for refiguring filtration and exposure when changing from one batch of paper to another (see text).*

Making a Test Print to Determine Exposure

Once the starting filter pack and your negative are inserted in the enlarger, you are ready to make a test print to determine exposure and color balance. In color printing it is important to establish a correct exposure *before* evaluating a print for color balance. That's because color balance is difficult to judge when a print is too dark or too light.

To make four test exposures on one sheet of 8 x 10-inch paper, take a piece of 8 x 10-inch black cardboard, like that in the photo paper package, which is thick enough not to allow any light to get through it. After cutting a 4 x 5-inch rectangle from one corner, use the remaining cardboard for masking off areas of your test print.

Elevate the enlarger head until the color negative image is focused and projected as you like it in 8 x 10 size on the enlarging easel.

For later reference, remember to write down on the negative's filing envelope or in a notebook all important information: filtration, enlarger height, brand of photo paper, and exposure.

If you've decided to standardize exposure *time,* as suggested earlier, set the enlarger timer at 10 seconds.

Now you are ready to place a sheet of unexposed color paper into the enlarging easel, emulsion side up, and cover three-quarters of it with the cardboard mask. This will leave a 4 x 5-inch rectangle of paper exposed for your first test exposure.

By changing the position of the cardboard you can make four test exposures of your image on the 8 x 10-inch sheet of paper. Each test exposure will cover *one quarter of the total image; do not* readjust the enlarger to make the size of your projected image 4 x 5 inches.

If you are processing in trays, you could cut the paper into small sizes and make individual exposure tests. But with tube processing it is more efficient to process an entire 8 x 10 sheet that contains several test exposures.

With room lights out, remove a sheet of Ektacolor paper, handling it carefully by its edges, and put it in the easel emulsion side *up.* After covering the paper with the three-quarters mask, expose the first test area at f/5.6, the next portion at f/8, the third at f/11, and the final section at f/16.

These are only suggestions because exposure is affected by filtration, the type of enlarger and its light source, and the density of the color negative and its magnification (the greater the enlargement, the more exposure required).

An alternative method for making test exposures is to use the same f/stop but change the time of each exposure.

It's worthwhile to mention that after you have the experience of making a few prints, you can save time and materials by testing more than one color negative at a time. Do this by altering the cardboard mask. Take the leftover piece of cardboard and cut it into five strips that are one inch wide. Attach these flaps with tape to the edge of the cardboard mask so they will fold back individually.

This will enable you to make five separate exposure (or filtration) tests of one color negative within the 4 x 5-inch rectangle, which means four different negatives can be tested on one sheet of 8 x 10 paper. After a negative is used to expose the print paper five times, take the paper out of the enlarging easel to store in a light-tight box until you have changed negatives and are ready for the next series of test exposures. To keep track of which areas of the print paper have been exposed, snip off a corner of the paper where the first negative was exposed, and rotate the paper clockwise with each succeeding negative.

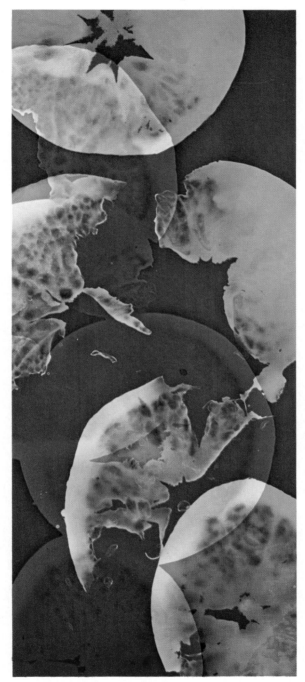

15. *Like the cover photograph, this is a photogram made in the darkroom. Thin slices of an orange were arranged on a piece of color negative paper. First it was exposed with light from an enlarger equipped with a red filter, then the orange slices were moved and a second exposure was made through a green filter. Red produced the cyan color and green produced magenta, and where the two colors overlapped, blue was produced. Also see Chapter 16.*

16. This is a straight and rather unexciting slide of a big tree with two strollers in London's Hyde Park.

17. It was made much more interesting by the Sabattier effect. To get this print, the slide was copied on color negative film, and that film was reexposed to light during processing (see Chapter 16). This affected the dark areas, as seen in this print made on color negative paper.

When prints or transparency films are given the Sabattier effect, which is commonly but erroneously called solarization, the bright areas are affected rather than the dark areas (note the sky and lady's light coat have remained nearly the same in both pictures).

18. *Color infrared film will give some interesting effects and can be processed in home darkrooms. This photograph was made on Kodak's Ektachrome Infrared film with photoflood illumination.*

19. *To produce this image, the infrared slide above was printed on color negative paper, which was then reexposed to light during development to get the Sabattier effect (see Chapter 16). A mask was used to create the oval frame, and the reexposure to light produced its gray tone.*

20. Multiple images can be created in several ways, as described in Chapter 16. To make this photograph, two slides were sandwiched together (one of the couple and one of the sun) and printed directly on color reversal paper.

21. To make this multiple image, the metal sculpture of a football player was shot against a white background on color negative film, using lights covered with magenta and green filters. The negative was then exposed five times on the same sheet of color negative paper, each time moving the paper to a different position and varying the exposure time.

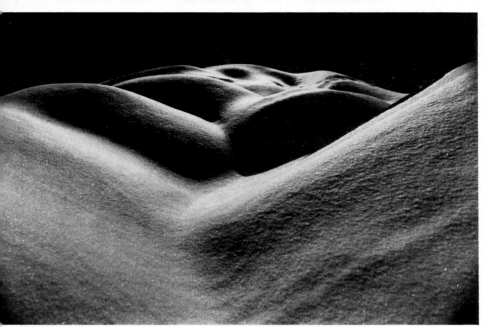

22. The impact of a black-and-white photograph, like this one of a snow scene, can be changed by toning.

23. After processing, this print was immersed in a bath of blue toner. The degree of toning can be easily controlled for dominant or subtle effects. Toning processes are described in Chapter 8.

24 and 25. A special effect was created with this black-and-white photograph (left) by prolonged toning. A darker than normal print was bathed in a concentrated solution of red toner for 15 minutes, which caused the silver to be eaten away in varying amounts. Then it was bathed in a blue toner to produce the final result below.

26 and 27. The black-and-white photograph of this cowboy slot machine (above) was given a duotone solarized effect by reexposure during processing. High contrast paper, special chemical steps, and a bright light are required to produce subtle reddish brown, green, or pink tones, as described in Chapter 16.

28. Hand coloring of prints is limited only by the photographer's imagination. In this photograph, cotton was used to apply light pink transparent oil color to some areas of the print, and then the subjects were outlined with a pen and India ink.

29. *Photographers have unlimited opportunities to be creative in their darkrooms. To make this photograph, two slides of the girl were sandwiched together and printed on color negative paper to give a negative image. During processing, the print was reexposed to light to cause the Sabattier effect and add other colors.*

Processing Color Test Prints

The procedures for processing color prints were discussed in the preceding chapter. You should especially read the section called "Processes for Making Color Prints from Color Negatives," outlining the steps for processing prints in tubes and in trays in specific chemistries: Kodak's Ektaprint 2, Beseler's 2-Step, and Unicolor's Universal A^r and Total Color. They can all be used to process Kodak's Ektacolor 74 RC and Ektacolor 78 papers.

The procedures for processing are the same whether you are developing a test print or your final print. There is a problem, however, when you try to judge the color balance of a wet Ektacolor print: it has an overall bluish cast. Dry the print before viewing it and deciding what changes in exposure and filtration may be necessary. Fortunately Ektacolor is a fast-drying resin-coated (RC) paper, and you can hurry the drying by using a hand-held hair dryer.

Analyzing a Color Print

To permit the most exacting evaluation of a *dry* print in regard to exposure and color balance, it should be viewed under adequate illumination that has good color quality. Deluxe Cool White 40-watt fluorescent lights work well for this purpose.

First check the density of the image on your test print to see which exposure is best. (You may have to remake the test print if your series of exposures were all overexposures or all underexposures.)

Now you're ready to judge color balance in the section of the test print that has the best exposure. If the colors do not seem true, you'll have to adjust the filter pack before making the next print. If you have a commercially produced print made from your own negative or a standard negative, use it for comparison.

The best way to judge color balance is to look for the color that seems to be in excess. Is there too much red or blue or green or yellow or magenta or cyan? Study color in the shadow areas. If there is a person in your picture, look at the skin tone to check for unnatural color cast. (If you have difficulty identifying magenta and cyan, refer to the color illustrations elsewhere in this book.)

Also, you may want to buy something called a *ring-around,* which is a series of identical color prints showing poor color balance in varying degrees. They surround a perfect print that has good color balance and exposure. The off-color images are marked by filter color and density, such as 10Y, 20Y, and 40Y. By studying the prints, you'll be able to see how much a color might be in excess, and use that information to make your filter corrections. A fold-out color ring-around can be found in Kodak's professional data book, *Printing Color Negatives.*

Figuring Filter Corrections

First review the material presented earlier in this chapter under the heading "Understanding Filtration." You must become familiar with the concepts of filtration that apply to printing color negatives (which are not the same as for printing color slides).

In brief, all colors in a print usually can be corrected by using filters of just one or two colors: yellow and/or magenta. Cyan filters occasionally may be required. When possible, *subtract* filters from the filter pack in order to keep exposure to a minimum.

After you identify the offending color in the test print, *subtract the filter or filters of its complementary color.* If there is no such filtration to subtract, *add* filtration of the same color that is offensive.

Use the chart below as a guideline. As you'll recall, and note in the chart, combining two complementary colors produces the equivalent of one primary color (i.e. yellow + magenta = red).

Excess color in a print (from a color negative)	Filters to subtract	Filters to add (only when unable to subtract filtration)
Blue	Yellow	Magenta + Cyan (= Blue)
Green	Magenta	Yellow + Cyan (= Green)
Red	Cyan	Yellow + Magenta (= Red)
Yellow	Magenta + Cyan (= Blue)	Yellow
Magenta	Yellow + Cyan (= Green)	Magenta
Cyan	Yellow + Magenta (= Red)	Cyan

Once you identify the offensive color in the test print that you want to eliminate—and figured what color of filter(s) to subtract or add—you must determine the *density* of the filters to use in the new filter pack.

As a general rule, when a *slight* change in color balance is needed, change filtration by 05 or 10 degrees of density. When a *moderate* change in color is required, change filtration by 15 or 20. And when a *significant* color change is called for, change filtration by 30 or 40 degrees of density.

Use the following three guidelines for making changes in filtration.

1) When filters are of the *same* color, you can subtract or add their density values directly.

For example, if your starting filter pack (see page 232) is 45M + 55Y and your test print seems to have a moderate excess of blue, you'd probably decide to subtract 20 degrees of yellow: 55Y − 20Y = 35Y. So your new filter pack for the second test print would be 45M (as before) + 35Y.

Similarly, if your first test print with a starting filter pack of 45M + 55Y showed a slight excess of magenta, you should subtract 10 degrees of its complementary color, green. Yellow and cyan filters produce green, but since there is no cyan in your starting filter pack, you cannot subtract it. So you must take the alternative and add 10 degrees of magenta: 45M + 10M = 55M. Thus, your new filter pack for the second test print would be 55M + 55Y.

2) When filtration of a primary color is required, convert that primary color to its equivalent in *both* filter colors. Remember that blue = magenta + cyan; green = yellow + cyan; and red = yellow + magenta.

For example, if your test print shows a significant excess of cyan, you should subtract 30 degrees of red from the starting filter pack. To do this, you actually would subtract 30 degrees of magenta and 30 degrees of yellow, because 30R = 30M + 30Y. So, if your starting filter pack was 45M + 55Y, your revised filter pack would now be *15M + 25Y* (45M − 30M = 15M; 55Y − 30Y = 25Y).

3) When your revised filtration requires all three complementary colors (which happens only occasionally), subtract an *equal* amount of density from *each* color until only two colors remain. This avoids neutral density and unnecessary exposure (see page 228).

For example, say you had a significant excess of blue in your first test print, so you subtract 40 degrees of yellow from the starting filter pack (45M + 55Y). The revised filter pack, with 45M + 15Y, yields a second test print that is still too blue by a significant amount. There's not enough yellow filtration remaining, 15Y, to enable you to subtract 40Y more, so now you must take the alternative and *add blue* filtration. Of course, blue must be converted to its filter colors (magenta and cyan), which means filters of 40M and 40C would be added to the pack of 45M + 15Y. This makes 85M + 15Y + 40C. Because using filters of all three complementary colors has *no* effect on color balance, you would remove 15 degrees of density from *each* color in order to end up with just two colors of filters. Thus, filtration you would use for the third test print is *70M + 25C* (85M − 15M = 70M; 15Y − 15Y = 0Y; 40C − 15C = 25C).

With experience you will become familiar with the color relationships and which filters to subtract or add to the filter pack in order to obtain good color balance in a print. Use the charts provided in this chapter, or just memorize the three abbreviations and a simple rule which follows.

To remember a primary color's complementary color, memorize BY, GM, and RC. *B*lue's complement is *Y*ellow, *G*reen's complement is *M*agenta, and *R*ed's complement is *C*yan.

Also remember that filters of the two *other* complementary colors will produce the equivalent of the primary color. Blue is created by using magenta + cyan filters, green is created by yellow + cyan, and red is created by yellow + magenta filtration.

Besides comparing their test prints with a color ring-around, some photographers use *viewing filters* to help them decide what changes in filtration should be made in order to get good color balance in a print. You can view prints through CP filters used in the enlarger or buy a special set, such as Kodak's Color Print Viewing Filter Kit. It has filters in six colors (yellow, magenta, cyan, red, blue, green) in three densities (10, 20, 40) that are mounted in viewing cards. You flick the filters back and forth in front of the prints to see which filter color and density improves the print's color balance.

Judge the effect on tones of the image that seem average in density, because viewing filters tend to overcorrect colors in the highlights and undercorrect colors in the shadow areas. Whatever filter color seems to improve the print, you would subtract that same color (or its equivalent) from the filter pack in your enlarger.

As examples, if the print looks better through a yellow filter (correcting for excess blue), subtract yellow filtration. Likewise, if a red viewing filter improves the color of a print (correcting for excess cyan), you would subtract yellow and magenta (which equal red) from the filter pack.

Also remember that a filter will make a greater change in a print's color balance than what it seems to make when you view a print through a filter of the same color and density. As a rule of thumb, alter filtration by *half* of the density of the filter used for viewing. For example, if a viewing filter of 20Y (yellow) makes the print look better, you would subtract only 10Y from the filter pack (½ of 20Y = 10Y) before making another print.

Figuring Exposure Corrections

When filtration is changed in order to improve a print's color balance, exposure probably needs to be changed in order for tne print to have proper density.

Since every filter has a *filter factor* that indicates how much additional exposure is required when that filter is used, you can use the factors to compute the revised exposure. Here's a list of filter factors of various densities of Kodak's yellow, magenta, and cyan CP and CC filters.

Filter	Yellow	Filter Factors Magenta	Cyan
05	1.1	1.2	1.1
10	1.1	1.3	1.2
20	1.1	1.5	1.3
30	1.1	1.7	1.4
40	1.1	1.9	1.5
50	1.1	2.1	1.6

If you are going to adjust exposure by changing exposure *time, divide* the old exposure time by the filter factor of any filter that is *removed* from the filter pack. If two or more filters are removed, first multiply the individual factors together and use their product to divide the exposure time.

For example, if the original exposure time was 10 seconds and you removed a yellow filter (of any density), divide 10 by 1.1—all yellow filters have a factor of 1.1—and the result is about 9 seconds for the new exposure time. Or, if you removed a yellow filter (of any density) and a 20M (magenta) filter, first multiply 1.1 by 1.5 (see chart above), then take their product (1.65) and divide it into 10 seconds. Your revised exposure time would be 6 seconds.

As for *adding* a filter to the filter pack, you would *multiply* the old exposure time by the filter's factor. If two or more filters are added, first multiply the individual factors together and use their product to multiply the exposure time.

For example, adding a 40M (magenta) filter to the filter pack, you'd multiply the original exposure time of 10 seconds by 1.9 (see chart above). The new time would be 19 seconds. Or, if you're adding a yellow filter (of any density) and 10M (magenta), multiply 1.1 by 1.3 (see chart) and take their product (1.43) and multiply it by 10 seconds. The revised exposure would be about 14 seconds.

Optionally, but somewhat less accurately, you can adjust exposure by changing the f/stop on the enlarger lens instead of the exposure time. This works best only with lenses that have enough space between f/markings to allow you to make exposure adjustments by 1/3 stops. The chart on page 240 suggests how much to open up or close down the lens opening when you add or subtract specific filters.

Special mention should be made regarding the *dichroic filters* that are part of enlargers with color heads. Filter factors do not apply to dichroic filters because they are interference-type filters that block only light of their respective complementary colors and do not affect the other colors of light. Therefore, unless there have been *major* corrections in filtration, a change in

| | | Exposure Adjustment by f/stops | |
Filter	Yellow	Magenta	Cyan
05	none	1/3	1/3
10	1/3	1/3	1/3
20	1/3	1/3	1/3
30	1/3	2/3	2/3
40	1/3	2/3	2/3
50	2/3	2/3	1

exposure normally is not required when dichroic filters are used. When exposure changes are needed, experience (or a color analyzer) will help you estimate the new exposure.

After a while, you will be able to confidently judge the color balance and density of a print, and then make filtration and exposure corrections. At the beginning you may need to make several test prints before you are happy with the results. Although trial-and-error test printing is the most common method for determining good color balance and print density, there are some alternative methods involving the use of electronic *color analyzers* and less expensive *color calculators* (both were already described, beginning on page 195).

Once you have a satisfactory test print, the final full size enlargement can be made. Remember, if you change the enlarger's height in order to print the image larger or smaller than it was in the test print, your exposure will change—the greater the distance the enlarger lamp is from the photo paper, the greater the exposure required.

Improving the Color Print

You should inspect the final print when it is dry to see if it could be improved. Careless handling or some processing errors may be evident (see page 207). The emulsions of color print papers are quite delicate, and you should take care to avoid bending the paper or smudging it with fingerprints. Many camera stores sell inexpensive thin white cotton gloves that can be used to handle color photo papers in the darkroom. You may want to wear a glove on only one hand, leaving the other hand free to do the other things that might get the gloves dirty or wet.

More critical analysis of your print may reveal areas that are too dark or too light. To improve the density of the image in such areas, you can use techniques called *dodging* and *burning-in*. Dodging holds back light from the enlarger so an area doesn't get too dark, while burning-in increases exposure so a light area will become darker in the print. (Tools and methods of dodging and burning-in were described in detail in chapter 7.)

You can also improve a color print by doing some *selective filtration* in areas where you want to alter color without affecting the rest of the print. By attaching filters to dodging and burning-in tools, you can decrease or increase a color, or change one color to another.

Have filters available in the primary and complementary colors: red, blue, green, magenta, yellow, and cyan. Use 30 or 40 degrees of density in order for the filter to have a significant effect on the color.

Often you'll have an excess of blue in the shadow area of an image. When you dodge that area with a blue filter during *part* of the print's regular exposure, the blue in the print will be reduced. Or, if a person's face is too red or too yellow, you would dodge the face with a red or yellow filter to achieve normal skin tone without changing any of the other colors in the print.

Or, let's say you burned-in a highlight area that's too bright but it picked up too much unwanted color because of the additional exposure. To correct this problem, you should burn-in with a filter that is the same color as the unwanted color. You can also alter the true colors in a print by using selective filtration. Experiment and you'll be surprised at the effects you can create.

One thing to be certain to do is keep a record of how you print *every* color negative. This can be written in a small notebook, or marked on the envelope in which you store the negative. Even if they are printing 35mm color negatives, some photographers buy 4 x 5-inch or larger size glassine negative envelopes so they will have space to record printing information.

This should include details of the enlarger height, print size, exposure time and f/stop, filter packs used, the color photo paper and its emulsion or batch number. If you did some cropping or dodging or burning-in, this should be noted too.

Such printing information will save you paper, chemicals, and time if you decide to reprint the negative in the future. And when you have another color negative with similar characteristics (same type of film, same light source, similar subject matter), this recorded data will give you a starting point for making a test print.

Always write down the print size and the enlarger's height, because a different height will mean a different exposure. When you want to reprint the same negative the same size later, just raise the enlarger to the height noted in your record. Some enlargers are equipped with a measuring scale attached to the support column, but if your enlarger doesn't have this feature, mark the enlarger yourself or attach a tape measure.

If you decide to control exposure by adjusting f/stops while keeping the *same* exposure time, and if there is enough space between the f/ numbers on your enlarger lens, mark lines or notches such as 5.6'''8. These marks will enable you to make exposure changes more accurately, which is important because the slightest change in exposure will make a difference in print density. If you mark two or three lines between each f/stop, you can easily set the exposure, and record it, by 1/3 or 1/4 stops.

For example, to record the exposure data, you would write down the lens opening like this: 5.6' when it is a quarter-stop past f/5.6; 5.6'8 when it is a half-stop between f/5.6 and f/8; and '8 when the lens opening is a quarter-stop before f/8.

The notes written on a negative's envelope, or in your notebook, might appear as below:

6/18/78 (printing date)
Neg. # 100240
15½ (enlarger height)
8 x 10 (print size)—crop bottom
Ektacolor 74 #597510 (paper and emulsion number)
10 sec. (exposure time)

f/16	25Y	45M	(starting f/stop and filtration)
f/16'22	25Y	30M	(second test print)
f/16'22	35Y	30M	(third test and final print)

By the way, a good idea is to save your test prints, marking their backs with the exposure and filtration you used. This information can help you improve your ability to judge correct color balance and density in future prints.

Making Color Contact Prints

Once you've made enough test prints to establish the proper filter pack and exposure to use with your first (standard) color negative, you can use the same filtration and exposure with similar negatives on the same type of film, as long as you keep the same enlarger height and use print paper with the same emulsion number.

It is also convenient to make *contact prints,* sometimes called a *proof sheet,* of the other negatives in the same roll, so you'll have a positive image of each one and can compare them for color and density. Include the color negative you've already test-printed to use as a standard.

An entire thirty-six-exposure roll of 35mm film will fit on one sheet of 8 x 10-inch paper, as will a twelve-exposure roll of 120-size film. If your setup was for making test prints on 8 x 10-inch paper, the enlarger height should not be changed.

Place the color paper *emulsion side up* on the enlarger baseboard or enlarging easel. On top, arrange the color negatives *emulsion side down,* then cover the negatives and paper with a piece of clear window glass to make sure they are in contact. Now expose and process the paper exactly as you did for the original print.

When dried, study the contact sheet carefully. If the image of your original (standard) negative looks good, use it to judge the other images for color balance and density. If they compare favorably, you can use exactly the same filtration and exposure when making 8 x 10-inch prints from the other negatives. Nevertheless, making at least one test print with a color negative that has been only contact-printed is probably a good idea before you go ahead with a final enlargement.

A contact sheet serves both as a guide for filtration and exposure, and a positive record of your color negative images, so consider making one with each roll of film you shoot.

Exposing Color Transparencies Step by Step

Much of the preceding explanation in regard to exposing color negatives also applies to exposing color slides. However, since you are using a positive image instead of a negative image to make a print, the color print papers and chemical processes are different, and the concepts regarding filtration are reversed. Making a print directly from a transparency is often called the *color reversal print process,* or Type R printing.

Photographers like to make color prints from transparencies for a number of reasons. One is that a slide is a positive color image and can be compared easily with a print. Also, there are fewer exposure and filtration changes required for slides than for color negatives. Once you get a good print from a particular type of transparency film, such as Kodachrome or Ektachrome, other transparencies of similar density shot on the same type of film can often be printed with identical exposure and filtration. Even though reversal print papers are more expensive than color negative papers, the amount of testing is less, and final enlargements can be finished with shorter spells in the darkroom.

Filtration itself is easier to figure, too. With transparencies, every color you change in the enlarger's filter pack has an *identical* effect on that color in the print. This means that determining filtration for correct color balance of a slide is *reverse* of the procedure described for figuring filtration for color negatives.

You use the same filters—yellow, magenta, and cyan—but to change a specific color, you *subtract a filter of the same color,* or its equivalent. For example, if your color reversal test print shows an excess of magenta, you would subtract magenta filtration. Or, if there is too much red in the print, you would correct this by subtracting yellow and magenta, the equivalent of red.

One problem in reversal printing is that prints made from color slides often have too much contrast. Color transparencies inherently have more contrast than color negatives, and when they are printed directly on reversal paper, contrast increases. This is because it is impossible for slides to have a built-in color mask (the orangish tint) that is part of some types of color negative film. Consequently, even if you have a slide with a wide range of contrast, with details in both shadows and highlights, its image will look better when projected than when printed.

To a limited extent you can lighten or darken areas in a reversal print by using burning-in and dodging techniques. When that doesn't solve a contrast problem, some photographers copy the slide to make a *color internegative* for printing on color negative paper, which permits better control of contrast.

Currently there are two popular ways to make color prints directly from color transparencies. One features Kodak's Ektachrome 2203 print paper, which can be processed in various brands of chemistry, including Kodak's Ektaprint, Ektaprint R-1000, Beseler's 3-Step, and Unicolor's RP-1000 chemistry.

The other positive-to-positive print process is called Cibachrome, and it requires Cibachrome Type A (Pearl-RC or Hi-Gloss) paper to be used in Cibachrome's Process P-12 chemistry, or Type D paper in P-18 chemistry. Since the Kodak and Cibachrome papers are quite different, including filtration and exposure characteristics, they will be discussed separately. The differences in their respective chemical processes were explained in the preceding chapter.

First, there are several things common to Cibachrome and Ektachrome RC papers.

Both can be used to make prints from all types of color transparency films, including Kodachrome, Ektachrome, Fujichrome, Agfachrome, and GAF color slide film. Filtration will vary according to the type of film.

Both require that a heat-absorbing glass and an ultraviolet (UV) filter be placed in the enlarger, as was necessary for printing color negatives. You can use the same No. 2B UV filter, although Kodak recommends a No. 2A UV filter be used with Ektachrome 2203 paper. Enlargers with color heads have ultraviolet filtration and heat-absorbing features built in.

Both Cibachrome and Ektacolor papers should be handled in *total* darkness.

The same filters used for color negative printing are also used with Cibachrome and Ektachrome color reversal papers: yellow, magenta, and cyan. As a filtration guide for changing the color balance of a color reversal print, the following chart (opposite page) indicates what to do in order to get rid of a color that is excessive.

With this background information, you are ready to make your first test print from a color slide. It is important to pick a transparency that has good exposure and is not too contrasty. There should be detail in the highlights and a variety of rich colors. Try to use the type of film you shoot with most often, such as Ektachrome.

Remember that a slide will always seem to have more brilliance than a print

Excess color in a print (from a slide)	Filters to subtract	Filters to add, only when unable to subtract filtration
Yellow	Yellow	Magenta + Cyan (= Blue)
Magenta	Magenta	Yellow + Cyan (= Green)
Cyan	Cyan	Yellow + Magenta (= Red)
Blue	Magenta + Cyan (= Blue)	Yellow
Green	Yellow + Cyan (= Green)	Magenta
Red	Yellow + Magenta (= Red)	Cyan

made from a slide. The reason is that you view a transparency by light transmitted through the slide, and you view a print by reflected light. For print viewing, light must pass through the color dyes, reflect off the base of the paper, and go back through the dyes before reaching the viewer's eyes. Also, surface reflections tend to reduce the brillance of a color print. So details that were apparent in a slide, especially in shadow areas, are often lost when you see a print of the same image.

One way to judge a slide before printing is to view the slide against a sheet of white paper that is reflecting light from a bulb of normal wattage. (Do not place the slide directly on the paper or let its shadow fall on the paper.) This will give you an indication of how the slide image will reproduce in a print, although its shadow detail will turn out somewhat better than what you see.

Place the selected transparency or slide in the enlarger's negative carrier with the emulsion (dull) side *down* so it faces the enlarger baseboard or enlarging easel. It is not necessary to remove a slide from its cardboard, plastic, or glass mount unless it does not fit into the enlarger easily, or causes light from the enlarger to leak around the negative carrier. You can use black masking tape or black paper masks to keep stray light from leaking onto the photo paper, which it will fog. The transparency should not come into contact with the enlarger's condensor lenses, so you may have to tape mounted slides to the bottom of the negative carrier. You may want to purchase a special negative carrier that is designed to hold mounted slides. Be sure your transparency is free of dust or black spots will appear in the print.

Choosing the starting filter pack and test exposures are the next steps, and these depend on the type of paper you are using. There are descriptions of Cibachrome and Ektachrome color reversal papers in the preceding chapter. Both have delicate emulsion surfaces, and you should protect them from fingerprints by handling the papers by their edges only, or preferably by wearing thin white cotton gloves that are sold in many camera stores.

With Ektachrome 2203 paper, to enlarge a 35mm slide to 8 x 10 inches, Kodak's instructions recommend specific filtration to start with in your enlarger depending on whether the transparencies being printed are Kodachrome, Ektachrome, or a random mix of slides. Set the enlarger lens to f/8 and make test exposures at 4, 8, and 16 seconds, with a No. 212, No. 302, or tungsten-halogen enlarger bulb. The paper is exposed in sections by using a cardboard mask (see page 234).

With Cibachrome Type A paper, a label on the back of each package lists Basic Filter Pack information for that specific batch of paper. The suggested filtration to start with is given for Kodachrome (which also can be used with GAF slides), Ektachrome, Agfachrome, and Fujichrome.

Expose each test section for 10 seconds, but change the enlarger lens opening to f/4.5, f/5.6, f/8, and f/11. This is with a 100- or 150-watt enlarger bulb, as Cibachrome recommends.

Process the test prints in their respective chemistries (for Ektachrome 2203, see pages 213 through 217, and for Cibachrome Type A, see pages 217 through 224).

Analyzing the Test Print

As with color negative papers, color reversal papers must be dry before you can accurately judge them for density and color balance. Wet Ektachrome RC prints have an overall bluish cast, while wet Cibachrome prints have a reddish magenta cast. You can speed up the drying process of both papers by using a hand-held hair dryer.

Kodak recommends viewing dry Ektachrome prints under light of good color quality and intensity, such as 40-watt Deluxe Cool White fluorescent lights.

Do not try to compare a test print with its transparency to determine density. Instead, study the print's highlight and shadow detail and pick the test section that looks best. If none of the exposures are good, make another test print with different exposures before trying to judge color balance. Since this is a reversal paper, you must *add* exposure to *lighten* a print, and *subtract* exposure to *darken* a print.

To analyze color balance in a color reversal print, compare it with the transparency. Place a white piece of cardboard at an angle beneath the viewing light and the overhead transparency in the light reflected toward you.

Use the chart on page 245 to determine what filtration should be *subtracted* or *added* to improve color balance in the initial test prints on Ektachrome or Cibachrome papers.

You can also use viewing filters to help determine correct color balance (see page 238). *Add* to your filter pack the color of the viewing filter that improves the appearance of your test print.

One thing to keep in mind when altering color balance is that color reversal papers require a great amount of change in filtration than do color negative papers. Start with a change of at least 20 degrees of density.

Changes in filtration usually require changes in exposure, and you can compute the adjustment required by using filter factors. Dichroic filters used in enlargers with a color head are exceptions. (An explanation of how to figure exposure changes was given previously, beginning on page 238.)

Once a basic filter pack and exposure have been determined for a certain type of film, such as Kodachrome, they can be used for other transparencies of the same type of film—as long as enlarger height and paper emulsion remain the same.

Changes in exposure and filtration will usually be required when using a batch of Ektachrome paper with a different emulsion number. Printed on the paper package label, along with the emulsion number, is *Filter Correction* information, such as +15C −35M −10Y. Instructions packed with Ektachrome paper will tell you how to use this information to figure a revised filter pack and exposure for the new paper, without making another series of test exposures.

As previously mentioned, Cibachrome prints must also be *dry* before judging them for density and color balance. Viewing under fluorescent light or daylight is preferred to viewing with tungsten light.

If none of the exposures in your Cibachrome test print appear to give the best density, make another series. Remember, the longer you expose color reversal paper, the lighter the image becomes. And the shorter the exposure, the darker the print will be.

You will discover that Cibachrome has great latitude, which means you must make a significant change in exposure in order for it to be evident in the print. Sometimes you must change the enlarger lens opening by one or two f/stops, or alter exposure time by a factor of 2 to 4, to make an appreciable change in density.

Filtration changes to improve color balance also must be significant, usually by at least 20 degrees of density if you want to see much of a change in a Cibachrome print. Use the chart for color reversal papers on page 245 for determining what filters to subtract or add to make corrections in a print's color.

When filters are changed, exposure corrections are required, and Cibachrome suggests you make the following percentages of change, depending on the filter's density, as indicated on page 248. If filters are subtracted, decrease exposure by the given amounts; if filters are added, increase exposure by the listed percentages.

Other essential information that will help you make color reversal prints with Cibachrome will be found in the Cibachrome *Color Print Manual* sold with Cibachrome processing kits.

| Filter density | Percent (%) of change to make in Cibachrome exposure | | |
	Yellow	Magenta	Cyan
05	10	20	10
10	10	30	20
20	10	50	30
30	10	70	40
40	10	90	50
50	10	110	60

Improving the Color Reversal Print

Areas in prints that are too dark or too light can be improved by dodging and burning-in, but with Ektachrome and Cibachrome papers, the procedures are opposite of those used with color negative papers. Dodging is done to *darken* an area in a print (by holding back enlarger light from the paper), while burning-in will actually *lighten* a print area (by adding additional exposure). Make your own tools from cardboard; do not use the dodging and burning-in tools of red plastic sold in camera stores because they will change the print's color balance.

You can do some *selective filtration,* however, by using dodging and burning-in tools fitted with colored filters of magenta, yellow, cyan, red, blue, or green. Use filters of 30, 40, or 50 degrees of density in order for the effect to be evident. The amount of dodging time with a color filter may be considerable in order to achieve the desired change in color.

Use a filter that is *complementary* to the color you wish to reduce. For instance, if there is excess blue in a shadow area, dodge it with a yellow filter during part of the print exposure (yellow reduces the blue color; refer again to the chart on page 245).

As one consequence of being reversal papers, Ektachrome and Cibachrome papers produce prints with black borders rather than white borders. The enlarging easel's border masks prevent the enlarger light from reaching the paper's edges; to produce *white borders,* you must expose those edges with twice the amount of light used for the basic exposure.

First, cut an opaque mask (black cardboard from the paper package will do) that's the size of the picture area you want to keep. Expose your transparency, then remove it from the enlarger. Do not change the filtration. If your easel's border masks have been used to hold the paper in place, lift them away so they no longer cover the paper. Cover the picture area you want to preserve with the cardboard mask. Now make a second exposure that is *twice* as much as the first one (double the exposure time *or* open up the lens one f/stop). This will overexpose the print's edges and they will develop as white borders.

In order to make additional prints of the same slide without remaking test prints, don't forget to record all printing information on the transparency storage envelope or in a notebook (see page 241).

You can also make *contact proof sheets* of transparencies to use in determining exposure and color balance for groups of slides. It serves as a printed record of the images, too. Twenty mounted 35mm slides can be contact-printed on one sheet of 8 x 10-inch paper. Cover them with a piece of glass to keep the slides in contact with the paper. The enlarger height should be set for making an 8 x 10-inch print with a 35mm slide. Use the same filtration and exposure that produced a good enlargement from a slide of the same type of transparency film that you are contact printing.

Once you have made a print of which you are proud—whether from a color transparency, a color negative, or black-and-white negative—it's time for the finishing touches: spotting, mounting, and framing.

15

Finishing and Mounting
Black-and-White and Color Prints

Too many photographers give too little attention to print finishing. There are a number of things you can do before showing off your prints, like spotting, etching, corrective coloring, and mounting. If a photograph is worth making, then the print should be worth finishing. Unless otherwise noted, the information in this chapter applies to *both* color and black-and-white prints.

Ferrotyping Glossy Prints

Before you're ready to finish a print, proper drying is important. Several methods have already been described in chapter 5, and you'll recall that glossy surface papers have special considerations. Resin-coated (RC) print papers of the glossy type are self-glossing, but conventional paper-base papers require ferrotyping to add gloss to their surfaces. This is done by pressing the wet paper's emulsion against chrome-plated metal, which may be an individual *ferrotype tin* or a chrome-surfaced print dryer.

Before placing the paper on the shiny metal, air bells must be eliminated or the gloss will be uneven. Under running water, rub the emulsion surface gently with your hand. Place the print facedown on the ferrotype surface and squeegee it flat with a rubber-edged window wiper. Cover it with a blotter to remove excess water, then rub or use a roller over the blotter to press the print hard against the metal.

When the print is dry, it will pop off the chrome surface; do not pull a dry print away or it may tear. If a print sticks to the metal, or has a pitted gloss, the ferrotype plate may be dirty or the print was inadequately washed. If the gloss is unsatisfactory, you can thoroughly wet the print again and redo the ferrotyping procedure.

Prints of all types, glossy or not, should dry flat. There is little problem with resin-coated (RC) papers, but sometimes conventional paper-base papers will curl up, especially when the humidity is low, as in wintertime. There are several ways to *flatten a print*. The simplest is to rub the *back* of a print over the edge of a table, but be careful not to crack its emulsion. Another way is to dampen the print's *back* with a sponge, then place the print under weight for 24 hours. Or, you can bathe the print in Kodak's or another brand of *print flattening solution,* and then dry it as usual.

Spotting and Retouching Prints

Whether black-and-white or color, most every print will need some spotting, despite your efforts to have a clean darkroom and make sure negatives and transparencies are dust free. Even if you use an antistatic brush or a can of compressed air to clean the dust off your negatives before printing, there probably will be a few dust spots on your prints that need to be filled in. Photographers call this *spotting.* Spotting a print is not difficult, and it takes little time once you develop a steady hand with a *spotting brush* and learned how to use *spotting colors* and *spotting dyes.*

Besides cleaning up dust spots, your spotting technique can be used to enhance an image. Often an image that is slightly "soft" can be improved by subtle retouching to sharpen areas of the print. For instance, by brushing around the eyes, mouth, and a few other facial details, you can improve a portrait to the point that viewers won't notice its original lack of sharpness.

71. *Prints can be improved by "spotting" them with a fine brush and dry or liquid dyes to fill in dust marks and other blemishes.*

Beginning spotters often get impatient. But spotting must be approached slowly and with care. When touching up white spots in a print, caused by dust on a negative, you start by applying the spotting dye lightly, then slowly build it up to match the tone or color of the surrounding area.

A very wet brush, or one with too much dye, is hard to control. Use a dry brush that is moistened slightly by wetting it with your tongue or a sponge. A brush dipped in water will be too wet.

Use a stippling technique to spot a print, making dots with the tip of your brush until the error is covered up. Don't cover more than is necessary. Normally, a small amount of dye applied to the center area of a dust spot is all that's needed. If the edges around the error pick up some of the dye, a dark outline may form and create an even bigger problem. So just touch up the error until it appears lost when studied from print-viewing distance.

Spotting brushes are sold at camera stores. Many photographers prefer a brush that is small and thin, but a thicker brush won't have to be dipped into a dye as frequently. Best are pure sable brushes (try a No. 0 or No. 2), and make sure they have pointed tips and no stray hairs.

There are a number of spotting dyes commercially available for *spotting black-and-white prints*. Two types that are especially useful, and different in form, are Kodak's Spotting Colors and Spotone Dyes. Kodak Spotting Colors are dry pigments—black, white, and sepia—that come on three 3 x 3-inch cards per package. Spotone Dyes are liquid dyes that are available in a set of three or can be bought individually. They are numbered 1, 2, 3. Number 1 is for cold tone print papers; number 2 is for warm tone (but not as warm as sepia); and number 3 is a neutral dye that can be used on most papers. The dyes can be diluted with water and mixed together to match special tones.

Kodak's Spotting Colors, because they are dry, are easier to control than the liquid Spotone Dyes. Moisten the brush to pick up the pigment, blot it on white paper, and then lightly apply the pigment to the print. The black pigment is fine for all cold tone papers, while the sepia works well on warm tone papers, and they can be mixed with the white to match any print tone. Also, white can be used to touch up any dark spots that look out of place on the print. These may be caused by pinholes in the negative, or if you are printing direct positive images, dust spots will show up as black dots, too. It is wise to begin with the darkest errors, and as the pigment or dye is used up on the brush, move on to lighter mistakes.

Both types of spotting dyes mentioned above work with resin-coated (RC) and conventional paper-base black-and-white photographic papers. Since the dyes tend to stand up on the surface of resin-coated prints, you'll have to be more careful when spotting RC papers. Also remember that glossy papers reveal spotting errors and corrections more than do matte and other paper surfaces.

Spotting color prints is done much the same way you would spot a black-and-white print. Apply the dyes lightly, with a slightly moistened brush, and build the tone up slowly. With practice, black can be used to spot many mistakes on a color print, but other times a dye of a specific color is necessary. Light blues (as in skies), light greens, and yellows usually require the corresponding color dye be used.

There are a number of dyes that work well on both resin-coated (RC) and conventional paper-base color papers, and two are especially recommended. Marshall Retouching Colors are liquid dyes in a variety of colors, and are available in inexpensive kits at camera stores. These water-based dyes come in small bottles with eye droppers, and include colors like basic flesh and primary blue. Rather than dipping your brush into the liquid, put a few drops of each color onto a piece of glass. Once they dry, you can use a moistened brush to transfer the color from the glass to the print.

Kodak Retouching Colors, once called Flexichrome dyes, also are available in a kit, but they are more expensive. They come in waxlike cake form. For spotting Ektacolor RC prints, use a brush moistened in a solution of equal parts water and Kodak Ektaprint 3 stabilizer. For Ektachrome RC prints, mix water with Ektaprint R-1000 stabilizer. These Kodak dyes have a special appeal because they can also be rubbed on dry with cotton to add color to larger areas of a print.

Spotting with colored pencils, such as Eagle Prismacolor pencils, is easily done. Apply them by dotting or stippling, and keep their points well sharpened.

Spotting Cibachrome prints is more difficult than spotting the other color printing papers. Because of its plasticlike glossy surface, retouching dyes seem to stand out—so keep spotting to a minimum. Cibachrome has special retouching kits, including a set of water soluble transparent dyes. However, another kit gives the most satisfactory results because it contains liquid opaque dyes that are oil-based pigmented lacquers. They can be applied with a brush, and a lacquer thinner is supplied that will remove the dyes from the print if you make a mistake.

Retouching involves changes to larger areas of a print than covered by spotting. You can use the same color dyes and pencils. Pencils are easier to handle than dyes because they cover up, but dyes are translucent and are best for making color corrections.

Prepare the emulsion for color penciling by spraying it with a retouching lacquer. Use light strokes and build up the colors as desired. If considerable penciling is done, a secondary coat of retouching lacquer may be necessary. In case you make a mistake, the pencil colors can be removed by using cotton soaked in naphtha. Let it dry before repenciling.

Liquid dyes give little control in retouching because they are absorbed quickly by the emulsion. Kodak's Retouching Colors are in the form of dry cakes, however, and they can be used both wet and dry. When mixed in a solution, they can be applied by brush tip for spotting and detail work. But for tinting greater areas of a color print, they should be applied dry with cotton.

This enables you to change the bluishness that frequently appears in shadows, improve skin tones, add color to subjects that appear gray (neutral), and even improve a print's color balance.

Apply the dye by moving the cotton in a circular motion. You can decrease the density of a dye that has been applied by continuing to buff it with clean dry cotton. Also included in the dye kit is a cake of reducer that will remove the dye, and you can apply it to areas of the print where you made a mistake or overlapped another color. The dyes will lose their waxy appearance and become permanent only when steamed for 5 to 10 seconds. Use a steaming tea kettle or a room vaporizer, and hold the print's retouched area about 10 inches from the steam source.

When correcting colors in a print, remember to apply the appropriate dyes. To reduce red, apply cyan; apply red to reduce cyan. Change green with a magenta dye, and vice versa. To alter blue, use the orange dye; likewise, use blue dye to reduce an orange color. To change yellow, you need to apply a purple dye, which is made by mixing blue and magenta dyes; yellow dye will reduce purple color in a print.

Instructions for applying the dyes are packed with each set of Kodak Retouching Colors, or you can follow the advice in the Kodak pamphlet, *Retouching Ektacolor Prints,* which can also be used as a guide for retouching Ektachrome RC paper.

Etching Prints

Occasionally, small black spots may appear on the surface of a print or in a negative. One way to get rid of them, instead of spotting, is to scratch them off. This is called etching, and there are specially made *etching knives* with angled edges. An Exacto knife or sharp razor blade will also do the job, if you are careful.

You actually scratch the emulsion away until the black spot disappears. This can be done on any conventional print paper, black-and-white or color, and on the emulsion side of black-and-white negatives. Do not etch resin-coated (RC) papers or Cibachrome prints.

Color prints demand extra care because the paper has several layers of color dyes in its emulsion. The emulsion is relatively thick, and a spot can be etched away until the color value is similar to the surrounding area. But if you go too far, you will etch completely through the emulsion and create a white spot. Practice on an unimportant print.

So that etched areas will not show, wax the print with a clear liquid or paste wax, or coat it with a clear lacquer spray. With conventional glossy surface papers, etching should be done before the ferrotyping. Remember that etching is not recommended for resin-coated (RC) papers or Cibachrome prints.

Hand Coloring Black-and-White Prints

The hand coloring of black-and-white prints has been done since the early days of photography. Whether a portrait was made by a painter or a photographer, people wanted color. Until a decade or so ago, photography studios featuring color portraiture usually made black-and-white prints and then hand colored them. These days, actual color photography is so easy and inexpensive that hand coloring is more of a novelty and a means of special expression for those concerned with photography as art.

Unlike water-based retouching dyes applied to color prints, hand coloring of black-and-white prints traditionally involves *transparent oil colors*. The oils come in small tubes, and can be used straight or mixed to get intermediate colors. They are applied with cotton swabs or small tuffs of long-fiber cotton (to prevent problems with stray strands). Hand coloring kits, available at photo stores, usually include the oils, long-fiber cotton, an oil thinner, and a cleaner to help correct any errors you might make while working on the print.

Portraits intended for hand oil coloring most often are printed on warm tone papers. These are sepia-toned to make it easier to get good flesh tones. The paper surface should be matte; on glossy papers, the oils won't adhere properly. The oils can be applied thickly, or rubbed down to provide a pale, light cover. Remember, they are transparent and can be reapplied to get the color and intensity you want. The oils take several hours to dry, depending on how thickly they are applied, so be careful not to smear them as you work.

Hand coloring is not limited only to the transparent oils. There are many other things that can be used to color prints, depending on the effect you want. Among such items are felt-tipped ink pens, watercolors, chalk, India ink, and colored pencils. Use your imagination and experiment with hand coloring black-and-white prints.

Lacquering Prints for Protection

Print emulsions, black-and-white and color, can be protected by coating them with photo spray lacquers that are sold in camera stores. It is especially worthwhile to lacquer prints that have been spotted, retouched, etched, or hand colored. Lacquers enhance a print's appearance and protect it from scratches, fingerprints, dirt, and humidity. Lacquered prints can be cleaned safely with a damp cloth.

Prints that will touch glass or plastic in a frame should be lacquered to guard their emulsions; normally, framed color prints should be separated from the glass (see page 261). When framing without glass, use one of the spray lacquers containing ingredients that filter out much of the ultraviolet light that causes color print dyes to fade.

Lacquers are also sprayed on prints to give them a variety of surface textures (see below), and you can use them to change glossy prints to matte finishes, and vice versa.

Practice lacquering on unwanted prints until you are familiar with its application. Lay prints flat on a table covered with newspaper, and direct the spray can at a 30-degree angle about 12 inches from the print. Start at the edge of the print closest to you and spray in a sweeping motion. Be sure to spray past the edges so the coating will be uniform.

If the prints are going to be mounted by a heat process, they should be lacquered *after* mounting. As an alternative, black-and-white prints can be protected from scratches by applying a coat of clear paste wax or liquid wax, such as Simonize or Johnson's Glo-Coat. Rub in the waxes and polish the print surface with a clean soft cloth.

Texturing Prints

Besides texture screens that are used while enlarging, there are several methods for texturing a print surface after the photo paper has been processed. Lacquer sprays can be applied and brushed to give a painted look to color prints. Special sprays and brush work will even give an antique oil painting appearance to your color photographs. Another way to imitate the art look is to use a palette knife to apply a clear gelatin substance along the lines of your subject. One company that makes a variety of print-finishing products stocked by camera stores is McDonald Photo Products, Inc., 2522 Butler St., Dallas, Texas 75235.

Resin-coated papers can be embossed after processing to add unique surface textures to RC prints. Always use minimum pressure to avoid cracking the print emulsion. Among the manufacturers of texturing equipment are Coda, Inc., 45 N. Dean St., Englewood, New Jersey 07631, and B. F. Perkins, Inc., P.O. Box 366, Chicopee, Massachusetts 01021.

Mounting Prints

Mounting prints, especially enlargements, will give them extra support and durability, and prevent wrinkling and curling. When borders are included, mounts also enhance the prints by separating them from their surroundings.

There are several products that can be used for mounting prints: dry mounting tissue, either heat-sealing or self-sticking; photo spray glues; and mounting cement. Ordinary glues are not recommended for mounting photographs because they will eventually affect the print's image or bleed through the paper, and because their bonding is inadequate. Never use rubber cement to mount photographs. Kodak Rapid Mounting Cement can be used to secure small prints in photo albums, but there are better mounting methods for enlargements.

Probably the most popular and permanent bonding method is heat-sealed *dry mounting*. In order to dry-mount a print you must use dry mounting tissue, which looks like a piece of glossy waxed paper but contains an adhesive that melts when heated. A hot *dry mount press* does this best, but the tissue can also be applied with heat from a household iron. Brands of heat-sealing mounting tissue include Kodak's Dry Mounting Tissue, Type 2, and Seal's Colormount, MT5, and Fotoflat.

The self-sticking type of dry mounting tissue requires no heat, just pressure, and it is especially recommended for color prints because heat can change their dye colors and damage the emulsion, especially resin-coated and Cibachrome papers. It works well on nonporous mount surfaces. Two brands of self-sticking mounting tissue are Falcon's Perma/Mount 2 and 3M's Scotch Brand Positionable Mounting Adhesive Sheets.

Before describing the procedure for using dry mounting tissue, the types of *mounts* must be considered. The most common is mat board that is sold in art supply stores and many camera shops. Some are precut to standard photo paper sizes, such as 8 x 10, 11 x 14, and 16 x 20 inches, and these are fine for bleed or flush mounting. If you want a border around the print, buy an oversized piece of mat board.

Prints that are mounted with their edges flush with the mount board are called *bleed mounts* or *flush mounts*. When such prints are not framed, they can still be displayed in an effective way. Begin by bleed mounting the print on double weight mount board or Masonite, then sandpaper the edges to make them smooth. Next, blacken the edges with a felt-tipped marker so they don't stand out, and glue small pieces of wood as spacers onto the back of the mount. When the print is hung, the spacers keep it one-half to one inch away

 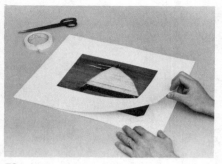

72. An easy way to mount Cibachrome and RC prints is to use an acid-free tape to secure the print to a backing board.

73. Afterward, a window mat is placed in position to cover the tape and frame the photograph.

from the wall, and this makes the display of the photograph quite impressive.

Prints are often mounted between two pieces of board—solid *backing board* and an *overlay board* or *window mat* that frames the photograph. Sometimes these can be bought as sets in camera stores, or you can cut your own overlay mats with a special mat cutter sold at art supply stores.

Colors of the mats are another concern, although white, cream, black, and gray boards are the most common. Sometimes you can match the dominating color in a color print to an appropriately colored mat board, which is a matter of personal taste.

The backing board can be of various thickness and materials, including mat board, Masonite, plastic, and smoothly sanded plywood. For archival permanence of mounted photographs, 100 percent rag, acid-free mounting boards are recommended, such as Bainbridge Museum Board and Stratmore Drawing Board.

If you are using heat-seal dry mounting tissue to mount prints to their backing boards, follow the procedures below.

First, attach a slightly oversized piece of tissue to the back of the print with a heated *tacking iron*. If you do not have a tacking iron, use a regular iron on the lowest synthetic setting and press its tip against the tissue near the center of the print. (Drain any water from the iron, if a steam type, to avoid steam that will damage the print.)

When the tissue is tacked to the back of the print, trim the print, if necessary, and the excess mount tissue together. A rotary blade paper cutter works best, although a razor and a straightedge ruler will do if you are careful. Be sure to hold the print down along the cutting edge, otherwise the tissue and the print might be trimmed unevenly.

Remove any moisture from the mount board by placing it in a dry mount press, or by ironing it. Use cover papers, such as brown kraft paper, or thin cardboard, which should also be dried out for use again later.

Once the mount board is dry and flat, align the print. Press the print in its center, then lift up one of its corners and use the iron to tack the tissue to the mount. Do this at each corner by tacking directly on the tissue; do not tack by pressing the iron on the print's surface.

When the print is tacked to the mount board, place it into a dry mount press between two cover papers. These protect the surfaces of the print from direct heat and dry mount press platen that might be dirty. Dirt or other particles that get between the surfaces of the print and the platen of the press will cause indentations in the print, while particles that get between the mount board and the print will cause small raised areas in the print.

For color and RC prints, the press should be preheated to a temperature range of 180° to 210°F (82° to 99°C); it can be hotter for black-and-white prints on conventional papers. Lower the press platen and apply pressure for 30 seconds for color and RC prints, and up to 60 seconds for black-and-white prints on conventional papers. Take the finished print out to cool, facedown.

If you mount the prints with a iron, use the cover papers and start in the

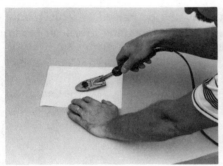

74. *To dry mount a photograph, first tack the heat-seal tissue to the back of the print with a hot tacking iron.*

75. *With a paper cutter, carefully trim the tissue and print together, using a piece of cardboard to hold them flat.*

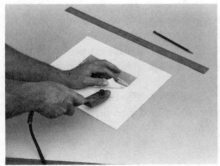

76. *Use a ruler to position the print on the mount board, and then tack each corner of the tissue to the board.*

77. *Finally, place the board and print in a preheated dry mount press which will smoothly bond them together.*

center of the print on the iron's lowest synthetic heat setting. Carefully iron out toward the edges of the print, trying to maintain an even pressure. Remember to preiron the cover papers, or moisture could cause them to stick to your print and ruin it. Dry mount presses do the job better than irons because they apply even heat and pressure. Ask at larger camera stores if they have a press available for customer use.

For photographers without access to a dry mount press, and for those who've had little success dry mounting with an iron, *photo spray glues* solve the problem of mounting prints. There are several brands available, including 3M's Scotch Brand Photomount Adhesive, and McDonald Photo Product's Lamin-All.

After trimming the print, spray the adhesive uniformly on the print's back. Be sure the coat covers the edges completely so the print will not peel up from the mount board later. Align the print after the glue is tacky, and press into position by beginning at one end. Cover the print with a clean piece of paper, then rub or roll over its surface to make sure there is good contact with the mount.

If desired, prints mounted with Lamin-All can be heated in a dry mount press to seal the bond. It can also be used for mounting prints on fabric, without heat. And by removing the bottom layer of resin coating from an RC print, you can use Lamin-All to mount a photograph on canvas or rough wood to give it a special texture.

Large prints, particularly photo murals, are usually *wet-mounted* on hardboard with water soluble glue. The procedure is described in detail in the following chapter.

Titling Prints

Some photographers like to title or to sign the prints they intend to display. Most often this is done with a pencil or India ink on the mount board rather than the print itself. If you write on the print, do it carefully so not to damage the emulsion, and coat the print afterward with a spray lacquer. Some portrait studios emboss their names on prints with a hand letter press and gold or silver foil. When writing on mount boards, titling usually begins flush with the left edge of the print; your name or signature should end flush with the right edge of the print.

Framing Prints

Once they are mounted, prints can be displayed impressively and safely by framing them. Frames protect photographs and also set them off from their surroundings. You have a wide choice of frames, from simple slip-in types to plexiglass boxes to aluminum and wood frames. Frames frequently cost more than the actual photographs being framed, so shop wisely or consider making the frames yourself.

Regardless of the type of frame you select for a particular photograph, there are other aspects of framing to consider. Prints should be mounted on a backing board so they won't wrinkle or curl. If a glass is not used in the frame, the photograph should be treated with a photo lacquer spray. When glass or a plastic-faced frame is used, the photograph should be separated from the glass or plastic with an overlay mount or window mat. If this is not done, the print should be lacquered to protect its emulsion and keep it from sticking to the glass or plastic.

Other than ordinary window glass, you can purchase *nonreflecting glass,* such as Tru-Site, which makes it easier to view the photograph. If such glass is used, the print must touch it or the image will be somewhat diffused; spray the print with photo lacquer before putting it in contact with the nonreflecting glass.

Framing behind glass absorbs the harmful *ultraviolet light* that causes color photographs to fade. Sunlight and fluorescent light are especially high in ultraviolet radiation, so try to use other types of light to illuminate your photographs. Air pollution is damaging to photographs, too, as are paint fumes. The peroxide in bleached, unpainted wood frames will also attack print images.

Art supply stores, portrait studios, and specialized framing shops carry the widest selections of ready-made frames and do-it-yourself framing materials. Especially popular are prepackaged pairs of aluminum molding in various lengths and finishes that can be assembled easily into most any size frame you desire. Wood frame moldings are also sold in precut lengths, which you can glue and nail together at home. To cut long molding strips to the precise angle for jointing together, use a miter box and saw.

While not really frames, there are *picture brackets* that will hold together a mounted photograph and its window mat and cover glass so they can be hung on a wall. These brackets attach at top and bottom, or slip over the corners.

Regardless of your framing methods, you should do the job carefully, after considering in advance where the photograph will be hung. Its intended location should help you decide the appropriate mat size, color, and what type of frame will show off your print to its best advantage.

16

Experimenting with Special Techniques

You will spend many fascinating and enjoyable hours in the darkroom while learning the procedures for processing and printing in black-and-white and color. After a while, however, developing films and making prints will become almost second nature, and undoubtedly you will be eager to try something new. Many ideas for expanding your processing and printing abilities are offered in this chapter, with how-to-do-it details. Included are a number of special techniques that are worth knowing. Remember that part of the excitement of photography is the chance to express your own creativity, so don't be afraid to experiment and to develop your own personal approach to producing images.

Making Black-and-White Prints from Color Negatives

Some photographers wonder whether they can expose color negatives on regular black-and-white photo paper, such as Kodabromide, and get an acceptable black-and-white print. Try it and you'll discover it works! However, close inspection of the print will show that the gray tones in the print seem unnatural. Usually, blues appear too light while reds and yellows seem too dark.

You can avoid this problem by printing color negatives on a special paper, Kodak's *Panalure*. It is sensitive to all colors, instead of just blue, the color of light to which regular black-and-white papers are mainly sensitive. That means Panalure papers produce a print from a color negative in appropriate gray tones, just as if you shot the picture with regular black-and-white film.

Another bonus with Panalure paper is that you change a print's tones by using filters with the enlarger during exposure, just as you can use them over the camera lens while shooting black-and-white films (see the chapter on filters in my companion Plume paperback, *The Basic Book of Photography*).

Use color printing (CP) filters in the enlarger's filter drawer for subtle changes or place regular camera filters over the enlarger lens to effect a

78. *Color negatives printed on regular enlarging papers do not produce tones identical to those produced by black-and-white negatives because the papers do not have the same sensitivity to colors.*

79. *The proper tones will be evident, however, when the color negative is printed on Kodak's Panalure paper. In this comparison, especially notice the improvement in facial tone, the baseball cap, and the uniform emblem and lettering. Even the bike in the background has changed tone.*

considerable change in the print's tones. To lighten a gray tone, use a filter color that is *similar* to the actual color you want to change; to darken a gray tone, use a filter color that is *complementary* to the actual color of the subject (see page 176). Beware, however, that filter correction for one color also changes the gray tones of the other colors in your picture.

There are three types of Panalure paper. Kodak's Panalure II RC is medium-weight with a water-resistant base, smooth, glossy (F) surface, and a warm-black image tone. It has a developer-incorporated emulsion and can be developed, fixed, and washed in trays in less than 8 minutes. Panalure F is single-weight, with a smooth, glossy surface, and a warm-black image tone. Recommended development is in Kodak's Dektol or Ektaflo, Type 1, developers for 1½ minutes at 68°F. Panalure Portrait E is double-weight paper, with a fine-grained lustre surface, and a brown-black image tone. Recommended development is in Kodak's Selectol or Ektaflo, Type 2, developers for 2 minutes at 68°F. The other processing steps (stop bath, fixer, wash, and dry) are done just as for normal black-and-white papers. Make a test print to determine proper exposure with your specific enlarger. If print contrast is too high, use Selectol-Soft developer.

A special consideration is that Panalure paper can be fogged by safelight because its emulsion is sensitive to all colors of light. For this reason, process in total darkness, or use a dark amber (No. 13) safelight filter with a 7½-watt bulb at least 4 feet from the paper. Keep Panalure prints submerged in the processing solutions when using a safelight, and do not develop them by inspection.

Making Black-and-White Transparencies

At one time or another, you may want to have black-and-white transparencies instead of prints. If you already have a black-and-white print, you can copy it with color transparency film and get a black-and-white slide.

More often, photographers use Kodak's Direct Positive Panchromatic, Type 5246 film or Panatomic-X film to shoot original pictures or copy an existing photograph. When these films are processed in Kodak's *Direct Positive Film Developing Outfit*, the images are chemically reversed from negative to positive to produce a black-and-white transparency.

Shoot these films as you normally do other black-and-white films. Direct Positive Panchromatic film is available only in 35mm 100-foot rolls, so you'll have to bulk-load it into individual 35mm cassettes. Its film speeds are ASA 80 for daylight and ASA 64 for tungsten.

Panatomic-X is available in twenty- and thirty-six-exposure 35mm cassettes. Or you can get 120-size, which is called Panatomic-X Professional film. Normal speed of Panatomic-X as a negative film is ASA 32, but directions with the processing kit recommend ASA 80 when shooting it as a transparency film. However, many photographers find their exposure results are best when rating Panatomic-X film at ASA 125.

The Direct Positive Film Developing Outfit will process eight rolls of thirty-six-exposure 35mm film or equivalent. It consists of four chemicals and complete instructions. Below is a summary of the procedure and processing times when solutions are at 68°F (20°C).

Step	Time (Min.)
1. First developer	6—9*
2. Water rinse	2—5†
3. Bleach	1
4. Clearing bath	2
5. Redeveloper	8
6. Water rinse	1
7. Fixer††	5
8. Wash	20**

*Actual first developer time depends on processing equipment and agitation; suggest giving "normal" agitation (30 seconds' initial agitation, then 5 seconds' agitation every 30 seconds thereafter), and use 6 minutes developer time.
†With running water and agitation, 2 minutes is adequate.
**When a clearing agent is used, wash time can be shortened considerably.
††Fixer is not provided in the processing outfit; use your normal fixer for black-and-white films.

Follow the processing kit's instructions carefully. Especially note that all steps must be carried out in total darkness until the bleach step is completed. After that, a greenish yellow (OA) safelight filter with a 15-watt bulb can be used 4 feet from the film. Do not turn on white lights until the film is out of the fixer.

To project your processed transparencies, cut them apart and put them in cardboard, plastic, or glass slide mounts, available at camera stores.

Making Photo Murals

Making a very large black-and-white print, often called a *photo mural,* is not as difficult as it may seem. You need more space than usual for exposing and processing, and some additional materials, but the excitement and satisfaction of producing an extra big print is worth your efforts.

Several companies manufacture mural-size photo paper. Very popular is Kodak Mural paper, which you can buy in 3½-foot-wide rolls that are 30 or 100 feet long. Despite being single weight, the paper resists abrasion caused by folding and wrinkling that may occur in handling. It has a rough tweed surface on cream white stock, and gives a warm-black image tone.

Your negatives must be of good contrast because the mural paper is only available in contrast grades No. 2 and No. 3. Normal OC (light amber) safelights can be used. Choose a developer designed for warm-tone papers, such as Kodak's Selectol or Ektonol.

Processing equipment and methods are special considerations. For occasional photo mural making, three makeshift trays (for developer, stop bath, and fixer) can be constructed on the floor of a light-tight room. Use 2 x 4-inch boards to form three frames a little larger than the size of your print, then line each of them with a durable piece of plastic. Use sponges or mops to make sure the mural paper gets thoroughly covered and agitated with chemicals during processing. You can wash the prints in a bathtub, or in a small plastic wading pool. This system is inconvenient but works well.

An alternate and easier method to use involves three wooden troughs covered and sealed with fiberglass. Each should be about 4 feet long, 7 inches wide, and 6 inches deep. These take less room and waste less chemistry than large makeshift trays.

To process a print, roll up the exposed piece of photo paper and insert the leading edge into the developer trough, emulsion side up. Then reroll the paper inside the trough until all of it has come in contact with the developer. Continue with this rerolling procedure throughout the developer time, and in the other processing steps. By rerolling from one end and then the other, the paper receives adequate agitation and even development. After the stop bath and fixer steps, bathe the paper in a clearing agent, using the same rerolling technique, and then follow with a running water wash in one of the troughs or in a large sink or bathtub.

You can buy processing tanks designed especially for large prints. One such product is the Maxwell Photo-Mural Tank, for processing prints up to 30 x 40 inches. These are available through camera stores, or you can write directly to Maxwell Photo-Mural Tanks, 999 E. Valley Blvd., Alhambra, California 91801.

Tanks like the Maxwell type are light-tight tubes with an apron. The photo paper is rolled up in the apron, which keeps the paper from sticking to itself and allows chemicals to cover its emulsion.

Your enlarger may need modification to project a mural-size image. Some models have an optional extension support column that enables the enlarger's head to be raised a greater distance from its baseboard. Other enlargers are designed so the head can be rotated 90 degrees to project onto a vertical plane, such as a wall. And some can be rotated at the baseboard so the image will project past the tabletop and on to the darkroom floor.

If you can not get enough distance between the enlarger and photo paper to produce an image as large as you wish, it is necessary to buy or make a right angle projection attachment. This is a *front-coated mirror* mounted at a 45-degree angle below the enlarger lens. When your negative is projected onto this mirror, the image reflects onto the mural paper secured to a vertical support, such as a wall. (Be sure to put the negative in the carrier emulsion side *up,* because the mirror reverses the projected image.)

For focusing and cropping, project the image on a piece of plain paper cut to the size of your intended print. Be sure to allow at least two extra inches on every side for use when mounting the print.

Cut a small piece of mural paper from the roll and make a test exposure. Remember that the enlarger's light has to travel a considerable distance for such large image projections, so expect a long exposure—perhaps even several minutes. Be careful your negative does not buckle from enlarger bulb heat during the long exposure, or else your image will pop out of focus; use a glass negative carrier if necessary. Also, any vibration during exposure will cause a fuzzy image; be sure your enlarger is sturdy and that you remain stationary during exposure.

For exposing the actual print, you can fasten the mural paper to the wall with pushpins. And it may be necessary to use a double-sided sticking tape behind the center area so that the paper stays flat. Once exposed, processed, and washed, lay the print on a smooth flat surface and squeegee away the excess water. Use clips to hang the print up to dry, and put weights along the bottom so it will not curl.

If you plan to *wet mount* the mural print, it's easier to begin right after the wash step. Since very few photographers have access to a dry mounting press large enough to mount photo murals, most photographers use a wet mounting process. You'll need a piece of one-half- or one-fourth-inch thick Masonite board cut to the size of the print. Also required are a white glue, such as Elmer's or Wilhold (or you can mix some wheat paste glue); a brush for applying the glue; a squeegee or print roller; 1 x 2-inch boards to make a framework for the Masonite; finishing nails and wood glue; knife or scissors; brown kraft paper; and a sponge with a container of water.

Once the Masonite is cut and its edges sanded, wipe it completely with a wet sponge. Then cut a piece of kraft paper to size for mounting on one side of the board. After applying glue liberally to the Masonite and wetting the kraft paper, lay the paper on the Masonite and begin squeegeeing out the excess glue.

The next step is to prepare the mural print. If it has dried, you must soak it in water. Once the paper is wet enough, squeegee away the excess water, and position the print on the Masonite. The print should be large enough to overlap the Masonite with a 2-inch border all the way around. Cut the paper at an angle at each corner so the borders will not overlap each other when folded over.

Remove the print and apply an even coat of glue to the Masonite. Then lay the print back in place and start to squeegee, from the center outward. Apply glue to the overhanging edges of the print and press them onto the back of the Masonite with a damp sponge. Be very careful not to get glue on the surface of the print, because it will show when it dries. Wipe off any excess glue and place the mounted print so that air can reach both surfaces at once in order to speed drying.

When the print is thoroughly dry, attach the 1 x 2-inch boards to the back of the Masonite by using wood glue. Strengthen the frame's corners with the finishing nails. Besides giving support to the Masonite and helping to prevent bowing, the frame sets off the photo mural from the wall and improves its display.

Working with the Zone System

By using the Zone System, you can calculate exposure and plan the development of a negative in order to get a black-and-white print that has the specific qualities you envisioned when taking the photograph. The Zone System is something that many photographers experiment with and then adopt. Beginning photographers especially hold the Zone System and its originator, Ansel Adams, in awe; many let his system totally control their photographic efforts. Whatever your feelings about the Zone System, its principles can improve the quality of your black-and-white work, and even your color photography.

In general, the Zone System takes the trial and error out of exposure because you learn to identify the tones of a subject or scene and previsualize how you want them to look in your print.

The Zone System was developed by Ansel Adams in the early 1940s as part of his personal method of photographing and printing. Basically, Adams adapted the photographic gray scale. The distinct shades of gray that range from black to white were called "zones" by Adams, and are identified by numbers (Roman numerals) 0 to IX.

As described by Adams, the zones form three main groups: Low Values (dark tones)—Zones 0, I, II, III; Middle Values—Zones IV, V, VI; and High Values (bright tones)—Zones VII, VIII, IX. His explanation follows.

Low Values	
Zone 0.	Complete lack of density in the negative image, other than filmbase density plus fog. Total black in print.
Zone I.	Effective threshold. First step above complete black in print. Slight tonality, but no texture.
Zone II.	First suggestion of texture. Deep tonalities, representing the darkest part of the image in which some detail is required.
Zone III.	Average dark materials. Low values showing adequate texture.
Middle Values	
Zone IV.	Recommended shadow value for portraits in sunlight. Average dark foliage. Dark stone. Landscape shadow.
Zone V.	Middle gray (18 percent reflectance). Clear north sky with panchromatic films. Dark skin. Gray stone. Average weathered wood.
Zone VI.	Average Caucasian skin value in sunlight or artificial light, and in diffuse skylight or very soft light. Light stone. Shadows on snow in sunlit snowscapes.
High Values	
Zone VII.	Very light skin. Light gray objects. Average snow with acute side lighting.
Zone VIII.	Whites with textures and delicate values (not blank whites). Snow in full shade. Highlights on Caucasian skin.
Zone IX.	Glaring white surfaces. Snow in flat sunlight. White without texture. (The only subjects higher than Zone IX would be light sources, either actual or reflected; but they would obviously be rendered in the print as maximum white values of the paper surface.)

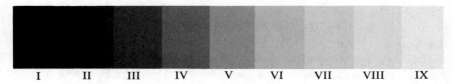

| I | II | III | IV | V | VI | VII | VIII | IX |

80. *A gray scale can be numbered to identify the various tones that are important in the Zone System.*

Knowledge and use of the Zone System will enable you to accurately control metering, film exposure, and development. This, in turn, gives you the potential to previsualize a subject or scene in terms of the final tonal values you want in the print.

Exposure meters read uniform tones as Zone V, even if the subject is all white or all black. (Zone V is *the middle value* of the gray scale, and represents an 18 percent reflectance value). This means if you took a meter reading of a white cat (or black cat) and exposed your film according to that meter reading, you will produce a negative that recorded the white cat (or black cat) as medium gray.

Of course, you can make a print from that negative which will show the cat as white (or black), because photo papers have various grades of contrast which offer enough latitude to make such corrections. However, to print the white or black cat with the medium gray negative, you'll sacrifice some of the other tonal values in the picture.

On the other hand, if you exposed the cat according to the principles of the Zone System, you would have gotten a negative that was much easier to print for the white (or black) cat, plus get a better range of tones and detail overall. Your approach, using the Zone System, would have been to study the scene and determine what zone (tone) the cat was, and what zone (tone) you wished it to be in the print. In other words, you previsualize the result you want.

Normally, a white cat that you want to record with texture and subtle values would be Zone VIII, while a black cat with similar texture would be a Zone III. Because you know your exposure meter will only indicate a Zone V when reading either cat, you have to do a little computation in order to make the best exposure.

For the white cat to record as Zone VIII, you have to make an exposure adjustment of three f/stops. If your meter indicates a Zone V reading of f/11 at 1/125 second, make your exposure at f/4 at 1/125 second. This is three stops more exposure, which means you build up density in the negative, and that will give you a whiter cat.

For the black cat, you would give two stops less exposure to put it in Zone III rather than Zone V, which means shooting at f/22 at /125 second instead of f/11 at 1/125 second.

What happens to the other values in the scene if you change the exposures that much? They will be affected in the same proportion as the cat. Consequently, it is important when using the Zone System to consider the tonal relationships of everything you consider important in your photograph. If some things in the scene would be changed too much by the exposure you choose for a specific zone, it may be necessary for you to make a compromise exposure.

However, photographers who are faithful to the Zone System will adjust their film developer time to either "expand" or "contract" the contrast ratio of the subsequent negative. They do this in order to achieve the zone they want in the final print without changing the other tonal relationships. This expansion and contraction amounts to understanding how to control exposures so you can increase or decrease development in order to compensate for photographic situations with unusual contrast or tone values.

Altering developer time to control contrast is easiest for photographers who use sheet film. For photographers using roll film, it is awkward to apply the expansion and contraction concept. That's because usually you have more than one shooting situation on each roll, and if you adjust for one situation you have to adjust for them all.

Regardless, you can make use of the principles of the Zone System because they make it easier for you to visualize how things will appear in the print. Also, after doing Zone System tests, you can reduce many exposures and

81. *Users of the Zone System learn to "read" a scene they are going to photograph and assign it various tonal values (i.e. zones) so they can previsualize how the final print will look.*

processing variables, and therefore systemize your methods in order to have more control of all your black-and-white results.

The tests will help you find the proper ASA to use with a particular film, exposure meter (hand-held or built in the camera), and film developer. Because a film's published speed (ASA) is only an average, using an ASA that is different than the normal rated speed of your film may give you better results.

The tests also will help determine the proper film developer time you should be using for that film. The times published for developers are only average times; to get the best results you should test for the time that is best for your equipment and working methods.

In addition, the tests will enable you to establish a method for making a proper proof print, and this in turn becomes a means for determining whether your film exposures were correct or not.

A standard printing time is another thing that these tests will help you establish. This means your properly exposed and processed negatives will always produce an acceptable print without additional exposure tests.

The discussion presented here was only a simple summary of the Zone System. For a detailed explanation, and directions for making Zone System tests, you should read Ansel Adams' *Basic Photo Series,* Minor White's *Zone System Manual,* or Fred Picker's *Zone VI Workshop;* the latter book is especially helpful for photographers who use roll films, including 35mm.

Copying Prints and Slides

Many times photographers want to copy a picture, artwork, map, document, or other flat, two-dimensional object. Or you may have a need for duplicate slides. Reflex or view-type cameras are preferred for *photocopying* because they make framing and focusing easy. For close-up copy work, a macro lens is ideal, or you may need extension rings or tubes, or a bellows, to use with your camera lens and/or supplemental close-up lenses.

Always aim the camera squarely at the flat subject so it is parallel to the film plane. This allows uniformly sharp focus and no distortion. A tripod is suggested to maintain framing and focus.

Material to be copied can be mounted vertically on a wall or laid flat on a table or the ground. Some tripods have elevator posts which can be reversed to allow the camera to be mounted underneath the tripod. This keeps the tripod legs out of your picture when shooting down on flat copy work.

Lighting of copied subjects must be uniform. Often outdoor illumination is very good, but be careful no shadows fall on your subject. If the object to be copied is shiny or covered by glass, use a *polarizing filter* to diminish or eliminate reflections and glare.

Inside, make your copies in a darkened room. If you still get reflections, hide your camera, tripod, and yourself behind a piece of black cloth. Cut a hole in the cloth for the lens to slip through. Another idea, when copying smaller items, is to use a piece of black cardboard instead of black cloth. Cut a hole for the lens, then secure the cardboard with tape or a filter holder that screws to the lens.

When copying indoors, use two *identical* studio or movie lights with a color temperature of 3200 *Kelvins (K),* photoflood lamps (3400K), or electronic flash units. Tungsten color films are color-balanced for 3200K illumination or you can use *light-balancing filters* so color tungsten films can be used with photofloods. (There are two types of photofloods—No. 1, and a bulb that's twice as bright, No. 2.) Electronic flash units are color-balanced for daylight color films.

Place the twin light sources at equal distances on either side of the camera at a 45-degree angle to the subject. As a quick check for evenness of illumination with the tungsten lights, hold a pencil, ruler, or a similar object perpendicular against the copy work and see if the shadows it causes are equal in density. If you are copying oil paintings and see tiny glare spots reflecting from dabs of paint, move your lights farther away from the painting while maintaining the 45-degree angle and equal distance. As the light broadens, glare is reduced.

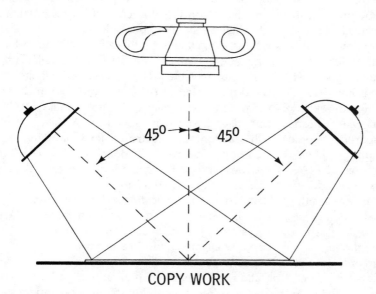

COPY WORK

82. Proper placement of lights for copying photographs or other flat artwork.

Always use a light meter to determine exposure, and make sure it reads only the subject area to be copied. Some photographers make readings off the standard 18 percent reflectance gray card. A hand-held meter gives you more freedom for making exposure than a meter built in a camera that's on a tripod.

There is a special film for copying line drawings, documents, books, newspapers, maps, and similar material that may be large originals and must be reproduced in smaller scale. Use Kodak's High Contrast Copy film, rated for tungsten light at ASA 64. It's available in 35mm thirty-six-exposure rolls. An alternative is another film with a relatively slow speed, Panatomic-X, rated at ASA 32. Both these films give good contrast and sharp detail with very little graininess.

Medium speed films, such as Plus-X (ASA 125), are preferred for copying photographs, paintings, and other artwork because they help preserve the shadows and highlights of the original.

For color copies with color negative film, try Kodak's Vericolor II Professional films. Type S, rated at ASA 100, is balanced for daylight or electronic flash exposures, with exposure times of 1/10 or faster. It is available in both 35mm and 120 sizes. For use with photofloods, use ASA 32 and a No. 80B light-balancing filter.

Type L Vericolor film is balanced for tungsten light of 3200K illumination. This film is for slower exposure times, ranging from 1/50 second to 60 seconds. Film speed varies according to exposure time; for shutter speeds from 1/50 to 1/5 seconds, use the ASA 80. With photofloods (3400K), use ASA 50 and light-balancing filter No. 81A. Vericolor II Professional, Type L film is available in 120 roll film and sheet film sizes only.

For copying with color transparency film, try these films with tungsten light, balanced for 3200K illumination: Ektachrome 50 Professional (Tungsten) with a film speed of ASA 50 and available in 35mm and 120 roll film sizes, or Ektachrome 160 (Tungsten) film, rated at ASA 160 and sold in 35mm size only. To use either Ektachrome tungsten film with photofloods (3400K), use a No. 81A light-balancing filter and a film speed of ASA 40. For color transparency copies with daylight or electronic flash illumination, use daylight-type films: Kodachrome 25 (ASA 25), Kodachrome 64 (ASA 64), or Ektachrome 64 (ASA 64). These are available in 35mm size, and Ektachrome 64 comes in additional sizes, including 120 roll film.

There are a variety of techniques for *duplicating slides*. For direct copying, a special *slide-copier* can be purchased to attach to your camera. Daylight, electronic flash, or tungsten lights are used for illumination. Other photographers simply copy a reflected slide image projected on a normal screen or a piece of white poster board.

Successful slide duplication takes experimentation and patience. To start, make sure the slide is clean and free of dust. Fingerprints or smudges can be removed by removing the slide from its mount and carefully applying a liquid *film cleaner* with cotton.

Copies of slides can be straight duplicates, with life-size one-to-one (1:1) copying ratio, or you can crop the original slide to improve it when you make the duplicate. With the use of filters, color balance can be improved or made bizarre, and you can increase contrast and the richness of the original colors.

The main problem, if you want the duplicate slide to be identical to the original, is getting good *color balance*. The film must be matched with the illumination you use. Some photographers copy with regular daylight-type film of slow speed, such as Kodachrome 25 or Ektachrome 64, and use daylight reflected off a white cardboard to provide color-balanced illumination. Others set up their electronic flash to provide color-balanced light for daylight films.

There is a special film for tungsten (3200K) illumination, Kodak Ektachrome Slide Duplicating Film 5071. It is available in thirty-six-exposure 35mm cassettes and 100-foot 35mm rolls for bulk loading. The film can be developed in home darkrooms with Kodak's Process E-6.

Some filtration may be required for correct color balance. Kodak suggests a 10M (magenta) filter between the transparency and light source when copying Kodachrome slides; a 20R (red) for older Ektachromes such as Ektachrome-X and High Speed Ektachrome; and 10R (red) + 10M (magenta) filtration when duplicating E-6 Ektachrome films. The ASA suggested when using this film with a 35mm single lens reflex camera equipped with a slide duplicating attachment is ASA 8. Electronic flash can be used as the illumination source, with appropriate filtration. Study the film's instruction sheet.

After processing, always carefully compare your duplicate slides with the original, and use the chart on page 245 for figuring filter corrections if the color balance is off.

Using and Processing Infrared Films

Infrared photography can be fun as well as practical, and both black-and-white and color infrared films are available. The first has long been used in aerial and landscape photography to penetrate and eliminate haze. Such film has also been applied to scientific, medical, and technical use, including the field of criminology. As such, infrared film helps detect bloodstains, fingerprints, and forgeries. Another use is the determination of authenticity of paintings by art galleries and museums. The reason is that infrared film "sees" what normal films do not.

To help detect military use of camouflage, color infrared film was developed. Living plants and trees give off infrared rays different from those of dead or fake foliage commonly used for camouflage. An aerial photograph on color infrared film will indicate what is real and what isn't. For amateur photographers, color infrared film produces startling colors unlike those recorded by ordinary color films. The results will surprise you.

Infrared films register nonvisible infrared and visible light rays. Therefore ASA film speed ratings do not apply as normally because exposure meters do not react to infrared rays as they do light rays. Only suggested exposure guides are given in the films' instruction sheets. Experience determines the best exposure for specific situations. Bracketing is always recommended. Shoot at least one f/stop on either side of the f/stop which you think will give the best exposure. Unless you are experimenting, infrared films should always be used with a filter—red for black-and-white and yellow or any other color for color. However, filter factors are not applied as with regular films. Here are more specific details for each type of film.

Infrared film that yields negatives for making black-and-white prints is Kodak High Speed Infrared film. It eliminates atmospheric haze and turns skies black while making grass green and trees white. It is available in twenty-exposure 35mm size only. A No. 25 filter (Kodak Wratten A) is recommended for general photography, although a No. 29 (Kodak Wratten F) can be substituted. The film can be used with daylight, electronic flash, clear flashbulbs, or photoflood lamps. With electronic flash, a No. 87 filter is best.

Pictures made in darkness without the subject being aware are possible when this infrared film is exposed by infrared flashbulbs. These bulbs provide no visible light but your subject will be recorded on film. Infrared bulbs usually must be specially ordered by your camera store. Without such bulbs, a special filter can be used over your regular electronic unit or flashbulb reflector. When using infrared flashbulbs or a filter on flash units, a No. 25 filter on the camera lens is not required.

With more normal illumination, the suggested guide for making trial exposures with Kodak's black-and-white infrared film is a film speed of ASA 50 for daylight and ASA 125 for tungsten light. But be sure to bracket. With two 500-watt reflector-type photoflood lamps, suggested trial exposures at 1/30 second are f/11 with lamp-to-subject at 3 feet, f/8 at 4½ feet, and f/5.6 when the lights are 6½ feet from the subject. Suggested guide numbers for electronic flash and flashbulbs vary according to the flash unit's light output. The film's instruction sheet lists these guide numbers and gives more details.

The film must be developed in *total darkness* according to instructions on the same sheet. The processing procedure is identical to regular black-and-white film processing: developer, stop bath, fixer, and wash. For general infrared photography, develop the film for 11 minutes at 68°F

(20°C) in D-76. To get negatives with maximum contrast, develop the film in D-19 for 6 minutes.

Because of the sensitivity of this film, be sure to open the film can and load and unload your camera in *total darkness* (a changing bag makes this more convenient).

Focusing black-and-white infrared film is different from focusing regular films, since infrared rays do not focus in the same plane as visible light rays. Some camera lenses have a special *infrared focusing mark,* usually a red line or R on the focusing scale. Focus your subject as normally, then move the focusing ring for that distance to the infrared focus mark. Without such a mark on your lens, focus on the closest point of the main subject. Or use very small f/stop openings at the normal focus mark.

For making infrared color pictures, use Kodak Ektachrome Infrared film. It is available only in twenty-exposure 35mm size cassettes and yields color slide transparencies. A yellow No. 12 filter is recommended, although the more common yellow No. 15 filter (Kodak Wratten G) will do just as well.

Actually the colors of your subjects on color infrared film are rather unpredictable—that's the reason amateurs find infrared photography fascinating. As examples, some black cloth photographs dark red, faces become green, and lips turn yellow. Scientists, however, have learned to read color distinctions carefully. For instance, to detect diseases in trees, forests are photographed with this film and studied closely. Healthy trees appear red, while those that appear magenta, green, or yellow indicate they are under stress.

Like its black-and-white counterpart, Ektachrome Infrared film should be stored until use in its original sealed package in a refrigerator at 50°F (10°C) or lower. For long periods of storage, keep the film in a freezer at temperatures from 0°F to −10°F. Before use, let the film warm up for at least 4 hours to room temperature to avoid moisture condensation.

As a guide for trial exposures, a film speed of ASA 100 is suggested. But for cameras with built-in through-the-lens light meters, set the ASA dial to 200 and align the exposure meter needles as normally. Bracket exposures on the initial roll of film until you've determined the best film speed setting for your particular subject and hand-held or built-in exposure meter. Besides using sunlight for illumination, exposures also are possible with electronic flash, blue flashbulbs, and photoflood lamps. Study the film's instruction sheet for suggested guide numbers and exposure settings.

Unlike black-and-white infrared film, color infrared film records its sharpest image when the camera is focused in the normal manner. In other words, the special infrared focusing mark on some camera lenses should be disregarded when color infrared film is used.

You can develop Ektachrome Infrared film yourself in E-4 chemistry (see page 168). *Total darkness* is required—also open the film can and load and unload in total darkness.

If you like to experiment, get a roll of black-and-white or color infrared film and be ready for some unusual results. With the first type you'll be surprised—haze is eliminated, the blue sky goes black, and green grass and trees become white. With the color type, any color rendition is possible, depending on the filter you use. Although No. 12 or No. 15 yellow filters are suggested, experiment with other filters, too. You'll see why many photographers find infrared films an exciting change of pace.

Adding Texture to Prints

Some photographers enhance their black-and-white and color pictures by adding texture to the images. You can use a textured paper stock, but the variety of textured printing paper is quite limited, so most photographers use *texture screens*. These are transparent films or plates printed or etched with a fine pattern.

The screens are sandwiched with the negative for projection by the enlarger, or they are placed over the printing paper during exposure. Besides

83. *Photographs sometimes can be enhanced by printing them through a texture screen.*

84. *This print was made with a fine linen texture screen held in contact with the paper in the enlarging easel.*

85. *Especially with portraits, take care not to use a texture pattern that will obliterate too much or conflict with the subject.*

the screens, a variety of other items can also be used to produce texture patterns: cloth, plastic wire screens, lens cleaning tissue, glass, netting—almost anything, as long as the material is translucent.

Texturing relieves the monotony of large areas in a print that have the same tone; it's not suited for subjects that are very intricate or have too much detail. Texture patterns are widely used for portraiture work, and to enhance pictorial effects in scenic pictures.

There are two approaches to using texture screens or materials. One is the *screened print method,* which means laying the texture screen on top of the printing paper when the exposure is made. A piece of clear glass should be used to hold them in good contact. To keep the texture pattern from becoming too dominant, sometimes it is best to keep the screen in place for just a portion of the exposure. This way the image retains its dominance and there is only a faint texture.

The *screened negative method,* the other way to add texture to prints, is done by placing the texture screen or textured material in contact with the negative in the enlarger's negative carrier. The screen may be a commercial one designed for enlarging, or you can use thin fabric like silk or muslin, lens tissue, or some special texture negative that you have made yourself. You can make a texture negative by photographing a pattern, like wood or stone textures, on Kodak High Contrast Copy film or Kodak Kodalith Ortho 6556, Type 3, a graphic arts film that eliminates gray tones to produce a clear negative with black pattern lines.

With a screen in contact with the negative, the texture effect may be softened by using the usual diffusion methods (see page 122). When very fine texture patterns are diffused in this way, they disappear in the shadow areas and show only in the highlight areas of the print.

Be sure that the texture complements the image and does not dominate it. The same texture pattern that you use on a small print will have a completely different effect when used on a large print. Commercially made screens are available for both the screened print and screened negative methods. The small ones used in the screened negative method are designed to be enlarged up to 20 x 24 inches, but give the most satisfying effects when used for 11 x 14, or 8 x 10-inch enlargements. These are inexpensive and easy to use.

Screens designed for the screened print method come in a variety of sizes up to 20 x 24 inches and are much more expensive, but they are preferred by many photographers because there is no loss of quality in the enlargement. A company that makes a wide variety of these products is Tecturefects, 7557 Sunset Blvd., Hollywood, California 90046. They will send you a free pamphlet that shows the various textures their screens create.

Some inexpensive texture screen material for the screened print method is available in art stores. One company, Letterset, which makes press-on type, has a wide variety of texture patterns. These come in 9 x 12-inch sheets, and they must be peeled off their backing sheets and transferred to a piece of clear acetate. Once this is done, you have an inexpensive contact printing texture screen. One caution: These are opaque patterns and will not allow any light to get through them. Consequently, you can keep the screen in place for only part of the exposure, or else it will completely overpower the image.

Remember that a texture screen may cause a slight loss in contrast, so you may want to use a grade of black-and-white paper with higher contrast than you normally would.

(Postprinting texturing methods were described in the previous chapter, including the use of photo spray lacquers and embossing resin-coated [RC] prints.)

Reticulating Films to Make Patterns

Another way to get an overall texture pattern in prints is to reticulate your films. This is usually done during processing by putting the film in hot and cold water baths and solutions, which makes the emulsion swell and shrink and form regular patterns.

86. Reticulation of the negative after initial processing created a number of unusual patterns in this emulsion. It was dipped in a boiling solution of sodium carbonate, then plunged into ice water. Notice that dense areas of the negative produced larger patterns than the less dense areas.

Years ago, reticulation was a common problem when developing films, but with today's films, it rarely happens accidentally. As long as you keep processing chemicals and wash water within a 5°F range, you needn't worry about reticulation. However, the texture effects that are created by reticulation can be quite interesting, and you may want to reticulate film on purpose. Reticulation works especially well with images that have a simple design and are without intricate details.

Any film can be reticulated, black-and-white or color, but once it is done, you cannot return the film to its original condition. So think twice before deciding to reticulate your irreplaceable pictures. One thing you can do is to make a copy of a normal negative or transparency and then reticulate the duplicate.

There are two methods of reticulation. One is to reticulate the film during its initial processing while the other is to reticulate later, after the negatives (black-and-white only) have been processed normally.

To reticulate *black-and-white films* during initial processing, follow these steps. Process the film in the developer as normally. Then rinse the film for 1 minute in a hot acetic stop bath at a temperature between 140° and 150°F. Next, immerse the film for 1 minute in a cold water bath that's below 40°F.

If you want to make reticulation patterns more noticeable, after this cold water step, immerse the film for 1 minute in hot water at 180° to 190°F. Then quickly immerse it in another cold water bath below 40°F.

Finish up by fixing the film as normally, being sure to use a fixer that contains a hardener. After washing, do not use a wetting agent, but dry the negatives quickly with a hand-held hair dryer.

When reticulating *color negative films,* you have a choice of producing a fine or coarse pattern. The fine pattern occurs when you reticulate *before* beginning the color processing steps. Do the following in *total darkness.*

With the color negative film loaded on the developing tank reel, immerse it for 2 minutes in hot water that's 135°F, and agitate gently. Next, plunge the film into ice water and soak it from 1 to 2 minutes. Finally, bring the film to the proper color developer temperature (100°F for C-41 process) by giving it a 15-second bath in water that's the same temperature (i.e. 100°F), then process the film as normally (see page 153).

For reticulation that has a coarse grain, process the color negative film through the developer and bleach steps (with the C-41 process) in *total darkness.* Then immerse the film for 2 minutes in hot running water at 135°F. Next, quickly plunge the film into ice water and soak it for 1 to 2 minutes. Finally, bring the film to proper temperature for the fixer step by giving it a regular water wash at 100°F, then continue the processing steps.

To reticulate *color slide films,* specifically the E-6 Ektachromes, the procedure is done in *total darkness* before beginning the normal processing steps. After loading the film on the developing tank reel, immerse it for 1 minute in a hot water bath at 125° to 130°F, with continuous and gentle agitation. Next, plunge the film into ice water and soak it for 1 minute. Finally, bring the film back to normal processing temperature by rinsing it in water at 100°F. Process as normal in E-6 chemistry (see page 164), but dry the film afterward as quickly as possible by using a hand-held hair dryer.

When you want to reticulate *processed black-and-white negatives,* follow these steps. Soak the negatives for 10 minutes in a 70°F water bath. Then plunge the film for 2 to 3 minutes in a hot alkaline bath at 125° to 130°F. (Dissolve three level tablespoons of sodium carbonate—not bicarbonate—in 8 ounces of water to make the alkaline solution.) Next, plunge the negatives into cold water about 40°F, and let them soak for several minutes. Finally, wash the negatives at 70°F for a few minutes, and dry them quickly with a hand-held hair dryer. By repeating this reticulation process either before or after drying, coarseness of the pattern will increase. Initially, it's a good idea to practice reticulation with negatives or films that are of no value.

Making Prints with Black Borders

Black borders on prints may seem odd, since white borders have been the "standard" for years. However, with some photographs they can be appealing, or serve as a frame to improve the picture.

An easy method for making black borders is the same as described previously for making white borders on color reversal prints (see page 248). After the print's initial exposure, an opaque mask (such as one cut from cardboard) is placed on the photo paper over the image you want to preserve. Remove the black-and-white or color negative from the enlarger's negative carrier, lift up the enlarging easel's border masks, and then reexpose the paper twice as long as the first exposure (double the exposure time *or* open up one f/stop). The borders will now develop black. Be sure the mask is in good contact with the paper or light will leak around the edges and make the black borders fuzzy, as well as fog the image. If necessary, cover the mask with an oversized piece of glass to weigh it down on the paper. If you are making color reversal prints, their borders are initially black, but you can follow the procedure above to make them white.

Having Fun with Photograms

Photograms are pictures you create without using a negative or slide. Opaque or translucent objects are placed in a clever arrangement on photo paper and exposed to light. When the black-and-white paper is processed in the usual way, the objects appear white or gray against a black background. Color print paper offers even greater potential for creative photographers, as shown by the color photogram on the cover of this book.

Historically, some of the first photographic experiments were photograms. But it wasn't until the 1920s that artists such as Christian Schad, Man Ray, and Moholy-Nagy started to make use of the photogram's creative potential. Each of them had his own name for the process: Schad referred to his images as Schadographs; Man Ray, called them Rayographs, and Moholy-Nagy called them light drawings or *photograms.*

The early photographers were confined to working with black-and-white materials. But with today's color processes that have been designed for home darkroom use, abstract expression in color photograms is possible for everyone.

The only items necessary—aside from an enlarger, color paper, and color chemistry—are a dark amber (No. 10) safelight and red, blue, and green gelatin or glass filters. These three filters, which are held under the lens during an exposure, are all you need to produce any color you may desire.

87. *For this simple photogram, a plant was placed on the print paper and exposed to light from an enlarger.*

88. *The photographer put Vaseline on his hand and arm and touched the print paper before arranging toilet paper on top and making an exposure. Various layers of toilet paper produced the various tones, while the Vaseline kept developer from acting on areas touched by his hand and arm.*

An exposure through any primary color filter, such as red, will produce its complement, in this case, cyan. When you expose through blue, you get its complement, yellow, and green produces magenta.

Exposures can be made only through *one* primary filter at a time. Combining any two in one exposure produces black, as no light will strike the paper. But by exposing two primary filters *one after the other,* with equal amounts of light, you can produce the third primary color. Thus by exposing equal amounts of light through red and green filters, you get blue colors in the print. Equal exposures with all three filters produce black on your print.

When making color photograms, process in trays. This gives you the opportunity to view the print as it's developing. It also makes it easy to use *solarization.* Use a color process, such as Beseler's 2-Step Chemistry, which allows processing at variable times and temperatures. Also, after the bleach-fix step, you can see the image almost as it will appear when dry.

Any light source can be used to make color photograms, but an enlarger is the easiest to control. Place an empty negative carrier in it, and position the enlarger at the top of its support column. Stop the lens down two f/stops from

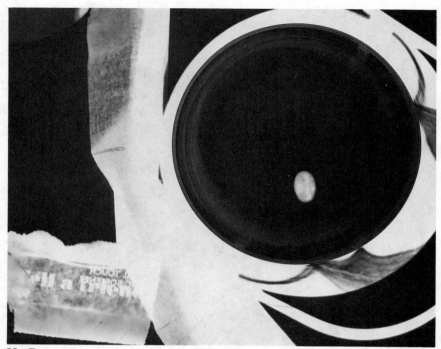

89. Exposure can vary the results of a photogram. A glass bucket, toilet paper, and a piece of newspaper were exposed at f/5.6 for 3 seconds.

its widest opening and then make a series of exposure tests for the primary colors and their complementary colors. Make a test strip of ten to fifteen 1-second exposures for *each* color. Hold the filters, one at a time, under the lens.

For the complementary colors, expose through a red filter to get cyan, a blue filter to get yellow, and a green filter to get magenta.

To make exposure tests for the primary colors, you'll have to make *separate* but equal exposures through two filters to get the third color. In other words, expose separately through red and blue filters to get green, red and green filters to get blue, and blue and green filters to get red.

The color scales produced by these tests will allow you to predict the proper exposure for any intensity of any color, provided the light source is the same.

Use your imagination when choosing objects for making your photograms. Literally anything can be used to form a design—cellophane, bent wire, string, kitchen implements, body parts, feathers, paper of various degrees of translucency cut or torn into different shapes, and organic materials such as parts of plants or food. Polished objects reflect light and make spots and lines of light on the print. Glassware reflects and refracts light in unexpected ways, producing unusual shapes and patterns.

Objects in direct contact with the paper yield sharp-edged silhouettes. Objects which don't come in complete contact with the print surface, such as eggs, allow the light to bleed around them to create subtle color tones, when given long enough exposures.

Photograms are usually considered one-of-a-kind images because it is hard to rearrange objects in the dark exactly as they were before. You can overcome this problem by arranging objects on a thin piece of glass and placing the glass over the photo paper. After exposing, you can remove the glass without disturbing the objects. If you want to make a duplicate photogram, just place the glass and objects on another sheet of photo paper.

You can also use glass to raise the objects above the paper. This will diffuse the image and allow light to bleed around the edges of the objects. Use an oversize piece of glass so it can be supported above the paper with some handy jars or other sturdy objects.

Glass also provides a means of controlling *multiple exposures*. Several pieces of glass are supported above the photo paper, with several inches between each layer, and objects are placed on each layer of glass so that some overlap. An exposure is made, and the top piece of glass is removed.

90. *The same objects gave this result when the exposure was reduced to f/16 for 3 seconds.*

Then another exposure is made which exposes areas previously covered. After removing the second layer of glass, a third exposure is made. The process continues until all of the glass layers have been removed.

When using this process, it is very important to calculate your exposure times before you begin. To do this, refer to your exposure tests and determine not only what colors you want but what will happen with the repeated buildup of exposure in the same areas.

If you expose through a red filter when making multiple exposures, the uncovered areas of the print become cyan. Then if you expose through a blue filter after rearranging the objects, you'll get yellow in the uncovered areas of the print which weren't exposed previously. Where the two exposures overlap, you'll get green in the print. If there is any white in the print, it means that no light struck the paper in that place.

Varying the direction of your light source is something else you may want to try. *Sidelight* will give you a completely different effect because of the shadows that are cast. However, when you change the light source, your exposure tests are no longer valid. In other words, you'll have to make a new series of tests or else guess at your exposures.

Some interesting effects occur when you lightly coat objects with Vaseline and put them in contact with the paper surface. The Vaseline impedes development, and the areas of the print which come in contact with it will remain white. When coated with Vaseline, surfaces with texture—such as skin, leaves, and flower petals—produce unusual results.

Use pages out of magazines and newspapers to create unusual images, too. By contact printing them, the photogram includes what is printed on both sides of the page.

Try combining regular photographic images from your negatives with the photograms by multiple printing. Or use solarization to add additional color to your images. By reexposing the print through a red filter after development but before the stop-fixer, you get its complement, cyan, in the areas which otherwise would be white.

All of these effects—color variations, multiple exposures, and even repeatability—can be controlled and predicted only if you are methodical and consistent in your approach to making photograms. As a result, you'll discover a unique form of creativity and personal expression.

Sandwiching and Multiple Printing

Sandwiching involves two or more negatives or slides that are put together to make a single image that can be printed or projected. By sandwiching, many times you can salvage a dull or ordinary shot and create a photograph that is much more dramatic. This also is the easiest way to produce multiple-image pictures.

With slides you can see the results immediately when the transparencies are placed together; with negatives you have to make a print before you can tell what the result will be.

Be careful that the combined density of the sandwiched images is not too dark or you may have trouble getting a satisfactory print. As a rule of thumb, when you are shooting with sandwiching specifically in mind, *underexpose* each negative a half-stop and *overexpose* each slide a half-stop.

Remove slide transparencies from their mounts so their images will be sandwiched in contact with each other and not with an air space that will cause one image to be out of focus.

Black-and-white negatives can be sandwiched and printed directly, but color negatives may present a filtration problem because their orange masks often produce a print with too much cyan. When you want to combine the images of two color negatives, it is better to double print them—expose each negative *separately* on the same piece of photo paper. By doing this, which is called *double* or *multiple printing,* you can emphasize one image more than the other, if desired, by giving it more exposure. It also allows you to enlarge the image of one negative more than the other.

Multiple printing is essentially the same for black-and-white and color negatives. No matter which you are printing, you have to test *each* negative for proper print exposure at its particular magnification (i.e. enlarger height). With color you also have to test for proper color balance. Because negatives can vary in contrast, variable contrast photo papers are useful when doing multiple printing in black-and-white; color papers are not available in various contrast grades.

When combining images, use the following remarks as guidelines. If you want to keep the illusion of the print being made from a single negative, make sure the images will blend in the print so the combination of negatives is not obvious. Select negatives that have similar texture and density along the lines where they will join together. The easiest multiple printing is blending the foreground of one negative with the background of another. One simple example is putting clouds in a scenic picture where there is only sky.

Once you have determined which negatives to combine, place each one in the enlarger—one at a time—and project it onto a piece of plain paper in your enlarging easel. Adjust the enlarger height, then make a sketch of the image that is to be part of the print.

Sometimes you can use your hand to mask off areas of the photo paper where you want the other negative to be printed, but using a *cardboard cut-out* is a more exacting way to block the light. With a piece of cardboard in the easel, draw a line where the images will join, then cut the board on this line. You'll use one section to partially mask off the image of one of the

91. *Multiple printing expands a photographer's creativity in the darkroom.*

negatives, and the other piece of cardboard to mask part of the other negative's image.

When blocking the light from part of the photo paper, it is necessary to hold the cardboard (or your hand) several inches above the easel and to keep this mask moving slightly during exposures so that the two (or more) images will blend smoothly without a distinct line. Draw a line on your sketch sheet to indicate the edge of the light-blocking cardboard cut-out, and mark that line on the side of the enlarging easel, too. As you hold the blocking card between the lens and easel, also mark its height on the enlarger's support column.

While the negative is in the enlarger, stop down the lens to its smallest opening, and make some test exposures (see page 109) to determine the correct exposure for that negative. Record all this information on the sketch sheet (enlarger height, blocking card height, exposure time, lens aperture, and variable contrast filter, if used for black-and-white prints).

Replace the negative in the enlarger with the other negative you plan to print. Use the sketch sheet as a guide for positioning the second image. Focus and stop down the lens as before, and position the other blocking card so the image from the second negative overlaps the area covered by the first negative by about 1 inch. Trace the image you plan to print, and also note the height of the blocking card on the enlarger support column. Tape the easel in position so it cannot be moved.

Once you've established the correct exposure for the second negative, expose it onto a piece of photo paper while keeping the blocking card moving slightly so a line will not be evident when the print is developed. If you want more than one print, expose additional sheets of paper. Mark the back(s) so you know which end is exposed. Return the paper to a light-tight storage box or envelope and change negatives in the enlarger.

Untape the easel and put the sketch paper back in it, then position the easel so the image fits the drawing. Focus, stop down the lens, and retape the easel.

Take the previously exposed photo paper from its storage box and return it to the easel, noting the mark on the print's back to be sure the paper is correctly oriented for the second exposure. Hold the other blocking card in the predetermined position, moving it slightly during exposure to prevent a line from appearing in the print.

After processing, examine the area in the print where the images overlap to make sure they blend together without being evident. This takes practice with the blocking cards. Save your sketch because if you wish to reprint the multiple image later, you can use the drawing to line things up, and follow the information you've written on the paper.

If multiple printing becomes a specialty, two or more enlargers will make the job easier because you won't have to continually change negatives; you place negatives in different enlargers and then just move your easel from one to another, exposing different portions of the paper as you go.

Combining photographs to form one image can be fun, and it's a good way to make use of negatives that don't quite make it on their own. You also might consider photographing subjects to use especially for multiple printing. Some photographers, for instance, shoot cloud formations of all types so they can be used later to improve cloudless scenic photographs.

92. *For this multiple print, a picture of an oil refinery was copied on high contrast litho film. Then that negative was used to expose the print paper four times, turning the enlarging easel each time to a premarked position.*

Subjects that are isolated against a dark or light background will be easier to use for multiple printing. If you shoot a subject against a white background, you can print it into a scene that has light tones, such as sky or snow, without affecting the surrounding area. When photographed against a black background, your subject can be printed into any part of a picture that is dark, without affecting the image around it.

If you want to put writing in a print, like a Christmas card greeting, or add silhouetted subjects, such as birds flying across a sky, make a negative of the words or silhouette subjects on Kodak's Kodalith film. This graphic arts film, generally called *litho film,* is a high contrast film that produces only blacks and whites (no gray tones).

For silhouetted subjects, you make a litho copy negative of the image, then print it over the first negative. Because the background of the litho negative is solid black, it acts as an opaque mask to protect the first negative's image; only the clear areas in the litho negative will print (black) on the photo paper, and these will appear as the silhouetted subjects.

You can use litho film in the same way to write over an image because the litho negative will mask out everything but the lettering. For black lettering, do your multiple printing as described above for silhouettes. To get white lettering in the print, the words must be black in the litho negative. Then it is printed as a sandwich with the main negative, using just one exposure. As you'll discover, experiments with multiple printing and sandwiching are limited only by your imagination and perseverance.

Making Negative Prints

You might enjoy making a print that has a negative image instead of the normal positive image. Sometimes you look at a negative and find its image is more interesting than a straight positive print of that image.

To make black-and-white negative prints from black-and-white films, first you must make a positive of the negative on film. This is really a black-and-white transparency which is sometimes called a *diapositive*. Contact print or enlarge your negative on Kodak Ektapan film, which comes in sheets of 2¼ x 3¼ inches and larger. The film's speed is ASA 100, and you'll have to run tests to determine proper exposure. Develop in a tray with D-76, HC-100, or Microdol-X developers.

Once processed, put this diapositive in your enlarger and make a print as you usually do—the image will be printed as a negative. Negative prints usually have greater clarity in shadow detail than positive prints, while some aspects of the subject tend to be more graphic and even abstract.

A simple way to get negative prints is by sandwiching a sheet of unexposed paper with a print and exposing it to light. The result is usually called a *paper negative,* and it can be used to make high contrast images without high contrast films or papers, or to do some quick retouching, as shown in the examples.

Place the print and paper with their emulsions facing together, and be sure the light is directed through the print onto the unexposed paper. When sandwiching a dry print with the paper, cover them with a sheet of glass so they will be in uniform contact. If a print is just processed and still wet, rinse it in running water for two minutes and then sandwich it face to face with the unexposed paper. Squeegee them together so they are in uniform contact. A wet or dry paper negative can be sandwiched by the same methods in order

93. The interior of this European ferryboat makes an interesting black-and-white photograph.

94. But it is even more striking when printed as a negative.

95. Paper negatives can be easily made, and will produce a variety of results. Begin by making a regular print, like this one, on contrast grade No. 2 paper.

96. Sandwich and expose the print with a low contrast paper, such as No. 0, in order to retain a good range of gray tones in the paper negative.

97. This print was made from the paper negative by sandwiching it with another sheet of No. 0 paper.

98. For high contrast results in the paper negative, sandwich and expose the regular print with a high contrast paper, such as No. 3.

99. Sandwiching and exposing the high contrast paper negative with another sheet of No. 3 paper produced this high contrast positive print. Paper negatives provide a quick way to make high contrast images without using high contrast film.

100. The photographer found streaks in the background objectionable in this informal portrait.

101. So he took a black felt tipped pen and painted them out (see text).

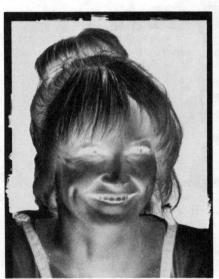

102. Then he made a paper negative by sandwiching and exposing another sheet of paper with the altered print.

103. Finally, the paper negative was sandwiched and exposed with another sheet of paper to produce a positive image without the disturbing background.

to make positive prints. Varying the contrast grade of paper will make remarkable differences in the images that result.

Another thing to try is making negative black-and-white prints directly from your color transparencies, which already are positives. Use normal black-and-white photo paper.

You can also make color negative prints from color transparencies. Print slides directly on negative-to-positive color paper, such as Ektacolor RC. The results will surprise you. Because transparencies do not have the orange mask that is characteristic of most color negatives, your print will be in vibrant colors that are complements of the colors in the transparency. For more control of color, you can sandwich a piece of unexposed but processed color negative film with the transparency to give it its own orange mask. Experiment.

Creating High Contrast Images

There are times when you might want to achieve special effects in your photographs by using high contrast films. Quite commonly, a *litho film* is used to eliminate all gray tones and produce just blacks and whites for graphic rather than realistic effects.

Normal black-and-white film is referred to as panchromatic, continuous-tone film, which means it is sensitive to all colors of light and a wide range of light values. Litho film is orthochromatic, high contrast line film, meaning it is not sensitive to red light and it records everything in blacks and whites, while eliminating gray tones.

Litho film is common to graphic arts and lithography. Photographers like to experiment with it for high contrast effects and use it for other creative techniques, such as posterization. It is also necessary for some of the so-called nonsilver process now popular with photographers, including photo silk-screen printing, blue printing (cyanotypes), and gum bichromate printing.

Many different brands of litho films are available, including Kodak's Kodalith, Cronar by DuPont, and Forolith from Ilford. Most camera stores carry at least one brand, usually the popular Kodalith Ortho film 6556, Type 3, available in 4 x 5- and 5 x 7-inch sheets, and 100-foot 35mm rolls. Because it is designed as a copy film, rather than for original photography, its film speed with tungsten light is ASA 6.

When litho films are processed in most ordinary developers, they produce a range of gray tones. However, they were designed to be processed in special litho film developers that produce high contrast black-and-white images only. These developers have two parts, usually referred to as A and B developers. First you mix stock solutions of A developer and B developer, and when

104. The impact of a regular photograph like this one can change when it is copied on litho film.

you're ready to process litho film, you mix the two solutions together. Life of this working solution is only a few hours.

Processing Kodalith film is simple. Develop it for 2¾ minutes in Kodalith Super Developer at 68°F (20°C), with *continuous agitation*. Rinse in a water stop bath for 15 seconds, then fix for 1 to 2 minutes in Kodak Rapid Fixer, with frequent agitation. Wash for about 10 minutes in running water, and speed drying with a wetting agent and a hand-held hair dryer. Processing can be done under a light red (No. 1A) safelight.

105. *That high contrast film eliminates gray tones and renders the subject in only blacks and whites.*

Underdeveloped film will not have solid blacks; you should be able to hold the film up to light and not be able to see through the black areas. More than likely there will be small *pinholes,* especially if agitation in the developer was inadequate, but these can be retouched later with *opaque,* a black-out paste applied with a small brush.

Consistent developer time and technique are important with litho films; if you pull the negative from the developer too soon, even though it looks developed, the negative won't produce a sharp, high contrast print.

106. Silhouettes can be rather dramatic.

To expose litho film to make a high contrast image from a normal continuous-tone black-and-white negative, color negative, or slide, place the negative or slide in the enlarger's negative carrier and project it on the enlarging easel as usual. Set the easel borders equal to accomodate the largest size negative that will fit in your negative carrier; the bigger you make the litho image, the easier it is to manipulate it later.

Litho film has an *antihalation backing,* but you may want to cover your

107. But this fishing pier scene has much more impact when copied on litho film to eliminate gray tones and produce a print in just blacks and whites.

easel bottom with black paper to avoid problems of light passing through the film's backing and being reflected back onto the film by a white easel—which will cause a loss in image definition.

You can bypass the easel and tape a piece of black paper to the enlarger baseboard. When the litho film is in place for the exposure, cover it with a piece of glass to keep the film flat. Several small negatives or transparencies, such as 35mm, can be contact printed on a single sheet of litho film, using the enlarger as a light source.

Be sure the litho film's emulsion side is toward the light source; it is lighter in color and not as shiny as the film base.

108. A regular photograph like this one that is copied on litho film offers several printing possibilities.

You'll have to make a series of test exposures to determine the proper exposure with your particular enlarger and light source. Beware of overexposing litho films because the image edges will be unsharp. Besides pinholes, if there are areas you don't wish to be printed black, fill them in by applying opaque with a brush. You can apply it to either side of the film.

If you used a negative to expose the litho film, the litho image will be positive and it can be used to make a negative print. To make a positive image print, contact print the litho image with another sheet of litho film. The result will be a high contrast litho negative, which can be used to make a positive image print. Actually since only blacks and whites are being printed, which are more graphic than realistic, frequently it doesn't matter whether the high contrast print is made from a negative or positive image—just as long as you like the result.

Positive images on litho film can be interesting when framed by themselves. Place an enlarged litho image between two pieces of glass and make a stand so the picture can be displayed on a table and viewed from either side.

Another idea is to add color to the image by dyeing the litho film with food coloring or toners (see page 126). Or sandwich colored filter material or cellophane between the litho film and the display glass. Litho images can be hand colored too (see page 255).

109. *It can be printed as a high contrast negative.*

110. *And it can be printed to give a bas-relief effect by sandwiching identical positive and negative images that are slightly off register.*

An enlarged litho film image can also be mounted with some sort of backing material, such as colored paper, and then framed for wall display. The black images should stand out from whatever background you select.

As described earlier, litho film can be used for making silhouette images to combine with normal negatives or slides and for making titles to add to your prints or slides (see page 292).

When multiple printing two litho images, you can make one image black, as usual, and then print the other image in a uniform gray tone by cutting its exposure in half. This gives a *duo-tone effect* and a feeling of depth to your print.

There are a variety of experiments you can make with high contrast images on litho film. For instance, you can contact print a negative on litho film, then sandwich that negative with the processed litho image so the images are just slightly off register. When printed, they will produce a *bas-relief effect* with the subjects surrounded by light or dark lines.

Images that are simple and have strong lines and separation of detail or tones usually work best with litho film. When you have a flat image and the tonal separation is slight, it is difficult to get a good litho image. However, you can try to build up contrast and separation by making a series of litho contact negatives and developing them in Dektol developer (diluted 1:3) for 1 to 2 minutes. This produces a continuous-tone negative, somewhat more grainy then the original and of higher contrast. Continue to contact print film after film, and develop in Dektol, until the image contrast and separation of detail have increased considerably. Then contact print on litho film again, but develop the film in litho AB developer to finally achieve a high contrast black and white effect.

You can create a photograph that resembles a pen-and-ink drawing by first making a *tone-line negative* that will outline the original image. Start by contact printing a normal negative with a piece of black-and-white film. After processing, place this diapositive (black-and-white transparency) and the original negative together in exact registration. If their densities and contrasts are similar, you should be unable to see through them—all the light will be blocked.

Now place a piece of litho film such as Kodalith Ortho film 6556, Type 3, in contact with the original negative, and sandwich all three in a contact printing frame: the positive transparency, original negative, and unexposed litho film. When light shines on this sandwich at a 45-degree angle, it passes through the thickness of the film where the positive and negative are in contact to create tone lines outlining the image. Once developed, the litho negative is enlarged to make your print.

To be successful in creating tone lines, the sandwich must be exposed at the 45-degree angle. Some photographers place the contact printing frame on a record turntable or lazy susan and spin it slowly about 3 feet from a 100-watt bulb that's at a 45-degree angle to the rotating platform. An alternative is to use your enlarger as the light source and hold the printing frame at the 45-degree angle to the baseboard. Turn each side toward the light and expose for equal amounts of time; you'll have to make exposure tests. If you want to make the lines in your print thicker, include a piece of clear film in the sandwich, placing it between the positive transparency and the original negative to separate them slightly.

Reexposing for the Sabattier Effect (Solarization)

More than a century ago, French doctor and scientist Armand Sabattier discovered what he called a pseudo-solarization reversal effect. Today it is more commonly, but erroneously, referred to as just *solarization*. But there is a distinct difference between solarization and what is really the *Sabattier effect*.

Technically, solarization is reversal of an image on film that occurs with extreme overexposure—an exposure about one thousand times more than normal. The Sabattier effect is reversal of an image that occurs when the film or photo paper is reexposed to light while in the developer. Only partial reversal of the image occurs, so the result is part negative and part positive.

One characteristic of the Sabattier effect that distinguishes it from solarization is a narrow band, called a *Mackie line* or *bromide line,* that is formed between highlight and shadow areas. Such lines are more evident in films than in prints; in fact, films reveal the Sabattier effect much better than prints. Most often, prints that are reexposed to light while in the developer have the appearance of being fogged instead of being partially reversed to a negative image, unless you print on the highest contrast grade of paper, a No. 5 or No. 6.

Films produce the most impressive results, but you are advised to make duplicates of negatives and slides instead of trying the Sabattier effect on the original film. If your reexposure during development is incorrect, only the duplicate will be ruined, and you can make another copy of the original negative or slide.

Besides a more pronounced result, another advantage of using the Sabattier effect on films rather than photo paper is that the negative can be used to make a number of identical prints; creating the same Sabattier effects by individually reexposing prints in the developer is rarely successful.

You can make continuous-tone copies of your original images on regular black-and-white films or on Kodak Commercial film 6127 (or make high contrast copies on Kodalith Ortho film 6556, Type 3). Commercial film is available on 4 x 5-inch and larger sheets, and you can contact print several negatives or slides on it at one time. Processing can be done under a red (No.

111. High contrast film litho film was solarized by deliberate overexposure while copying a normal negative. By necessity, the litho film's development was reduced from its normal 3 minutes to just 20 seconds (see text).

1) safelight in DK-50, HC-110, and other developers. Make exposure tests to get the best copies before attempting the Sabattier effect.

Once the best exposure for duplicating your negative is determined, expose another sheet of Commercial film, cut it in strips, and use them to determine the best exposure for creating the Sabattier effect.

Actually, your results depend on three things: the amount of development before reexposure, the amount of reexposure, and the amount of development after reexposure. As a guideline, follow these suggestions for Kodak Commercial film. Plan to use full strength DK-50 developer in a tray (at 68°F) for a total developer time of 2 minutes. Process with continuous agitation, except just before and during reexposure.

First place the exposed film in the developer and agitate continuously for 30 seconds. Allow 10 seconds for the negative to settle to the bottom of the tray, then reexpose the film for a few seconds to dim light from your enlarger (stop down the enlarger lens). Test strips will determine the best reexposure.

After reexposure, start agitation again until the total 2-minute developer time has elapsed. Finish the process with stop bath, fixer, and washing. After reexposure, the film will turn almost black, but continue to process it for the full developer time. You'll be able to analyze the Sabattier effect only after the film is in the fixer.

If you're going to copy on regular black-and-white film, like Plus-X Pan, or use it to make original negatives, follow these guidelines for creating the Sabattier effect. Plan to develop the film for a total of 3 minutes in HC-110 developer (at 68°F) that is diluted 1:16. After being agitated in the developer for 80 seconds, allow 10 seconds for the film to settle to the bottom of the tray, emulsion side up. Reexpose it for a few seconds to dim white light (stop down the enlarger lens), then continue agitating the film until the total 3-minute developer time is up. Finish processing with stop bath, fixer, and wash.

A test series of reexposures will determine the proper exposure for the Sabattier effect you like best; the more reexposure, the more the reversed image becomes evident. Don't give up easily when you begin experimenting with the Sabattier effect, because considerable testing for proper exposure may be required. Be sure to keep processing procedures constant, so you'll be able to judge the reexposure tests.

If you want to try the Sabattier effect on prints, here are some suggestions. Use a negative that has good contrast and print on the highest contrast grade of black-and-white paper, at least No. 5 or better yet, No. 6. Expose the print as normally, then develop it with constant agitation for about *one-third* of its recommended developer time in your normal developer. Reexpose the print with a dim light while it is still in the developer, then resume agitation and complete development for the total recommended time. Plan to do several tests to determine the proper amount of reexposure.

It's also fun to alter color prints with the Sabattier effect. Choose a process that can be used at variable temperatures, such as Beseler's 2-Step Color chemistry. Develop in trays rather than a processing tube so you can control agitation and move the print quickly from one solution to another.

With color prints, unlike black-and-white prints, to get the Sabattier effect you should *complete* the developer step before reexposure. Then place the

112. *These palm trees can be altered with some interesting variations by the Sabattier effect.*

113. *Reexposing the print during development produced almost uniformly gray palm fronds.*

114. A greater amount of reexposure created an entirely different result in the print.

print in the next tray, a shallow water bath, allowing it to settle on the bottom. Now *flash* a 250-watt bulb placed about 2 feet above the tray and allow the print to continue developing in the water bath.

The main areas of the print are completely developed at this point and are only slightly affected by the reexposure, but the highlight and less dense areas react to the light and develop rapidly. Any movement of the print in its water bath during reexposure will give a wavy or mottled look, because the light will shift as the water moves. Also Mackie lines will not form very strongly unless the print remains still.

After at least 10 seconds of continuing development, place the print, *without* draining, into the bleach-fix, and you can turn on the room lights to see your results. If you drain the print, streaks will occur. Wash and dry the prints as normally.

Be sure to make notes of your exact procedure so you can repeat or improve the results. You don't have to restrict yourself to white light for reexposure. Flashing through a colored filter will produce the filter's complementary color and alter the impact of the Sabattier effect. You can print from either color negatives or transparencies. The more contrast your image has, the more pronounced the Sabattier effect.

Another approach to adding color with the Sabattier effect is called *duo-tone solarization,* and the process produces color in black-and-white

115. For best results with the Sabattier effect, do not print on normal contrast paper like this.

116. Instead, use a high contrast grade of paper, like Nos. 5 or 6.

117. *A very brief reexposure of the print to light from the enlarger caused this effect.*

118. *A longer reexposure altered the print in a different way. Results are almost impossible to predict or control unless tests are made.*

119. A special solarizing developer, called Solarol, makes it easy to get a variety of Sabattier effects in prints by varying the initial and reexposure times. A short initial exposure gives complete reversal and the image appears negative; No. 6 high contrast paper was used.

120. A longer initial exposure causes less of a negative appearance.

121. And longer initial exposure but less reexposure produces an entirely different result. Full instructions come with packages of Solarol developer.

prints. Different combinations of developers and brands of photo papers create different colors. For instance, by developing Kodabromide No. 5 paper in Dektol developer, a print will have green, pink, and brown images. As usual, you must experiment, but here are some suggestions for the duo-tone procedure.

Use high contrast paper, at least grade No. 5, and dilute the stock Dektol developer one-to-one (1:1) to use at 68°F. Prepare a tray of acetic acid stop bath and two trays of fixer: the first is diluted one part fixer to one part water (1:1) and the second tray has regular full-strength paper fixer. Pick a negative without much detail, preferably with some dense areas, such as sky. Rig up a 150-watt light bulb for the reexposure step. And get ready to work fast.

After the initial exposure of the negative with your enlarger, develop the paper until an image begins to appear. Now dip the print quickly for 1 second in the stop bath and transfer it to the diluted fixer for another quick 1-second dip. Lay the print out flat about 2 feet beneath the 150-watt bulb and make the reexposure. The amount of exposure time will vary the effect on your print; start with an exposure between 10 and 25 seconds.

Because the paper receives only very brief stop bath and fixer treatments, the developer is still working. It reacts with the reexposure light, causing the image on paper to turn various colors. When you like what you see, place the print in the regular fixer, then wash and dry it as normally. Effects will vary if you squeegee the print before reexposure, or tilt it so the solutions run off. Try your own approach and experiment with different developers at different strengths.

Sensitizing Materials for Printing

Most photographers are content with printing on the usual photographic papers, but there are others who would like to make images on other materials. You can do this by making your own emulsion or by purchasing a commercially made emulsion that can be applied to practically anything.

Concocting your own emulsion is quite a project, although inexpensive, and the Eastman Kodak Company, Rochester, New York 14650, has two customer service pamphlets that tell you how to do it. Order *Making Your Own Emulsion,* pamphlet AJ-12, and *Photographic Sensitizer for Cloth and Paper,* pamphlet No. AJ-5.

It's much easier to buy and apply a premade emulsion, such as the ones manufactured by Rockland Colloid Corp., 599 River Rd., Piermont, New York 10968. They can be coated on brick, canvas, ceramics, cloth, concrete, eggs, glass, leather, metal, paper, plastic, rock, tile, wood, and countless other materials.

Rockland's basic product is called Print-E-Mulsion, and it comes in several types: CB-101, a medium-speed emulsion for enlarging; BB-201, a fast-speed emulsion for making large off-easel images; and BX-201, a slow-speed emulsion for contact printing. Print-E-Mulsion comes in half-pint, pint, quart, and gallon sizes; one quart covers about 40 to 50 square feet.

The emulsion can be handled under red or amber safelights. It is not as sensitive as regular photo paper emulsion, so exposures will be at least 1 minute or longer. BX-201, the emulsion for contact printing, can be handled under dim white light, and it requires exposure with bright incandescent or fluorescent light.

The emulsion is a gelatin that must be heated in a hot water bath before applying it with a brush, or by pouring or spraying. Glass and ceramics must be pretreated with a special powder before the emulsion is applied, and metal and plastic must be primed with polyurethane. Coat a few white note cards to use as test strips for determining exposure. The emulsion must dry before exposure is attempted.

Processing is the same as for black-and-white photo papers. Develop in Dektol, diluted 1:2, by immersing the sensitized material or by applying developer with a sponge. Rinse in water (or a stop bath) and apply fixer for 5 minutes. Wash for 15 minutes in cool running water, then dry and display your unique photograph.

Because fabrics will stiffen when Print-E-Mulsion is applied, Rockland also makes a fabric sensitizer, FA-1, that allows cotton or linen cloth to remain supple. Frequently it is used to make photo pillowcases. Cloth sensitized with FA-1 requires contact printing and exposure (1 to 2 minutes) with a sunlamp or sunlight. The image develops in cool running water in less than a minute, then the cloth is transferred to fixer for about 15 seconds until the image becomes gray brown. Afterward it is washed for 10 minutes, then dried. FA-1 comes in powder form to make 1 gallon of fabric sensitizer.

The Rockland Colloid Corp. also makes presensitized metal sheets called Photo-Aluminum that give a black-on-silver image from negatives that are enlarged or contact printed.

Other sensitizing products are available from Diversy Creation Corp., P.O. Box 8167, Wichita, Kansas 67208, which offers a Sensitiz-Sur kit, and from Luminos Photo Corp., 25 Wolfee St., Yonkers, New York 10705, makers of a presensitized cloth called Photo Linen.

There are a number of other unique processes that are attracting the interest of more and more photographers. *Posterization* is one example. After normal print tones are separated by using high contrast films, they are recombined to produce images that have the look of posters made by graphic artists rather than photographs created in a darkroom. Posterization can be done in black-and-white or color.

Also, there is a myriad of other new and old photographic methods, often call *nonsilver processes,* that do not make use of the traditional black-and-white or color print materials. Actually, most of the processes start with a negative that is produced on a light-sensitive silver emulsion, but the final images are normally much different than what we generally term photographic prints.

Among the so-called nonsilver processes are photo silk-screen printing, gum bichromate printing, blue printing (also known as cyanotype printing), photo sculpture, image transfer processes, photo etching on metal, and some of the newer electronic image-making methods, such as the Xerox color copier, which are sometimes referred to as *generative systems*.

Detailed discussion of these various approaches to photographic imagery would require another volume and are not within the intended scope of this book. Check your library for publications that deal in depth with such topics. An easily obtained reference book, especially regarding posterization, gum bichromate printing, and photo silk-screen printing, is Kodak's *Creative Darkroom Techniques*. Also research current and back issues of photographic magazines, including *Darkroom Magazine, Petersen's PhotoGraphic, Popular Photography,* and *Modern Photography.*

Whatever your special interest, remember that photography is a very personal medium of expression. Using the material in this book for guidelines, you can be as traditional or avant-garde as you wish in your approach to processing and printing. Perhaps your approach will be similar to that of W. Eugene Smith, a master behind the camera and in the darkroom, who once revealed: "My formula for successful printing remains ordinary chemicals, an ordinary enlarger, music, a bottle of Scotch, and stubbornness."

Appendix A
A Glossary of Photographic
Processing and Printing Terms

ASA A system of numbers determined by the defunct American Standards Association to indicate the relative speed of films; see also Film Speed.

ANSI A system of numbers determined by the American National Standards Institute to indicate the relative speed of printing and enlarging papers; see also Paper Speed.

Acetic Acid A chemical that is commonly used in a stop bath to quickly halt the action of developer on the emulsion of film or photo paper.

Acid Rinse See Stop Bath.

Additive Color Printing An uncommon method of color printing requiring three separate exposures of a color negative or transparency through filters of each primary color: red, blue, and green; also called Tricolor Printing.

Additive Primaries In photography, the three colors that make white light: red, blue, and green.

Adjustable Camera A camera where the shutter speed, lens opening, and focus can be adjusted by the photographer.

Agitation The movement of chemicals over photographic film and paper to insure uniform processing.

Air Bells Bubbles of air that occasionally form on the emulsion of film or photo paper, preventing action of the developer or other chemicals and causing spots; can be avoided with proper agitation.

Angle of Acceptance The area included in a light reading by an exposure meter; measured in degrees (°); see also Averaging Meter and Spot Meter.

Antihalation Backing A light-absorbing layer on the back of film that prevents light rays from reflecting back to the emulsion.

Antistatic Brush Counters the electrical charge that attracts dust to negatives or transparencies; used to clean negatives or transparencies before printing.

Aperture The lens opening, the size of which is usually indicated by f/stop numbers; also called Diaphragm.

Archival Processing Special care given films or prints to insure long-lasting results; usually involves two fixer baths, thorough washing, and selenium or gold toning of prints.

Autochromes Early color transparencies that involved the additive system of color photography.

Automatic Aperture A lens that automatically closes down to the preselected f/stop when the shutter release is pressed, and then reopens to its widest f/stop.

Automatic Camera A camera that automatically adjusts the lens opening or shutter speed, or both.

Available Light Existing illumination that is not supplemented with artificial light by the photographer.

Averging Meter An exposure meter that has a wide angle of acceptance; sometimes referred to as a meter that gives "overall" or "integrated" exposure reading, see also Angle of Acceptance and Spot Meter.

Back Lighting Term used when the main source of illumination is behind the subject and shines in the direction of the camera.

Basket-and-Tank Processing A method used by some professional print processors involving tanks of chemicals which hold "baskets" of exposed photo paper to permit quick, quality processing.

Batch Number See Emulsion Number.

Batch Processing Refers to processing prints in a group rather than singly; sometimes called Gang Processing.

Bellows A flexible, accordionlike light-tight chamber; part of an extension device used for making close-ups; part of most enlargers connecting the lens to the enlarger body; part of some cameras connecting the lens to the camera body; see also Extension Bellows.

Black-and-White Transparency See Diapositive.

Bleach A chemical commonly used in processing color films and color prints; sometimes combined with the fixer.

Bleaching See Reducing.

Bleed Mounting A method of print mounting where the print runs to the edge of the mount board; also called Flush Mounting.

Blix A name for a chemical solution in certain color processes that combines the bleach and fixer steps.

Blotters Special lintless, absorbent papers sometimes used for drying prints or removing moisture from their surfaces.

Blue Printing See Cyanotype.

Bracketing Making two or more exposures in addition to the one thought to be correct; can be done by changing either the f/stop or exposure time.

Brilliance A characteristic of photo paper having good range of tones and bright highlights; see also Paper Surface.

Bulk Film Long rolls (often 100 feet) of 35mm film that are cut to desired lengths and loaded into cassettes by the photographer; a money-saving but less convenient way to purchase film.

Burning-in A technique used during enlarging to darken certain areas of the image on photographic paper by exposing those areas for an additional amount of time; with color reversal print papers, burning-in lightens selected areas of the image.

CC Filters See Color Compensating Filters.

CP Filters See Color Printing Filters.

Cadmium Sulfide (CdS) Cell A light-sensitive cell used to make light readings; sometimes part of print exposure meters; see also Print Exposure Meter.

Calotype The first process in photography using a "negative," which was then a piece of chemical-coated paper; patented in 1841 by William Henry Fox Talbot, who is considered the father of modern photography.

Camera Obscura Originally the name for a dark room with a small opening (sometimes fitted with a lens) that formed an image on the opposite wall; later, the name for a camera that could be fitted with tracing paper on its back so a sketch of the image could be made.

Cartridge A light-tight film container used in Instamatic and subminiature-type cameras.

Cassette A light-tight film container used in 35mm cameras; called film magazines by Kodak; exposed film must be rewound into the cassette before removing it from the camera.

Celsius (C) A temperature scale being slowly adopted in North America to replace the Fahrenheit (F) scale; identical to the Centigrade (C) scale.

Centigrade (C) See Celsius.

Changing Bag A light-tight bag with access for the photographer's arms; used any time complete darkness is required, such as when opening a jammed camera to retrieve film without exposing it or when loading a daylight developing tank.

Chemical Capacity The amount of film or prints that can be processed in a specific chemical before it must be replaced or replenished.

Chromogenic General description for processes that use color dye couplers to produce color images; common to all current color print processes except Cibachrome.

Cinch Marks Parallel scratches on a film's emulsion, often caused when the roll of film is wound too tightly.

Clearing Agent A chemical solution used to remove fixer from film or prints and thus speed up washing time; also called Hypo Neutralizer or Hypo Eliminator.

Close-up A picture made with the camera close to the subject.

Close-up Lens A lens attached in front of a camera lens to allow the camera to get closer to the subject than otherwise possible; see also Diopter.

Coated Lens A coating on the lens surfaces that improves picture quality by reducing the flare caused when light strikes the lens directly; most camera and enlarger lenses that have been manufactured in recent years are coated.

Cold-Light Enlarger Type of enlarger illumination system that uses gas-filled tubes or a fluorescent lamp instead of a tungsten bulb for the light source.

Collodion A syrupy chemical coating originally applied to glass plates, allowing them to be sensitized with silver nitrate and exposed in a camera to make an image; see also Wet-Plate Process.

Color Analyzer An electronic device that measures the color components of a projected color negative or slide; after initial programming, the analyzer indicates the correct filtration to use to achieve color balance in a print; most models also indicate the proper exposure to use.

Color Balance The ability of a color film or paper to reproduce colors as the photographer sees them; color films are designed by the manufacturer to reproduce colors accurately when used with the type of light for which they were balanced, either daylight or tungsten; in color printing, filtration in the enlarger determines the color balance in the resulting print.

Color Calculator A nonelectronic calculator for determining the proper filtration and exposure to use when printing color negatives or transparencies; intially, test prints are also required.

Color Compensating (CC) Filters Filters that are used to control color balance in a color print; for white-light (subtractive) printing, the filters are yellow, magenta, and cyan; for tricolor (additive) printing, the colors are red, green, and blue; usually refers to glass or gelatin filters placed beneath the enlarger lens; see also Color Printing (CP) Filters.

Color-corrected Lens A lens designed and ground to reduce chromatic aberrations that distort colors; modern camera and enlarger lenses are color corrected.

Color Developer A second developer commonly used when processing color reversal films or papers.

Color Dye Couplers Components in the emulsion layers of color films and papers that react with the processing chemicals to produce dyes that give color to photographic images.

Color Head General term for an enlarger equipped with an illumination system that includes built-in dichroic filters for making color prints; see aiso Dichroic Filters.

Color Mask Often refers to the overall orangish tint that is incorporated in some color negative films to help provide correct color balance when making prints.

Color Negative Film Color film which produces a negative image; commonly called color print film.

Color Positive Film Color film which produces a positive image; commonly called color slide film or reversal film.

Color Print Viewing Filters Used for viewing color test prints to determine what changes, if any, need to be made in filtration in order to improve the color balance of the print.

Color Printing (CP) Filters Technically these are color compensating (CC) filters, but they are made of acetate instead of glass or gelatin, and are used in the enlarger's filter drawer instead of beneath the enlarger lens; the most common type of filters used for color printing, unless the enlarger is equipped with a color head; see also Color Compensating Filters and Color Head.

Color Reversal Film See Color Positive Film.

Color Reversal Paper Color paper that produces a positive image direct from a color transparency; sometimes called Type R color paper.

Color Sensitivity Films and photo papers are designed to be sensitive to certain colors, i.e. wavelengths of light; black-and-white films that are sensitive to all colors of visible light are called panchromatic; see also Orthochromatic Film and Infrared Film.

Color Temperature A system of numbers used for measuring the color of light, which varies according to its temperature; expressed in Kelvins, abbreviated K.

Complementary Colors The colors produced when two primary colors are mixed: yellow (from red and green), magenta (from red and blue), and cyan (from blue and green); sometimes called secondary colors; see also Primary Colors.

Composition The arrangement of the subject or elements in a picture; carefully considered composition is the key to an effective photograph; see also Cropping.

Condenser Enlarger Features a pair or more of opposing pieces of convex optical glass condensers that yield sharp, high contrast results; also shows all flaws in the negative.

Condenser-Diffusion Enlarger Most common type of enlarger illumination system; twin condenser lenses used with a diffused light source or diffusion screen provide a sharper image than does a diffusion enlarger, but not as sharp as a condenser enlarger.

Condenser Lenses A pair of lenses used to concentrate a light source; common in condenser enlargers, condenser-diffusion enlargers, and slide projectors.

Conditioner A chemical used in the E-6 film developing process.

Contact Print A print that is the same size as the negative; made by placing the negative and photographic paper together and exposing them to light.

Contact Printer A boxlike device with a light source for exposing contact prints.

Contact Printing The process of making a contact print or negative.

Contact Printing Paper Photo paper that is specially designed for making contact prints; slower in speed than enlarging paper; see also Enlarging Paper.

Contact Sheet See Proof Sheet.

Continuous-Roll Processing Machine Processes rolls of photo paper (instead of sheets); used by commercial labs doing a large volume of print making.

Continuous-Tone Film A film that produces a wide range of tones, from light to dark; see also Litho Film.

Contrast The range of brightness of a subject; also, the range of density in a negative, print, or slide.

Contrast Grade Indicates different contrasts of photographic paper designed for different contrasts of negatives; paper grades are numbered 0 through 6; grade 0 has the lowest contrast and is used with high contrast negatives to produce a print of normal contrast; grade 6 has the highest contrast and is used with low contrast negatives; grade 2 is for normal contrast negatives.

Contrast Ratio Refers to the range of dark and light tones; the greater the range, the greater the contrast ratio.

Contrasty Usually describes a negative or print where the differences in tones are greater than when a negative or print is of normal contrast; occurs with overdevelopment.

Copy Negative The negative that results when a print is photographed or when an original negative is duplicated.

Corner-to-Corner Illumination and Sharpness Refers to uniform illumination and sharpness of a negative or slide projected by an enlarger; dependent upon the enlarger's particular illumination system and lens focal length.

Cropping Eliminating unwanted parts of a picture; a photographer crops with his viewfinder by framing only the subject he wants in his picture, or he crops during the enlarging process to print only the best portion of the negative.

Cyan A color produced by mixing blue and green light; complementary to the primary color red; one of the three complementary color filters used in white light (subtractive) printing.

DIN Abbreviation for Deutsche Industrie Norm, and refers to the European standard for film speeds.

Daguerreotype The earliest commercial photographic process (about 1839); an image that is formed by mercury vapor on a silver-coated copper plate.

Darkroom A light-tight room used for developing film and making contact prints and enlargements.

Data Sheet The instructional information packed with films and photo papers.

Daylight Developing Tank A light-tight plastic or stainless steel container in which roll film is loaded in the dark, after which processing can be carried out with the room lights on.

Daylight Film A color film designed to give good color balance when used with daylight, electronic flash, or blue flash illumination.

Definition The relative sharpness of a lens, negative, or print; the quality of detail evident in a photograph; sharpness of the image, graininess of the negative or print, and the resolving power of a film or lens contribute to a photograph's definition.

Degrees of Density Refers to the amount of filtration selected for making a color print; indicated by a number followed by the filter color, i.e. 30M means 30 degrees of magenta filtration; the higher the number, the greater the filter density and thus the greater amount of filtration.

Dense Negative A negative that appears darker than normal, usually with no details in the highlights; occurs with overexposure.

Density The relative darkness of a negative or print; a dense negative will not allow much light to pass through it; a dense print will not reflect much light.

Depth of Field The area in a photograph that is in sharp focus; figured as the distance between the nearest and farthest objects in focus.

Developer Chemical which acts on exposed film or paper emulsion to produce an image; its ingredients commonly include a developing agent, accelerator, preservative, and restrainer.

Developer Tones Developers for black-and-white papers can affect the image tone of a print, so they are described as cold tone, neutral tone, or warm tone developers; see also Image Tone.

Developing by Inspection Refers to viewing films by safelight while they are being developed to see if developer time should be increased or decreased.

Developing Reel The plastic or stainless steel reel on which roll film is loaded and placed in the developing tank.

Diaphragm The aperture mechanism, adjusted according to f/stop, which determines the size of the lens opening.

Diapositive A black-and-white transparency; can be produced by contact printing a negative with another piece of film, or by developing film in direct positive film processing chemicals.

Dichroic Filters Interference-type filters built in an enlarger color head; used to determine color balance when making color prints and determine contrast when printing with variable contrast black-and-white papers.

Diffusion Enlarger Enlarger illumination system which scatters the light reaching the negative, resulting in an image less sharp than that possible with a condensor-diffusion enlarger.

Diopter An optical term used to indicate the strength of magnifying power of a close-up lens; such lenses range from +1 to +10 diopters.

Direct Positive Printing Refers to making color prints directly from color transparencies; sometimes called Type R (for reversal) printing; see also Internegative.

Distortion Used to describe an unnatural or imperfect image; the enlarger lens or enlarging easel can be tilted to correct some image distortion that may be evident in a negative or transparency.

Dodging A technique used during enlarging to lighten certain areas of the image on photographic paper by allowing less exposure of those areas than the rest of the print receives; with color reversal photo papers, dodging darkens selected areas.

Double Exposure Two separate exposures made on one film frame or piece of photographic paper; see also Multiple Exposure.

Drum Processor A motorized device for processing color prints that works well for small volume color printing; see also Tube-Type Processor.

Dry Area An area in the darkroom where film is loaded in a daylight developing tank or prints are exposed; a space away from the darkroom's wet area (where chemicals are mixed and films and prints are processed).

Dry Down Factor Prints that are wet appear lighter than when they are dry, which is a factor to consider when deciding when to remove a print from the developer.

Drying Cabinet A dust-free place to dry film; can include a fanless electric heater to speed drying.

Dry Mounting Press A device incorporating heat and pressure to mount prints to a mat board or other support.

Dry Mounting Tissue Special heat-activiated tissue placed between a print and the board or other material to which the photograph will be mounted; self-sticking types of dry mounting tissue do not require heat.

Duo-Tone Solarization A method of adding color to black-and-white prints by an adaptation of the Sabattier effect; see also Sabattier Effect.

Dustless Negative Carrier See Negative Carrier.

Easel Used in the enlarging process to hold photographic paper flat, to crop the negative's images, and to make white borders on the print.

Effective Film Speed The actual speed of a film rather than the speed (ASA) the film is normally supposed to be; see also Professional Film.

Electronic Flash A flash unit that is capable of giving repeated flashes without changing the bulb; power for units vary from dry cell or rechargeable batteries to household (AC) current.

Emulsion The light-sensitive chemical coating of film or paper, usually silver halides held by gelatin on an acetate or paper base; most often identified as the dull side of a piece of film, and the shiny side of a piece of photo paper.

Emulsion Number A manufacturer's code number that indicates the batch in which the film or photo paper was made; also called Batch Number.

Enlargement A print that is larger than the size of the negative.

Enlarger A device for projecting images from a negative or transparency onto a piece of photo paper in order to make a print the size desired by the photographer.

Enlarger Baseboard The flat base to which the enlarger's support column is attached; should be large enough to accommodate easy alignment of the enlarging easel.

Enlarger Head Houses the illumination system of an enlarger; see also Color Head.

Enlarger Lens A removeable lens with adjustable aperture; lens focal length depends on the size of the negative or transparency being enlarged; see also Coated Lens and Color-Corrected Lens.

Enlarging The process of making an enlargement.

Enlarging Easel See Easel.

Enlarging Magnifer Optical device placed on the enlarger baseboard or enlarging easel to aid in focusing the projected image of a negative or transparency.

Enlarging Meter A photometer that reads a negative image projected by the enlarger and helps determine the correct exposure and contrast grade of paper to use when making a black-and-white print; also called a Print Exposure Meter.

Enlarging Paper Photo paper designed for images that are projected by an enlarger;

more sensitive to light and thus faster in speed than contact printing papers, but frequently used for making contact proof sheets.

Enlarging Timer An electric timer calibrated in seconds that can be preset to turn on an enlarger to make an exposure for a selected amount of time.

Etching Usually refers to scraping small unwanted spots or marks from the surface of a print.

Existing Light See Available Light.

Expiration Date The date printed on photographic film and paper boxes or packages indicating the time after which the manufacturer no longer guarantees the characteristics of the film or paper.

Exposure The amount of light acting on the emulsion of a film or paper; with cameras, exposure is controlled by the lens opening and shutter speed; with enlargers the lens opening and enlarger timer control exposure.

Exposure Factor A number listed on certain brands of color photo paper which indicates the difference in emulsion speed between that batch of paper and other batches.

Exposure Latitude The range of exposures, from underexposure to overexposure, that still will produce an acceptable picture; black-and-white film has more exposure latitude than does color film.

Exposure Meter A device, hand-held or built in a camera, that reads the intensity of light falling on or reflected from a subject; calibrates the light intensity into f/stops and shutter speeds for the photographer; also called a light meter; see also Enlarging Meter.

Extension Bellows An adjustable accordionlike device attached between the camera lens and camera body to increase lens focal length and magnify the subject; used for making close-ups.

Extension Tubes One or more rigid tubes or rings used for making close-ups; inserted between camera lens and body to increase lens focal length and magnify the subject.

f/stop Number indicating the relative size of the lens opening; the larger the number the smaller the opening.

F Synchronization Cameras or flash cord sockets sychronized for use with F class bulbs, which are fast-peaking flashbulbs no longer in common use.

FP Synchronization On cameras with focal plane shutters, the flash cord socket or switch synchronized for use with FP (focal plane) flash bulbs; can also be used with more common M class bulbs.

Fahrenheit (F) A scale of temperatures that is slowly being replaced in North America by the Celsius (Centigrade) scale.

Fast Film Film with emulsion that is very sensitive to light, such as one with a film speed of ASA 400 or more; see also Slow Film.

Fast Lens See Lens Speed.

Ferrotype Plate or Tin Chrome-plated steel sheet used for drying glossy prints, except resin-coated (RC) papers.

Fill-in Flash Light from a flash unit used to augment the existing illumination or main flash unit; often used to lighten or eliminate shadows in a picture.

Film Acetate material coated with light-sensitive chemicals, usually silver halides in a gelatin base, that registers the images formed in a camera by its lens.

Film Cassette Opener Device for popping off the clamped end of metal cassettes containing 35mm film prior to processing; frequently a bottle top opener is used.

Film Cleaner A special solvent used to eliminate fingerprints and other marks from the film's surface without harming the film itself.

Film Clips Plastic or metal clips used to hang up roll or sheet film for drying; spring clothespins can be used instead.

Film Code Notch A notch or notches on one edge of sheet film that indicates the type of film it is; can be felt in the dark to identify the emulsion side of the film.

Film Hangers Stainless steel or plastic hangers for holding sheet films in tanks during processing.

Film Leader The narrow portion of 35mm film that extends from its cassette and is attached to the camera's take-up spool; should be cut off before processing film.

Film Pressure Plate A broad metal or plastic plate in the back of the camera designed to keep the film flat and in the proper plane for sharp focusing.

Film Speed A system of numbers, commonly called ASA, to indicate a film's relative sensitivity to light; the greater the ASA number, the more sensitive the film; see also ASA.

Film Take-up Spool A built-in or removeable spool in cameras to which the leader of film is attached when loading the camera.

Filter Colored or coated glass or acetate placed in front of the camera lens that alters the light reaching the film; incorporated or placed in an enlarger to give proper color balance to a color print; see also Color Compensating Filters, Color Printing Filters, Dichroic Filters.

Filter Density Indicates the relative amount of light the filter absorbs; in color printing, the density is indicated by a number followed by the filter color, i.e. 30Y (Yellow); see also Degrees of Density.

Filter Drawer Compartment in the enlarger head in which color printing (CP) filters are placed when exposing color negatives or transparencies.

Filter Factor A number that indicates the increase in exposure required when a filter is used; the filter factor is expressed with a times sign (X).

Filter Pack The combination of filters in the enlarger, usually chosen to produce correct color balance in a color print.

Filtration The filter colors and densities selected for use in the enlarger when making a color print.

Fine Grain Refers to films or developers that yield images with little evidence of grain; see also Grain.

Fixer A chemical, often called hypo, which removes undeveloped silver halides from film and photo paper and which fixes the image on the film or paper so it does not change density by fading.

Flash Guide Number A number used when determining exposure with a flashbulb or electronic flash unit; varies according to the film's speed and type and size of flash unit or reflector and bulb.

Flash Synchronization Internal electrical and mechanical camera controls that insure the shutter is open when the flash goes off.

Flat Lighting Term used when the main source of illumination is coming from the direction of the camera and falling on the front of the subject; offers uniform illumination that is relatively shadowless, and thus lacks a feeling of depth.

Flat Negative A negative with less than normal contrast; often the result of underdevelopment.

Focal Length Technically, the distance from the optical center of a lens to the point behind the lens where the light rays from an object at infinity are brought into focus; indicates the relative image size produced by a lens; the greater the focal length the greater the image size.

Focal Plane Shutter A shutter built in the camera body just in front of the film plane; usually two flexible curtains which travel in the same direction; capable of shutter speeds to 1/2000 second; common in single reflex cameras.

Focus Adjusting a lens so the light rays transmitted by it are sharply defined on the photographic film or paper.

Fog Usually stray light that registers on film or photo paper and reduces the contrast of the image; photographic films and papers can also be fogged chemically.

Fog Density Inherent but limited amount of fog in films and photo papers caused by developer acting upon unexposed silver halides; see also Silver Halides.

Front Lighting See Flat Lighting.

Full Stop Indicates a change in the lens opening from one f/stop number to the next closest f/stop number, which either doubles or halves the amount of light.

Gang Processing See Batch Processing.

Glassine Envelopes Negative envelopes of translucent paper.

Graduate A plastic or glass vessel marked for liquid measurement and used when mixing chemicals.

Grain The sand grain or pebblelike appearance of some negatives, slides, or prints caused by the clumping of silver particles in the photographic emulsion; more evident in films with faster ASA speeds, films which have been overdeveloped, or prints which have been greatly enlarged.

Graphic Arts Film Commonly refers to high contrast film that produces blacks and whites but no gray tones; see also Litho Film.

Gray Card A piece of cardboard with 18 percent reflectance when measured by a reflected-light meter; serves as a standard medium tone; corresponds to Zone V in the Zone System; see also Zone System.

Guide Number See Flash Guide Number.

Gum Bichromate Printing An image-forming process where light hardens gum arabic sensitized with potassium bichromate; images are transferred to paper by contact printing.

Half-Moons Dark crescent shapes in a negative that occur when the film is wrinkled or creased, which can occur when loading film onto a developing reel for processing.

Half-Stop An intermediate lens opening between two major f/stops; half of a full stop.

Hardener A chemical sometimes required in processing to limit the softening of film or paper emulsion in order to protect it from damage.

Heat-absorbing Glass Used in an enlarger to protect color negatives and transparencies from heat produced by the enlarger lamp.

High Contrast A term used when there is an extreme difference in brightness between the lightest and darkest parts of a subject, negative, or print.

High Contrast Film A film that has a limited range of gray tones between white and black and produces a contrasty image.

High Energy Developers Special black-and-white developers that produce negatives of fine grain and good contrast from film exposed at a higher effective film speed than its normal ASA.

Highlight Detail Detail that is evident in the highlight (bright) areas of a picture; a consideration when making an exposure meter reading; see also Shadow Detail.

Hypo Common but erroneous name for fixer; see also Fixer.

Hypo Eliminator or Hypo Neutralizer See Clearing Agent.

Image Tone The tone of the silver image produced in a black-and-white photo paper; described as cold tone, neutral tone, or warm tone.

Incident-Light Meter An exposure meter designed to read the light falling on the subject; placed at the subject position and pointed toward the camera.

Infinity The point or distance beyond which everything will be in focus; indicated by the symbol ∝ on a camera lens.

Infrared Film Special film which records heat intensity as well as light intensity; available in black-and-white and color films; for best results, filters are required while shooting such films.

Integrated Reading Describes an overall light reading made by an exposure meter, enlarging meter, or a color analyzer; see also Averaging Meter and Spot Meter.

Intensifier A chemical solution used to increase the density and contrast of a negative that was underexposed or underdeveloped.

Interleafing A method of agitating two or more sheet films of photo papers in a tray by rotating the bottom sheet to the top in a continuous pattern.

Internegative A negative made from an original color or black-and-white transparency; frequently an intermediate step in making prints or additional transparencies.

Kelvins The system of numbers used to indicate the relative color temperatures of light sources; abbreviated K; see also Color Temperature.

Latent Image The invisible image caused by light which registers on a film or paper emulsion when an exposure is made; the image cannot be seen until the film or paper is processed.

Latitude The extent of a film's or paper's ability to produce an acceptable negative, slide, or print from a wide range of exposures.

Lens Optical pieces of glass designed to focus rays of light into an image on film, photographic paper, or a projection screen; adjustable lenses feature focusing and f/stop controls.

Lens Cleaner A special solvent used sparingly with lens tissue to clean fingerprints and other residue off the surfaces of a lens.

Lens Opening The light-regulating control in a lens indicated by f/stop numbers; also called Aperture and Diaphragm.

Lens Speed Refers to the largest f/stop opening of a lens; a lens with a very large opening (such as f/1.4) is called a fast lens because it transmits more light than a lens with a smaller maximum opening.

Light-balancing Filter Used to alter light reaching the film in order to color balance it for the type of film being used.

Light Meter See Exposure Meter.

Lighting Usually refers to the type or direction of illumination falling on a subject.

Litho Film High contrast film that eliminates gray tones and represents the image only in black and white.

Long Lens A lens with a focal length that is greater than a normal lens; a general name for a telephoto lens; see also Normal Lens.

M Class Flashbulb The most commonly used type of flashbulb, which reaches its maximum brilliance at a medium speed.

M Synchronization The camera flash socket or switch position for synchronizing the shutter when M class flashbulbs are used.

Mackie Line A characteristic of the Sabattier effect; a narrow band formed between the highlight and shadow areas in an image; also called Bromide Line.

Macro Lens Primarily designed for close-up photography, but also capable of serving as a normal lens; allows close lens-to-subject focusing without accessory equipment.

Magazine See Cassette.

Magenta A color produced by mixing red and blue; complementary to the primary color green; one of the three complementary color filters used in white light subtractive color printing.

Mask An opaque material that protects portions of light-sensitive film or paper from exposure; a dye color used in some color negative films to assist in correct color balancing when making a print.

Modular Enlarger General name for an enlarger that can be adapted with different illumination systems or a color head.

Mottle Blotchy, uneven development caused by improper agitation or under-development.

Mounting Cement Special adhesive or glue that is not harmful to photographic prints when used to mount them to mat board or other display materials.

Multiple Exposure Two or more exposures made on the same film frame or piece of photographic paper.

Multiple Printing Using two or more negatives or transparencies to make a single print.

Natural Light Existing light, usually sunlight, that is not supplemented with additional light by the photographer.

Negative Film that has been developed in which the light and dark areas of the subject are reversed.

Negative Carrier A glass or glassless device in the enlarger used to hold negatives and transparencies flat and in position for making enlargements; glassless carriers sometimes are called dustless carriers.

Negative Print A print in which the image appears as a negative; the light and dark tones are reversed.

Negative Sleeves Plastic or paper covers or envelopes in which negatives are stored.

Negative-to-Positive Paper Color photo paper that produces a positive image when printed with a color negative; see also Positive-to-Positve Paper.

Neutral Density Absorbs wavelengths of light equally; does not alter colors; when filters of all three complementary colors (yellow, magenta, cyan) are used together, they create neutral density and will not affect the color balance of a print.

Neutralizer A chemical required in some color processes.

Newton's Rings Distracting rainbowlike circles or patterns that occasionally appear in a print when negatives or transparencies, heated by the enlarger bulb, come in irregular contact with a glass negative carrier.

Non-silver Processes Image-making processes that do not make use of black-and-white or color print materials in the traditional manner; examples are gum bichromate printing, blue printing, and photo silk-screen printing.

Normal Lens The lens designed for a particular camera that produces an image similar in perspective to what the photographer sees with the naked eye; the focal length of a normal lens varies according to the film size and is approximately equal to the diagonal of the film frame; a normal lens of a 35mm camera is usually 50mm, of a 2¼ x 2¼ camera, 80mm; lenses of the same focal lengths are used in enlargers when printing negatives of those respective sizes.

One-Shot Developer A developer designed to be used one time only and then discarded.

Opaque Blocking all light; a pigment applied with a brush to cover certain portions of a negative or transparency to keep light from passing through.

Orthochromatic Usually used to describe black-and-white film that is sensitive to all colors of light except red; see also Panchromatic.

Overexposure Excessive exposure of photographic film or paper; overexposed negatives are too dense, overexposed prints are too dark, and overexposed slides or reversal prints are too light.

Oxidation Generally refers to loss of a chemical's strength or activity because of exposure to air (oxygen); developers especially should be stored in full, tightly capped bottles in order to avoid oxidation.

Oyster Shell Marks Circular ripples that sometimes occur on ferrotyped glossy prints which are dried too quickly by heated print dryers.

Panalure Paper Brand of Kodak enlarging paper designed for use with color negatives to make black-and-white prints in a full range of gray tones.

Panchromatic Usually describes black-and-white film that is sensitive to all colors of light; all films for general photography today are panchromatic.

Paper Backing The paper wrapped with spools of roll and cartridge film that prevents light from exposing or fogging the film before and after it is used in the camera.

Paper Base Material used to support the emulsion of a photo paper; conventional papers have an ordinary fiber base, while RC-type papers have a liquid-resistant base because they are resin coated, plastic coated, or polyethylene coated.

Paper Safe A light-tight box designed to hold photographic papers and protect them from exposure by room lights or safelights.

Paper Speed A system of numbers, established by ANSI, to indicate a photographic paper's relative sensitivity to light; the greater the ANSI number, the more sensitive the paper's emulsion; see also ANSI.

Paper Surface Photo paper surfaces vary according to their brilliance (such as glossy, lustre, and matte) and texture (such as smooth, silk, and tweed).

Paper Tint Actual color of the photo paper stock, such as white, warm-white, and cream-white.

Paper Weight Indicates the relative thickness of a photo paper, ranging from light weight (LW) to single-weight (SW), medium-weight (MW), and double-weight (DW).

Perspective The appearance of objects relative to their distance and position; a necessary consideration to suggest depth in photographs, a dimension the human eye sees but which the camera lens does not.

Perspective-Correction (PC) Lens A camera lens that can be rotated to correct distortion, such as parallel lines that appear unparallel.

Photocell A light-sensitive cell commonly a part of exposure meters, enlarging meters, and color analyzers, as well as automatic or electric-eye cameras, and remote or automatic flash units.

Photoflood Lamp A bright source of illumination that looks like an ordinary household-type bulb; normally used with a metal reflector; available in two brightnesses, and in blue; has a limited life of 3 to 6 hours.

Photogram A photograph made without a negative by placing objects on photographic paper and exposing it to light before processing.

Photography Literally means "to write with light."

Photo Mural Large photographic print; may consist of several sheets of photo paper joined together.

Photo Sensitizer Light-sensitive solution or substance applied to various materials, including metal or cloth, for the purpose of making photographic images on the material by enlarging or contact printing methods.

Photo Silk-Screen Printing A method of transferring a photo image to a silk screen, and then printing that image onto paper by forcing inks through the screen with a squeegee.

Photo Spray Glue A special adhesive for mounting prints; will not bleed through the photo paper or cause the image to deteriorate.

Pinholes Small clear spots in a negative's emulsion that produce black marks in a print; sometimes caused by air bubbles and improper agitation, or by dust particles that are especially attracted to litho film.

Polarizing Filter An adjustable filter that blocks some light rays to diminish or eliminate glare or reflections from shiny surfaces, except unpainted metal; also darkens blue skies in color photographs.

Positive Film A film, such as that used for making slides, that produces a positive image rather than a negative image; sometimes called Reversal Film.

Positive-to-Positive Paper Color photo paper that produces a positive image when printed with a transparency; sometimes called Type R (for reversal) paper; see also Negative-to-Positive Paper.

Posterization A printing method involving high contrast separation negatives that limits the number of tones in a black-and-white or color photograph and gives the resulting image the look of a poster created by a graphic artist.

Prehardener A chemical required in some color processes.

Presoak or Prewet A water bath that prepares film or photo paper for processing and prevents uneven development; required in some color processes, especially when a tube-type processor is used.

Primary Colors In photography, the three colors that combine to make white light: red, blue, and green; see also Complementary Colors.

Print A piece of photographic paper with a positive image produced by contact printing or enlarging.

Print Diffusion Refers to the use of a special filter or other translucent material to diffuse an image projected by the enlarger and reduce the sharpness of the image in a print.

Print Dryer A device, often heated, used to dry photographic prints.

Print Drying Screen Plastic or fiberglass screen on which prints are placed for drying by forced air or room air; especially satisfactory for drying color or other resin-coated papers.

Print Exposure Meter See Enlarging Meter.

Print Flashing Exposing areas of a print emulsion with a small light in order to darken limited portions of the image or reduce contrast.

Print Flattener A solution in which conventional paper base prints are bathed in order to reduce or prevent curling while they dry.

Print Lacquer A clear coating sprayed or brushed on prints to protect them from dust, fingerprints, scratches and humidity; can also be used to change a print's brilliance (i.e. glossy to matte finish) or to add texture to the print surface.

Print Tongs Plastic or wooden tongs, often rubber tipped, for transferring prints from one processing chemical to another; must be used carefully to avoid scratching the print's emulsion.

Print Washer Device for washing prints thoroughly that provides complete changes of water and sufficient agitiation.

Printing-Out Paper (POP) Produces an image upon exposure to light; no chemical processing is required, but the image eventually fades; sometimes used by portrait photographers for proof prints to show customers a selection of poses.

Printing Paper A light-sensitive paper that produces an image when exposed to light during the contact printing or enlarging process; also called enlarging or photo paper.

Processing Drum or Processing Tube See Tube-Type Processor.

Professional Films Films with limited latitude and tolerances which are designed for more exacting results; professional color films must be refrigerated and processed promptly; some data sheets give the film's effective speed, which is more precise than the film's intended ASA; see also Effective Film Speed.

Proof Print Generally, a test print or a print to be filed for reference; can be a contact print or an enlargement.

Proof Sheet Usually refers to a contact print of a group of negatives; used as a positive record of the negatives and for reference.

Protective Toning Toning, usually with selenium or gold toners, to protect the metallic silver image in black-and-white prints from fading or other ill effects.

Push Processing Developing film for a longer period of time than usual; allows the film to be rated at a higher ASA film speed than normal, which is termed "pushing" film.

RC Paper See Resin-Coated Paper.

Rangefinder An optical device used for focusing images in a rangefinder camera; generally produces twin or split images until the lens is adjusted to bring such images together to indicate the subject is in focus.

Reciprocity Effect A characteristic of most photographic films and papers when subjected to abnormally long or short exposures; the increase or decrease in exposure is no longer directly proportional to an increase or decrease in the density of the image registered on the emulsion.

Reducer A chemical solution used to reduce the density of black-and-white negatives or prints that have been overexposed or overdeveloped or to reduce the density of color transparencies that have been underexposed or underdeveloped; can also alter color balance; see also Selective Reducer.

Reducing Using a reducer to cut the density of a negative, print, or transparency; sometimes called Bleaching.

Reflected-Light Meter An exposure meter that reads the light reflected from the subject; pointed at the subject from the camera position.

Reflex Camera A camera that uses a mirror or other optical device to present the scene or subject to the photographer exactly as the camera's film will record it; a single-lens reflex camera uses one lens for both viewing and photographing, while a twin-lens reflex camera uses one lens for viewing and another for filming the image.

Replenisher Chemicals added to a processing solution, particularly developer, to keep its chemical activity constant.

Resin-Coated (RC) Paper Photographic paper that is liquid-resistant and absorbs little of the chemical solutions during processing, thus permitting shorter washing and drying times; may be treated with a resin, plastic, or polyethylene coating.

Resolution See Resolving Power.

Resolving Power Refers to the ability of a lens to form sharp images; also refers to the ability of a film to record fine detail.

Reticulation Wrinkling or cracking of film or photo paper emulsion, caused by extreme differences in the temperatures of the processing solutions, which produces regular patterns in the image; rarely occurs with modern films and papers unless intentionally done.

Retouching Changing portions of a negative or print by applying pigments, dyes, or pencil colors to the emulsion; see also Spotting.

Retouching Colors Dyes used for retouching color prints.

Ring-Around A series of prints that are variations of a normal print and are used for comparison in judging other prints; ring-around prints may vary in exposure, contrast grade (black-and-white prints), or filtration (color prints).

Reversal Film Produces a direct positive image (i.e. transparency); often called slide film; identified by the suffix "chrome" in the film name.

Reversal Paper Produces a positive print directly from a transparency; sometimes called Type R paper; identified by the suffix "chrome" in the paper name.

Roll Film Film on a spool that usually utilizes an opaque paper backing to prevent exposure when not in the camera.

Sabattier Effect Partial reversal of an image that occurs when film or photo paper is reexposed to light while in the developer and characterized by Mackie lines; frequently it is incorrectly called solarization; see also Mackie Line and Solarization.

Safelight A light with special filters used to illuminate the darkroom without exposing photographic film or paper.

Safety Filter A red filter attached to the enlarger beneath the lens and used to prevent exposure to black-and-white paper while aligning the projected image and the enlarging easel.

Sandwiching Combining two or more negatives or transparencies for printing or projection.

Secondary Colors See Complementary Colors.

Selective Development Increasing development of certain portions of a print by locally applying stock developer or hot water or rubbing the print surface.

Selective Filtration Using color filters with dodging or burning-in tools in order to alter color balance in certain areas of a color print.

Selective Reducer A reducer that acts on a specific color (yellow, magenta, or cyan) to change the color balance of a print or transparency.

Shadow Detail Detail that is evident in the shadowed (dark) areas of a picture; a consideration when making an exposure meter reading; see also Highlight Detail.

Sheet Film Individual pieces of film normally used to make a single exposure; loaded in special holders for camera use; see also Roll Film.

Shirley Nickname for a standard negative because the subject in the picture traditionally is a girl; see also Standard Negative.

Shutter A device, built in the lens or a camera, that regulates the length of time that light reaches the film to make an exposure.

Shutter Speed Indicates the precise length of time that light exposes the film; usually in marked fractions of a second.

Side Lighting A term used when the main source of illumination is at the side of the subject.

Silver Halides The chemical components that are sensitive to light and make up the emulsion of a photographic film or paper.

Single-Lens Reflex (SLR) Camera Uses a mirror and prism to allow the photographer to see the subject through the same lens that presents the image to the film; the most popular type of 35mm camera.

Slide A color film transparency mounted in a cardboard, plastic, or glass mount for use in a slide projector; can also be used to make color prints.

Slide Copier A device used with a camera for copying slides; usually is adjustable to allow cropping and has a light source and provision for inserting filters to permit color balancing.

Slow Film Film with emulsion that is not very sensitive to light, such as one with a film speed of ASA 25 or ASA 32; see also Fast Film.

Snip Test Refers to cutting a short length of film from a roll in order to test develop it before processing the entire roll.

Solarization Reversal of an image caused by extreme overexposure; frequently confused with the Sabattier effect; see also Sabattier Effect.

Spot Meter A type of exposure meter that has a limited angle of acceptance; see also Angle of Acceptance.

Spot Reading Describes a light reading of a small, limited area made by an exposure meter, enlarging meter, or color analyzer; see also Integrated Reading.

Spotting Covering small defects in a print by applying spotting colors or dyes with a fine-tipped brush.

Squeegee A rubber-edged implement for removing water from surfaces of negatives or prints in order to promote uniform and fast drying.

Stabilization Processing Use of a special tabletop machine that processes prints in about 15 seconds, plus drying time; requires two chemicals, activator and stabilizer, plus a special photo paper containing a developing agent; images are not permanent unless the paper is treated with fixer and then washed.

Stabilizer Chemical solution used in some color processes and in stabilization processing.

Standard Negative Usually a color negative of correct exposure and color balance that is used in judging the density and color balance of other color negatives; see also Shirley.

Stand Bath A tray of water used to hold prints as they are removed from the fixer, prior to the prints being washed collectively.

Static Marks Irregular, lightninglike black lines in a negative caused by static electricity when a film is wound or unwound too rapidly under conditions of low humidity.

Stock Solution Liquid chemical that must be diluted or mixed with another chemical before use; see also Working Solution.

Stop Bath A chemical solution in film and print processing used to stop the action of the developer and prevent contamination of the fixer; usually acetic acid.

Storage Life Refers to the period of time a chemical can be kept before it loses its potency and should be discarded; sometimes known as a chemical's keeping properties.

Subminiature Camera Small camera which uses 16mm or smaller film.

Subtractive Color Printing The most common method of color printing, requiring a single exposure through filters of one or two of the three complementary colors: yellow, magenta, and cyan; also called White-Light Printing.

Subtractive Primaries Yellow, magenta, and cyan; complementary colors of the additive primaries.

Surge Marks Short dark streaks, caused by excessive agitation, that appear at the sprocket holes of 35mm film or along the edges of sheet film processed in film hangers.

Synchronization See Flash Synchronizattion.

Tacking Iron A hand-held heating device for initially attaching dry-mounting tissue to a print and then its mount board; see also Dry Mounting Press.

Telephoto Lens A lens that has a greater focal length and a narrower angle of view than a normal lens; produces a larger subject image than a normal lens when both lenses are the same distance from the subject.

Test Print Usually a small print that is made to determine whether exposure, contrast grade, or color filtration is correct before making the final print or enlargement.

Test Strip A single print that has a series of different exposures, or varied color filtration, to use in selecting the correct exposure or filtration for the final print.

Texture Screen Commercially made or personally devised screen material placed in contact with a negative or photo paper in order to produce a pattern on the print image.

Thin Negative An underexposed negative with less than normal density; lacks detail in shadow areas.

Through-the-Lens Meter An exposure meter built in the camera that reads the light coming through the camera lens; common with single-lens reflex cameras.

Time Exposure Usually an exposure longer than 1 second; the camera's shutter is kept open by setting it at the "B" or "T" position.

Timer A clock for timing each processing step or for controlling exposures made by an enlarger or contact printer.

Tintype An early type of photograph that is a direct positive image made on a sensitized piece of enameled tin or iron.

Tone-Line Printing A photographic procedure that produces a print image resembling a pen-and-ink drawing.

Toning A process for adding color to enhance the image of a black-and-white photograph; sometimes done to protect the print image; see also Protective Toning.

Transparency A color or black-and-white film that is viewed by light transmitted through it; see also Slide and Diapositive.

Transparent Oil Colors Oils that are used for hand-coloring black-and-white photographs.

Tricolor Printing See Additive Color Printing.

Tube-Type Processor A plastic tube or drum which allows color prints to be processed in room light after the photo paper is loaded in the dark; solutions are poured in and out through light-tight openings in the tube's end; agitation is done manually by rolling the tube on a tabletop or automatically by placing it on a motorized base.

Tungsten Light Light from sources other than the sun; color films designed for use with artificial light sources are often called tungsten films, while those balanced for sunlight are called daylight color films.

Twin-Lens Reflex (TLR) Camera A camera which uses two lenses—one to project the subject to the photographer through the viewfinder and the other to record the image on the film.

Type R Print A photograph made directly from a color transparency on color reversal paper; see also Reversal Paper.

Ultraviolet (UV) Filter In color printing, a filter used in the enlarger to prevent color imbalance in the print caused by ultraviolet light produced by the enlarger bulb; in camera work, a filter used in front of the lens to help eliminate the ultraviolet light to which all films are sensitive.

Underexposure Insufficient exposure of a photographic film or paper; underexposed negatives are not dense enough; underexposed prints are too light, and underexposed transparencies or color reversal papers are too dark.

Universal Developer A developer that can be used for processing both black-and-white films and photo papers.

Variable Contrast Filters Used during enlarging to produce black-and-white prints of various contrast on a single type of paper; see also Variable Contrast Paper.

Variable Contrast Paper A single photographic paper that is capable of producing normal contrast prints from negatives having a wide range of contrasts; must be used with appropriate variable contrast filters; eliminates the need for papers of different contrast grades.

Variable Focal Length Lens A lens adjustable to different focal lengths but which must be refocused after each focal length change is made; see also Zoom Lens.

Viewfinder An optical device on a camera used by the photographer to view the subject to be photographed.

Viewing Light A white light for viewing prints or transparencies; for color transparencies, it should be of about 5500K color temperature, such as a cool white deluxe fluorescent light.

Vignetting Used to emphasize the subject of a print by creating a white or black background around it during the enlarging process.

Voltage Regulator/Stabilizer Electrical device for maintaining a constant voltage to the enlarger so exposure time or color balance will not be affected by fluctuating current during print exposure.

Water Bath A tray of water of a certain temperature in which processing tanks, tubes, or bottles of chemicals are kept in order to maintain the solutions at a constant temperature.

Water Marks Gray spots that occur where water drops dry on the emulsion or back of a negative.

Wet Area An area in the darkroom where films and prints are processed; a space away from the darkroom's dry area (where films are loaded in developing tanks or prints are exposed in the enlarger).

Wet Mounting Refers to mounting prints, usually large photographs or photo murals, while they are wet; requires a strong mounting surface, such as Masonite.

Wet-Plate Process Early photographic process involving glass or metal plates that were coated with a light-sensitive solution and then exposed and developed before the emulsion dried; see also Collodion.

Wetting Agent A solution in which negatives are bathed after processing in order to promote uniform, spotless drying.

White Light Data Information on some color paper packages that indicates the changes in filtration required when switching from one batch of paper to another.

White Light Printing See Subtractive Color Printing.

Wide-Angle Lens A lens that has a lesser focal length and a greater angle of view than a normal lens; produces a smaller subject image than a normal lens when both lenses are the same distance from the subject.

Working Solution Liquid chemical that has been diluted, or mixed with another chemical, and is ready for use; see also Stock Solution.

X Flash Synchronization The camera flash socket or switch position for synchronizing the shutter when an electronic flash is used; see also FP and M Synchronization.

Yellow A color produced by mixing red and green light; complementary to the primary color blue; one of the three complementary color filters used in white light subtractive printing.

Zone System A system to help determine camera exposure, devised by well-known photographer Ansel Adams; an adaptation of the gray scale in ten zones, from Zone 0 (black) to Zone V (middle gray) to Zone IX (white).

Zoom Lens A lens that can be adjusted to varied focal lengths while keeping the subject in focus; see also Variable Focal Length Lens.

Appendix B
Weights and Measures

Most of the weights and measures in this book have been given as used customarily in the United States (i.e., inches, feet, ounces, quarts, Fahrenheit), except in discussions of lens focal length, which is known almost universally in terms of millimeters (mm). Conversion to the metric system of weights and measures is imminent in the U.S. The following equivalents will guide you in converting the weights and measures given in this book. Some figures have been rounded off.

For photography, the major units of the metric system are the *meter* (m) for linear (length) measurement, the *liter* (l) for liquid measurement, and the *gram* (g) for weight measurement. Unit abbreviations are in parentheses.

EQUIVALENTS WITHIN THE METRIC SYSTEM

Linear Measure

1 millimeter (mm)	= 1/1000 meter
1 centimeter (cm)	= 1/100 meter, 10 millimeters
1 decimeter (dm)	= 1/10 meter, 100 millimeters, 10 centimeters
1 meter (m)	= 1000 millimeters, 100 centimeters, 10 decimeters
1 kilometer (km)	= 1000 meters

Liquid Measure

1 milliliter (ml)	= 1/1000 liter
1 centiliter (cl)	= 1/100 liter, 10 milliliters
1 deciliter (dl)	= 1/10 liter, 100 milliliters, 10 centiliters
1 liter (l)	= 1000 milliliters, 100 centiliters, 10 deciliters
1 kiloliter (kl)	= 1000 liters

Weight Measure

1 milligram (mg)	= 1/1000 gram
1 centigram (cg)	= 1/100 gram, 10 milligrams
1 decigram (dg)	= 1/10 gram, 100 milligrams, 10 centigrams
1 gram (g)	= 1000 milligrams, 10 centigrams, 10 decigrams
1 kilogram (kg)	= 1000 grams

EQUIVALENTS FOR THE U.S. AND METRIC SYSTEMS

Linear Measure

U.S. — *Metric*

1 inch	= 25.4 millimeters, 2.54 centimers, .25 decimeters, .025 meters
1 foot	= 304.8 millimeters, 30.48 centimeters, 3.04 decimeters, .30 meters
1 yard	= 914 millimeters, 91.4 centimeters, 9.14 decimeters, .91 meters
1 mile	= 1609.34 meters, 1.61 kilometers

Metric — *U.S.*

1 millimeter	= .039 inches, .003 feet, .001 yards
1 centimeter	= .39 inches, .032 feet, .011 yards
1 decimeter	= 3.93 inches, .328 feet, .109 yards
1 meter	= 39.37 inches, 3.28 feet, 1.09 yards, .0006 miles

Liquid Measure

U.S. — *Metric*

1 ounce	= 29.57 milliliters, 2.95 centiliters, .29 deciliters, .029 liters
1 quart	= 946.35 milliliters, 94.63 centiliters, 9.46 deciliters, .946 liters
1 gallon	= 3785.41 milliliters, 378.54 centiliters, 37.85 deciliters, 3.78 liters

Metric — *U.S.*

1 millileter	= .033 ounces
1 centiliter	= .33 ounces, .01 quart
1 deciliter	= 3.38 ounces, .105 quart, .026 gallon
1 liter	= 33.81 ounces, 1.05 quart, .26 gallon

Weight Measure

U.S. — *Metric*

1 ounce	= 28.35 grams
1 pound	= 453.59 grams

Metric — *U.S.*

1 gram	= .035 ounce, .002 pounds

TEMPERATURE CONVERSION

Temperatures have been indicated in the U.S. by a Fahrenheit scale (F), while most of the world uses the Celsius (also called Centigrade) scale (C). Two methods of converting one to the other follow.

To figure Celsius, subtract 32 from Fahrenheit and divide by 1.8, OR subtract 32 from Fahrenheit, multiply by 5, and divide by 9.

To figure Fahrenheit, multiply Celsius by 1.8 and add 32, OR multiply Celsius by 9, divide by 5, and add 32.

Because correct temperature is important for successful processing, a list of some temperature equivalents for Fahrenheit and Celsius is given below. The freezing point of water is 32°F and 0°C, and the boiling point is 212°F and 100°C.

The Celsius figures have been rounded off to the nearest ½ degree.

F	=	C		F	=	C		F	=	C
45		7		81		27		117		47
46		8		82		28		118		47.5
47		8.5		83		28.5		119		48.5
48		9		84		29		120		49
49		9.5		85		29.5		121		49.5
50		10		86		30		122		50
51		10.5		87		30.5		123		50.5
52		11		88		31		124		51
53		11.5		89		31.5		125		51.5
54		12		90		32		126		52
55		13		91		32.5		127		52.5
56		13.5		92		33.5		128		53.5
57		14		93		34		129		54
58		14.5		94		34.5		130		54.5
59		15		95		35				
60		15.5		96		35.5				
61		16		97		36				
62		16.5		98		36.5				
63		17		99		37				
64		18		100		37.5				
65		18.5		101		38.5				
66		19		102		39				
67		19.5		103		39.5				
68		20		104		40				
69		20.5		105		40.5				
70		21		106		41				
71		21.5		107		41.5				
72		22		108		42				
73		23		109		42.5				
74		23.5		110		43.5				
75		24		111		44				
76		24.5		112		44.5				
77		25		113		45				
78		25.5		114		45.5				
79		26		115		46				
80		26.5		116		46.5				

Index

(Page numbers set in bold refer to black-and-white photographs. See page 346 for references to the two color inserts.)

Color Section 1

1. Colors, in photographic process
2-4. Test prints, of color casts
5. Color balance, in final print
6. Test prints, four on one sheet
7-8. Color transparency, on reversal and negative paper
9. Selective filtration, on color print
10. Hand coloring, with felt-tipped pen
11-12. Retouching, of color print
13-14. Color transparency, on reversal and negative papers

Color Section 2

15. Photogram
16-17. Sabattier effect, on color negative slide
18. Infrared slide
19. Sabattier effect, on infrared slide
20-21. Multiple color images
22-23. Color toning, of black-and-white print
24-25. Toning, special effects of
26-27. Duotone solarization, of black-and-white print
28. Hand-colored photograph, with india ink outline
29. Sabattier effect, on sandwiched slides

The Basic Darkroom Book

Today there is no single hobby more popular than amateur photography. In terms of sheer numbers of stores, suppliers, manufacturers, school courses, exhibits, and publications, it is No. 1. Now, THE BASIC DARKROOM BOOK and its companion volume, THE BASIC BOOK OF PHOTOGRAPHY, together form a total reference library for photographing, processing, and printing.

TOM GRIMM is a free-lance photographer and writer based in Laguna Beach, California. He is also a photography instructor at the University of California, Irvine. His work has taken him on assignments to more than a hundred countries and has appeared in numerous leading magazines and newspapers. With his wife, Michele, he has illustrated six other adult and children's books. His acclaimed THE BASIC BOOK OF PHOTOGRAPHY is also available in a Plume edition.

The cover shows a color photogram created from nasturtiums and a tin can by Jerry Burchfield, an artist in the darkroom as well as with a camera. He is responsible for the majority of photographs in this book. His work has also appeared in numerous galleries, museums, and universities. My heartfelt thanks for all his help. (For details about photograms, see Chapter 16.)

—T.G.